THERE WERE 70,000 PEOPLE

- some were pious
- some were atheists
- some were journalists
- some were illiterate

**THEY ALL AGREED ON ONE THING...
THE THING THEY SAW WHEN THEY
LOOKED SKYWARD!!!**

Jacques Vallee, born and educated in France, holds degrees in mathematics and astronomy. He is a consultant on NASA's "Mars Map" project and has been a research assistant at MacDonald Observatory.

UFO's IN SPACE:
Anatomy of a Phenomenon

Jacques Vallee

BALLANTINE BOOKS • NEW YORK

Copyright © 1965 HENRY REGNERY COMPANY

All rights reserved under International and Pan-American Copyright Conventions. Published in the United States by Ballantine Books, a division of Random House, Inc., New York, and simultaneously in Canada by Ballantine Books of Canada, Ltd., Toronto, Canada. Originally published as *Anatomy of a Phenomenon: Unidentified Objects in Space—A Scientific Appraisal*.

Library of Congress Catalog Card Number: 65-19161

ISBN 0-345-34437-5

This edition published by arrangement with Henry Regnery Company

Manufactured in the United States of America

First Ballantine Books Edition: December 1974
Fifth Printing: May 1987

Cover photo by Don Landwehrle/The Image Bank

PREFACE

Ever since the amazing series of sightings of unidentified flying objects in France in 1954, I have been deeply interested in the problem of the origin, behavior and physical nature of the UFO phenomenon. When I was authorized to study the general files of the United States Air Force I welcomed this opportunity to clarify my ideas concerning the official approach to the sightings and to understand better the attitude of the scientific and military authorities toward this problem.

In the course of this research I had access to many interesting reports which had never been made public. Simultaneously, I was able to conduct a thorough analysis of the European files kept up-to-date by a number of researchers, some of whom worked in collaboration with professional scientists acting privately. This resulted in the accumulation of a unique collection of data, the volume of which is at present double that of the official files.

I soon reached a point in my personal research at which I realized that I was rapidly approaching the limits of my competence, and that it was becoming increasingly important for me to receive the advice of specialists of other disciplines. Unfortunately, communication between scientists still follows medieval patterns and any attempt on my part to bring the subject into the open would have resulted in misunderstanding. Thus I determined to restrict my work to a few specific points which could be investigated with scientific instruments without resulting in sensational interpretations or exaggerated publicity. But the reactions to some earlier publications on the subject led me to realize that by considering the scientific issue alone and trying to avoid a public debate I was seeing only part of the problem. I then came to believe that one should not try to "prove" that UFO's constitute a new phenomenon of an unknown, possibly artificial, nature before one has made an attempt to understand why such violent reactions are provoked by the thought of extraterrestrial intelligence.

My writing this book in a popular form is deliberate, because it is my opinion that my subject is important and concerns not only the scientist, but the military man, the philosopher, the man of the cloth and the general public as well.

It would be unrealistic on my part not to expect this book to be misinterpreted. It seems certain that any mention of the problem of extraterrestrial intelligence by a professional scientist (even if he insists that this is only a convenient hypothesis among others which he plans to study) will be commented upon by groups of enthusiasts as an indication that new evidence, unknown to the general public, has been obtained. I can categorically state that such is not the case. Furthermore, the position I am taking here is purely individual. It does not reflect the viewpoint of a group, nor the opinion of the research institution with which I am associated, nor that of any of the groups with which I have been associated in the past. In bringing my opinion into the open I simply make use of a privilege every scientist has, namely, the right to publish his views even when they are in opposition to generally accepted ideas.

I have endeavored to write a book that will help interested researchers become seriously acquainted with the problem, and I have tried to be objective in presenting summaries of all current theories related to the main points in the discussion. This book is documented with references,* and illustrated with pictures designed to aid the reader in visualizing a difficult problem—one which is unsolved after twenty years of analysis by outstanding scientists. Every statement of importance is supported by documentary authority. On several occasions I have had to admit that I could not commit myself to any particular point of view, but I have always kept an open mind and have been careful not to reject extreme hypotheses merely on the ground of their "fantastic" character, for nothing can be more fantastic than a natural phenomenon not yet recognized and classified by the human mind. In so doing, however, I have not lost sight of the fact that "an open mind does not mean credulity or a suspension of the logical faculties that are man's most valuable asset" (Menzel, [121]).

The interest of research is not solely what prompted me to take this frightening step; I was impressed by the deep emotion and the cry of anguish in many of these reports, which should be viewed as a challenge by all scientists; any citizen who becomes so concerned by the events he witnesses that he writes a detailed account of them has the

---

* Numbers in parentheses within the text refer to the Bibliography at the end of the book.

right to ask us to study this report as a piece of scientific information, and with an open, objective mind. We must view with contempt and irony those who will continue to call the problem ridiculous only because they do not know the solution. "Ridicule," wrote one of the eminent researches in this field, "is not part of the scientific method, and the public should not be taught that it is" (Hynek, [176]).

This book is not intended to convince; the author himself is far from having reached a definite opinion as to the nature of the puzzling phenomenon he studies. The numerous observations quoted in this work are not there to prove, but to illustrate only. They are taken from reliable, but not exceptional, reports, because our purpose is neither to shock nor to demonstrate, but to lead the reader to the idea that the phenomenon, whatever its nature and origin, can only be studied in terms of classes, not as a collection of individual oddities. Dr. Menzel's work has indicated that the average report could often be explained, assuming the witnesses had been the victims of some combination of physical or mental aberrations. As the number of reports of higher than average reliability becomes larger and larger, however, this approach loses its appeal to the scientific mind, and one is led to the idea that either an entirely new type of mental aberration, indeed most extraordinary, has taken an important place in the life of our civilization, or that the UFO phenomenon is unique in nature, is of large amplitude and thus deserves a special investigation.

How to progress in such an investigation with the greatest guarantee of scientific accuracy is the subject of this book. The phenomenon under study is not the UFO, which is not reproducible at will in the laboratory, but *the report written by the witness.* This report can be observed, studied and communicated by professional scientists; thus defined, the phenomenon we investigate is obviously real. Our problem is no longer to explain, but to analyze. We are dealing with "the science of structure, not the science of substance" (Eddington). The question, then, is no longer to believe or disbelieve, since we do not have elements of comparison upon which to base such a judgment; the question is rather how to derive proper methods of investigation, classification and control which will satisfy all guarantees necessary in the rational progress of knowledge to which science is devoted, without refusing to consider certain hypotheses. Among these, of course, is the possibility that the UFO phenomenon is an attempt at contact with our civilization by nonhuman knowledge for nonhuman purposes, possibly prompted by nonhuman emotions and perceptions.

This possibility has been neglected because, in the present context, its discussion involves a danger of seeing "metaphysical" considerations reintroduced into scientific reasoning. This is a danger we will try not to avoid, but to oppose and defeat as well. We will show that only rational analysis on the basis of actual facts can guide an attempt to understand possible manifestations of extraterrestrial intelligence, and that possible connections with traditional interpretations or legends should be considered only on a speculative basis.

I should thank many persons for having helped, guided or stimulated this work. I will mention only a few in this long list. My wife has certainly done more than anybody else to give me the confidence I needed to undertake such a book. The comments of air force officials, especially Dr.

Preface

Allen Hynek's, on my classification system and project of revised catalogue have been invaluable. And I wish to express my gratitude to Dr. Donald Menzel for having criticized and helped clarify several ill-defined points in our early attempts at rationalization of the UFO phenomenon. Without Aime Michel's remarkable contribution to the clarification of the UFO problem it would be impossible today to attain a good understanding of the important European sightings, and we owe to him much of the recent progress made in the constitution of the files. I am indebted to Harvey Plotnick and Samuel Randlett, whose work on the manuscript served greatly in making this book presentable to the public. The authorization given by A. M. Rener to use one of his paintings, published here for the first time, is gratefully acknowledged.

CONTENTS

Preface ... v

ONE **The Legend of "Flying Saucers"** ... 1
As Old as Man Himself?
Hast Thou Seen Ye UFO?
Scientific Reports of UFO's in the Nineteenth Century
Observations Made between 1900 and 1946
Statistical Aspects of UFO History before the Modern Period

TWO **Probability of Contact with Superior Galactic Communities** ... 40
A Philosophical Issue
Life in the Solar System
Contact with Other Civilizations in Space

THREE **Modern UFO Reports and Their Reliability** ... 54
Sources of Documentation
A Moment of History
The American Period (1947–1952)
The French Period (1953–1960)
The Unfinished Symphony

Contents

FOUR **The Scientific Problem** 105
  An Unusual Scientific Puzzle
  The Dangerous Precautions
  The Need for a New System of
    Analysis
  The Harvard Syndrome
  Specialists and Analysts
  Requirements for an Objective
    Analysis of UFO Reports
  Reliability of the Sources of
    Information
  The Search for Invariants
  Criticism of the Official
    Classification System
  The Myth of "Unidentified" Objects
  Basis of a Scientific Classification
  Comments on the Various Types of
    UFO Reports
  The Myth of Absolute Reliability
  Proposed Reorganization of UFO
    Research

FIVE **Flying Saucers and Human Reason** 154
  The Scientist's Emotional Reaction
    to UFO's
  Society's Reaction to UFO's
  Enthusiasm and UFO Groups
  The Witnesses' Reaction after a
    Sighting
  Dream and Hoax as Emotional
    Expressions
  Metaphysical UFO's

SIX **Typical Phases of UFO Behavior** 177
  The General Type I Event
  The "Operators"
  The June 1959 New Guinea Episode
  Fatima: The Miraculous UFO

Contents

Type II Sightings: Cloud Cigars and
the Generation of UFO's
Hovering and Special Maneuvers:
Type III Sightings

SEVEN **Theories and Hypotheses** 222
Agrest's Theory of Extraterrestrial
Visitation in Prehistoric Times
Misraki's Theory of Extraterrestrial
Intervention in Religion
Fletcher's "Scientific Theory"
Michel's Hypotheses and the
Feasibility of Contact
The Landing at Kelly
Oberth's Theory of the Extrasolar
Origin of UFO's
The Relay on the Moon and Sagan's
Hypotheses
A New System of Working
Hypotheses

**Note on the Probability of Contact with
Superior Galactic Communities** 248
The Formation of Solar Systems:
Theoretical Data
Planetary Systems: Observational
Data
Contact with Superior Galactic
Communities
Galactic Exploration in the Vicinity
of the Sun
Limitations of this Model

Bibliography 262

Index 275

CHAPTER ONE

THE LEGEND OF "FLYING SAUCERS"

AS OLD AS MAN HIMSELF?

On January 24, 1878, John Martin, a Texas farmer who lived a few miles south of Denison, saw a dark flying object in the shape of a disk cruising high in the sky "at a wonderful speed," and used the word "saucer" to describe it (1). John Martin seems to have been a true pioneer; seventy years later another man, Kenneth Arnold, spoke of "flying saucers." This time the word was here to stay.

The legend of the flying disks has existed throughout history. Apparitions of strange objects in the sky have for centuries stirred popular emotion and have at times caused crises and panics. Some writers have gone so far as to try to attribute them to "unknown civilizations" said to have preceded us on this planet (2). Such past societies, they argue, could have reached a very high level of evolution and developed space travel; or they could have remained at a stage of low technology under the domination of extraterrestrial "visitors," who are said to have departed from our planet for some unknown reason, leaving almost no traces. According to the same writers, some of our religious texts might have been inspired by such contacts with a supercivilization. Psonansky and Kiess, as well as Epstein, have studied the Tiahuanaco monuments and have interpreted some of their features as possible indexes of extraterrestrial "visitations" in prehistoric times. Tschi Pen Lao, of the University of Peking, has also discovered remarkable drawings on a Hunan mountain and on an island in Lake Tungting. Possibly made in 45,000 B.C., these granite carvings depict people with large trunks, and cylindrical objects in the sky on which similar beings are seen standing. In 1961, the Russian astronomer Alexander Kazantsev brought to the attention of the readers of the Soviet magazine *Smena* a discovery made by Henri Labote in the Tassili plateau in Sahara of sculpted rocks showing human beings with strange round heads, and other mysterious scenes. These sculptures were dated 6,000 B.C.

Along the same line, the prophet Ezekiel's vision has often been commented upon in books dealing with unidentified flying objects. This description (Ezekiel, chapter 1) of a strange machine coming from the sky and landing close to the Chebar River in Chaldea (now part of Iraq) in 593 B.C. includes expressions said to be similar to those commonly used by witnesses of modern sightings of UFO's.

Ezekiel says that out of a whirlwind from the north appeared a fiery sphere. As remarked in (3, and 4):

> Ezekiel's narrative in the Bible is mainly concerned with describing this incident in his own phraseology, however vague it may seem to us today. Ezekiel lived in an era of few metals and no machines. The war chariot

and the plough were the last word in their "technology." For this reason it was extremely difficult for Ezekiel to portray with his vocabulary the event he witnessed.

According to the same sources, an attempt to reconstruct from Ezekiel's words a model of the phenomenon in modern terms would lead to the conception of a machine rather than a natural phenomenon such as a mirage:

> The Vehicle which Ezekiel observed had four distinct pillars. From each pillar protruded two wings, eight in all, which moved about. At the base of each column there were rings with circular openings. The four columns formed a cubic body over which there was a transparent dome. For lack of any better term Ezekiel defined it as a "firmament." A throne of sapphire stone crowned the dome, encircled by a rainbow. The reference to sapphire, amber, crystal and beryl may be allusions to plastics which certain parts of the ship were made of.
>
> The prophet describes the workings of this extraordinary craft. Except for the wings no other parts moved. The wings produced a sound "like the noise of great waters." A fiery and thunderous exhaust issued from the base of the engine.
>
> The incident is so objectively depicted that it could hardly be considered a tale to impress superstitious listeners. The ship had other unusual features—it could extend a "hand" giving Ezekiel a roll with inscriptions "within and without." Then the prophet was taken on board the craft to Tel Abib Mountains. There he remained "speechless" for seven days....

This is a type of interpretation commonly found in the literature that deals with our problem. The terminology also should be noted. The words "ship," "craft," "engine" are used without justification. The scientist, obviously, will not be guided by situations thus presented. But the explanation given by Dr. Donald Menzel (that Ezekiel observed a sun dog) is equally unconvincing.

Wilkins and Drake (5, 6) have given numerous indications of luminous disks in the sky at day, or lights at night, under the Roman Empire. Some of these accounts describe beings associated with the objects. (In Ezekiel's story the figure of a man surrounded with a blinding light was mentioned.) In Julius Obsequens' book, *Prodigiorum Liber*, as well as in Livy, it is said that in many places there appeared men in white clothing coming from very far away; in Arpi a shield flew through the sky; two moons were seen at night; ghost ships appeared in the sky; luminous lamps were seen at Praeneste—all this is 218 B.C. If the Romans had had a more developed communications system, they would probably have interpreted this series of observations as a "UFO wave" similar to the celebrated series of sightings in the United States which we will review later.

In 213 B.C. in Hadria an "altar" was seen in the sky, accompanied by the form of a man in white clothing. A total of a dozen such observations between 222 and 90 B.C. can be listed, but we have eliminated many more sightings reviewed in the literature because we felt that they could best be explained as misinterpretations or meteors or atmospheric phenomena.

We will not attach much weight to rumors of such antiquity as far as the reliability of the description is concerned. As Sagan remarked (7):

The Legend of "Flying Saucers"

We require more of a legend than the apparition of a strange being who does extraordinary work and lives in the sky.... A description of the morphology of an intelligent non-human, a clear account of astronomical realities for a primitive people, or a transparent presentation of the purpose of contact would increase the credibility of the legend.

It is, however, interesting to find that such reports were made, and in practically the same terms as the modern ones, concerning strange vehicles flying across the sky long before the advent of Christ. B. Le Poer Trench, for instance, quotes in his book (182) from a papyrus found damaged, with many gaps in the hieroglyphics, among the papers of the late Professor Alberto Tulli, former director of the Egyptian Museum at the Vatican, and translated by Prince Boris de Rachewiltz, who stated that the original was part of the annals of Thutmose III, *circa* 1504–1450 B.C.:

> In the year 22, of the third month of winter, sixth hour of the day... the scribes of the House of Life found it was a circle of fire that was coming in the sky... it had no head, the breath of its mouth had a foul odor. Its body one rod long and one rod wide. It had no voice. Their hearts became confused through it: then they laid themselves on their bellies... they went to the Pharaoh... to report it. His Majesty ordered... has been examined... as to all which is written in the papyrus rolls of the House of Life. His Majesty was meditating upon what happened. Now after some days had passed, these things became more numerous in the sky than ever. They shone more in the sky than the brightness of the sun, and extended to the limits of the four

supports of the heavens.... Powerful was the position of the fire circles. The army of the Pharaoh looked on with him in their midst. It was after supper. Thereupon, these fire circles ascended higher in the sky towards the south....

These facts are certainly worthy of study. Unfortunately, we have no chance to gather more information today concerning the "men in white clothing," and it would be of little help to go now collecting samples on the shores of the Chebar River. But we can at least be sure that these reports were not provoked by a psychological reaction to atomic fear, or to mass hallucination typical of overcrowded cities. Certainly no explanation based on the assertion that the alleged UFO's are misinterpreted conventional objects could be consistently correct over such periods of time.

HAST THOU SEEN YE UFO?

A plain near Mortimer's Cross—Herefordshire.*

EDWARD: Dazzle mine eyes, or do I see three suns?
RICHARD: Three glorious suns, each a perfect sun,
Not seperated with the racking clouds,
But sever'd in a pale clear-shinning sky.
See, see! They join, embrace and seem to kiss,

---

* Quoted in B. Le Poer Trench (182).

The Legend of "Flying Saucers"

> As if they vowed some league inviolable:
> Now are they one lamp, one light, one sun,
> In this the heaven figures some event.
>
> Shakespeare,
> *King Henry VI*, Part III, Act II, Scene I

We have on file more than three hundred UFO sightings prior to the twentieth century and, although it is difficult to comment upon them in the light of scientific analysis, we feel they should be treated exactly as modern reports in respect to their psychological and sociological aspects. Many of these accounts were written during the nineteenth century, but this should not be presumed to favor the "modern" character of the UFO myth, for some of the older reports indicate that series of objects had been witnessed much earlier; but most of the accounts were lost and resulted only in a few general notes in some very rare manuscripts.

Of sightings before the year 1800, after eliminating a large number of descriptions too vague to be included in our catalogues, we have finally retained sixty observations manifesting a fair degree of homogeneity with the balance of our files. Remarks worth studying, for instance, are those presented by Drake (8):

> Agobard, Archbishop of Lyons, wrote in "De Grandine et Tonitrua" how in 840 AD he found the mob in Lyons lynching three men and a woman

accused of landing from a cloudship from the aerial region of Magonia. The great German philologist, Jacob Grimm, about 1820 described the legend of a ship from the clouds, and Montanus, an eighteenth century writer on German folklore, told of wizards flying in the clouds, who were shot down. The belief of Beings from the skies who surveyed our Earth persisted in human consciousness throughout the Middle Ages.

Several drawings and engravings clearly depicting phenomena treated in the same way in which the modern public interprets UFO's should be added to the lists of historical documents to be studied in this context, as Professor C.G. Jung pointed out (9). Amateurs in Europe could easily find many more documents and reports simply by consulting the innumerable local libraries in castles, churches, monasteries throughout Great Britain, France, Holland, Belgium, Germany, Poland, Russia, Switzerland, Italy, Portugal and Spain. Our selections were not accumulated through direct research and therefore represent only a small sample. We hope that researchers with advanced knowledge of history will examine more carefully this mine of information.

Their attention, for example, should be directed to the ship that was often seen speeding across the sky, at night, in Scotland in A.D. 60. In 763, while King Domnall Mac Murchada attended the fair at Teltown, in Meath County, ships were also seen in the air. In 919, in Hungary, spherical objects shining like stars, bright and polished, were reported going to and fro in the sky. Somewhere at sea, on July 29 or 30 of the year 966, a luminous vertical cylinder was seen; this may well have been the first report made in a very fascinating series which we will discuss later. In Japan, on August 23, 1015, two objects were seen giving birth to smaller luminous spheres. At Cairo in August, 1027, numerous noisy objects were reported. A large silvery disk is said to have come close to the ground in Japan on August 12, 1133.

Drake gives in (183) a translation of the *Annales Laurissenses* for the year A.D. 776, which reads:

> Now when the Saxons perceived things were not going in their favor, they began to erect scaffolding from which they could bravely storm the castle itself. But God is good as well as just. He overcame their valour, and on the same day they prepared an assault against the Christians, who lived within the castle, the glory of God appeared in manifestation above the church within the fortress. Those watching outside in that place, of whom many still live to this very day, say they beheld the likeness of two large shields reddish in colour in motion above the church (*et dicunt vidisse instar duorum scutorum colore rubeo flammantes et agitantes supra ipsam ecclesiam*), and when the pagans who were outside saw this sign, they were at once thrown into confusion and terrified with great fear they began to flee from the castle.

These sightings sometimes come in series, affecting selected areas. We translate from (10) this account, which contains a confirmation of the remarks by Drake quoted above:

> In 927 the town of Verdun, like the whole eastern part of France, saw fiery armies appearing in the sky. Flodoard's chronicle reports that they flew over Reims

on a Sunday morning in March. Similar phenomena happened several times under King Pepin the Short, under Charlemagne, under Louis I, the Debonair. These sovereigns' capitularia *mention penalties against creatures that travel on aerial ships*. [Italics mine—Author.] Agobard, the archbishop of Lyons, is said to have freed three men and a woman who had come down from one of these spaceships, and were accused by the mob of being emissaries sent by Grimoald, Duke of Benevento, to spoil the French harvests and vintage by their enchantments. Emperor Charlemagne's edicts forbid the perturbing of the air, provoking of storms by magical means and the practicing of mathematics.... Agobard's manuscript, which can be consulted at the National Library, mentions that the astronauts captured in Lyons were obviously foreigners and that "by an inconceivable fatality, these unfortunate people were so insane as to admit they were wizards." The mob killed them, and their corpses were fastened to boards and thrown into the rivers.... In March, 842, multicolored armies were seen marching in the sky.... These sightings of infernal armies were nocturnal. They several times accompanied the siege of Jerusalem.

A similar occurrence took place in Thann, Alsace, where a chapel was built in 1160 after three lights had been observed over a fir tree. A luminous cross was seen in 1188 between Gisors and Neaufles-Saint-Martin; a cross carved in stone still marks the spot.

We observe here that the appearances of lights or phenomena interpreted as objects, seen in the sky, were not in general associated with the idea of "visitors" or with the possible arrival of fantastic creatures, but rather with religious beliefs, and were treated as manifestations of supernatural forces. After the twelfth century, reports become more documented; religious chronicles give more space to local events and a larger quantity of information is recorded by monasteries. On January 1, 1254, at Saint Alban's Abbey, at midnight, in a serene sky and clear atmosphere, with stars shining and the moon eight days old, there suddenly appeared in the sky a kind of large ship, elegantly shaped, well equiped and of a marvelous color. (Matthew of Paris, *Historia Anglorum,* quoted in Wilkins [5], with numerous other good reports.) The observation made in 1290, at Byland Abbey, Yorkshire, of a large silvery disk flying slowly is a classical one and can be found in a number of books. On November 1, 1461, a strange object shaped like a ship, from which fire was seen flowing, passed over the town of Arras in France (5). Jacques Duclerc, a chronicler, and counselor to Duke Philip the Good, writes a detailed account of this sighting in his *Memoirs of a Freeman of Arras*: "A fiery thing like an iron rod of good length and as large as one half of the moon was seen in the sky for a little less than a quarter of an hour."

An incunabulum made in 1493, which belonged to the Saint Airy Library and is now visible in a museum in Verdun, may contain the earliest example of the representation of UFO's in Europe. The author of the manuscript, the German Humanist Hartmann Schaeden, describes a strange sphere of fire sailing through the sky, following a straight path from south to east, then turning toward the setting sun. An illumination depicts a cigar-shaped form in a blue sky, surrounded by flames, flying over the green, hilly countryside. The date of the sighting seems to have been 1034.

A round shape with a rotating light or beam was described, accompanied by two fiery suns, in the sky of Erfurt in 1520. A "cloud cigar" was possibly seen in France on October 12, 1527 (11).

With the observations of Nuremberg (April 14, 1561) and Basel (August 7, 1566), of which drawings were made and are preserved in Zurich, we reach a period analyzed in detail by Professor Jung. Again, the Nuremberg sighting involves large tubes shown in inclined positions, from which spheres originate, generally three or four. Spheres and disks were seen and appeared to fight each other in aerial dances. The same behavior was described in Basel, where the objects were large black spheres.

After the year 1600 many good references will be found in the books of Charles Fort, in addition to the reviews by Wilkins. It should, however, be pointed out that the accounts Fort seems to prefer concern luminous objects in the sky associated with earthquakes and cataclysms on the ground, and that these should be considered with extreme caution. An article (quoted in [12]) has discussed this possible connection between seismic phenomena and atmospheric perturbations. We do not seem to be dealing here with reports of the same nature, although it is understandable that Fort could be puzzled by such descriptions, at a time when the nature of earthquakes was not at all understood.

On March 6, 1716, the astronomer Halley saw an object which illuminated the sky for more than two hours in such a way that he could read a printed text in the light of this object. The time of the observation was 7:00 P.M. After two hours, the brightness of the phenomenon was reactivated "as if new fuel had been cast on a fire" (5).

Interesting reports are also given by Wilkins for March 19, 1718 (Oxford), December 5, 1737, and especially December 16, 1742 (London). But this book cannot possibly elaborate upon all of these cases; it can only be suggested that extensive studies be made to determine whether these old documents refer to phenomena of the same general type as the modern reports, as this preliminary study would seem to indicate. We will have to discuss, for instance, the sighting of "luminous spheres coming out of a bright cylinder" in Augermanland, Sweden, in 1752, in connection with similar sightings in modern times.

In the latter part of the eighteenth century and during the nineteenth century observations of UFO's made by astronomers were quite common. The modern gospel that "astronomers have never seen UFO's" is untrue. Old astronomical chronicles are very interesting in this respect. Every important observatory has its own collection of UFO reports made by professional observers. On August 9, 1762, an object was seen in front of the sun by two different observatories in Switzerland. On June 17, 1777, Charles Messier observed a large number of dark spots (13). On August 18, 1783, at 9:25 P.M., at Windsor Castle, Tiberius Cavallo, a Fellow of the Royal Society, described a peculiar luminous phenomenon. In Greenwich, on August 30, 1783, there was seen a very strange object giving rise to eight satellites which disappeared slowly toward the southeast.

SCIENTIFIC REPORTS OF UFO'S IN THE NINETEENTH CENTURY

After the year 1800 the reports of objects in the sky become so numerous and well documented that one can lay aside the popular rumors and study only accounts published in the scientific press. They represent a large amount of data, and their reliability is excellent.

In (5), for example, we find this observation by John Staveley on August 10, 1809, at Hatton Garden, London, published by the *Journal of Natural History and Philosophy and Chemistry*:

> I saw many meteors moving around the edge of a black cloud from which lightnings flashed. They were like dazzling specks of light, dancing and traipsing thro' the clouds. One increased in size till it became of the brilliancy and magnitude of Venus, on a clear evening. But I could see no body in the light. It moved with great rapidity, and coasted the edge of the cloud. Then it became stationary, dimmed its splendour, and vanished. I saw these strange lights for minutes, not seconds. For at least an hour, these lights, so strange, and in innumerable points, played in and out of this black cloud. No lightning came from the clouds were these lights were playing. As the meteors increased in size, they seemed to descend....

Concerning observations at Embrun, France, on September 7, 1820, François Arago writes in the *Annales de chimie et de physique*:

Numerous observers have seen, during an eclipse of the moon, strange objects moving in straight lines. They were equally spaced and remained in line when they made turns. Their movements showed a military precision.

We cannot use Pastorff's observations in 1822 (two alleged disks in front of the sun); Webb's observations in 1823; the unknown object seen by various other astronomers in 1826, 1828, 1831 (the latter in Geneva by a Dr. Wartmann and his staff), by Pastorff again in 1834, 1836 and 1837, by Cocciatore in 1835 and De Vico in 1837, by De Cuppis in 1839, by Glaisher in 1844, by Capocci, of Capodimonte Observatory in Naples (May 11, 1845)—which is related in *Nature*—by Schmidt in 1847, Brown as well as Sidebotham in 1849, by Inglis in Switzerland the same year; these reports cannot be studied in detail before a complete analysis of all accounts published in this period is made under scientific control. I suggest that such a study would show that several interesting points in the history of astronomy have been forgotten.

It certainly is audacious to declare that astronomers are unaware of any reliable observation of a UFO when so many computations have been made by some of the founders of modern astronomy in an effort to interpret coherently their observations of strange objects, seen in front of the sun close to Mercury, as the movement of an intramercurial planet. Le Verrier spent a large part of his scientific life working on such observations (14).

We are not, however, claiming that the alleged "objects" were of artificial construction, as Fort tried to demonstrate, or that they even existed at all. We do not consider descriptions involving *point sources*,* even those of Le Verrier, as sufficiently reliable for us to base upon them assumptions of this magnitude. But we do think that such reports should be assimilated into the general body of observations involved in the UFO problem; those who claim that nothing out of the "ordinary" has ever been seen in the sky by professional astronomers should be reminded of the existence of these data. If we had no other reason to think that strange phenomena are being observed around this planet such indications would be of very limited significance; but in the light of modern observations of UFO's in the atmosphere or close to the ground these old sightings are of interest.

A very large number of accounts of objects crossing the disk of the sun or the moon were reported in the middle of the last century, but cigars, disks, spheres seen closer to the earth were also described; these observations carry more weight, for the possibility that the strange objects seen in front of the sun or moon were ordinary birds or optical defects has been underestimated. For our part, we tend to attach more significance to detailed descriptions of closer objects:

In July, 1868, at Capiago, Chile, an aerial construction emitting light and giving off engine noise was interpreted locally as a giant bird with shining eyes, covered with large scales clashing to produce a metallic noise (15 and 16).

On March 22, 1870, an observation was made aboard the "Lady of the Lake" in the Atlantic Ocean at 5°47′ N. and 27°52′ W. The object seen was a disk of light gray

---

* Luminous sources which appear as points of light.

color. What appeared to be the rear part was surrounded by a halo and a long tail emanated from the center. This UFO was viewed between 20° and 80° elevation for half an hour. It flew against the wind and Captain Banner made a drawing of it.

On August 29, 1871, the astronomer of Trouvelot of the Observatory of Meudon observed a number of very complex objects and a scene comparable to the sightings at Nuremberg and Basel mentioned earlier. Among the UFO's he saw was a spot that first seemed about to fall, then descended like a dead leaf or "like a disk falling through water" (17). This is a type of UFO behavior often described.

On April 24, 1874, a Professor Schafarick saw in Prague "an object of such a strange nature that I do not know what to say about it. It was of a blinding white and crossed slowly the face of the moon. It remained visible afterwards...." (18) On March 23, 1877, we find another case of generation of UFO's by a "cloud cigar" at Vence, France, where "fiery speres, extremely luminous, came out of a cloud of a peculiar shape and went slowly toward the north for one hour" (19).

On January 24, 1878, John Martin used the word "saucer" to describe his UFO. On May 15, 1879, at 9:40 P.M., from the "Vultur" in the Persian Gulf two giant luminous wheels were observed spinning and slowly descending. They were seen for thirty-five minutes, had an estimated diameter of forty meters and were about four diameters apart. Similar "giant wheels" were seen the year after, again in May and in the same part of the ocean, but by another ship, the steamer "Patna" (20).

On June 11, 1881, at 4:00 A.M., between Melbourne

and Sydney, the two sons of the Prince of Wales, one of them the future king of England, saw a strange celestial object similar to a fully illuminated ship. (See *The Cruise of the Bacchante*, written by the two princes.)

In the last twenty years of the nineteenth century we have found eighty-four observations of interest, thirty-four of which were published in full detail in the scientific press. These alone would justify a systematic investigation. The proportion of witnesses with a high scientific standing is greater in these reports than, for example, those of 1947. They give more detailed descriptions, and by the precision and clarity of the accounts we know that they were not the products of mass hallucination or emotion. Among them, we find our second detailed account of a "landing," the first one being the Ezekiel incident. On April 10, 1897, at Carlinville, Illinois, an object landed in the fields but took off as soon as the witnesses came close to it. Its shape was that of a cigar with a dome (21).

During the night of January 8, 1888, luminous bodies were seen flying through the sky in lines for one hour, according to the *Memoirs* of the Minor Brothers of Ragusa, Italy.

A large number of the reports published in the scientific press concern objects of the general aspect of a bolide, but following strange paths, sometimes at very low speeds. Although we would like to think of these phenomena as peculiar, but natural, astronomical objects, it is difficult to do so in many instances, and Flammarion designated them under the new name of "bradytes." A typical example is found in *L'Astronomie*, the bulletin of the French Astronomical Society, for the year 1883. The report reads:

The Legend of "Flying Saucers"

On February 23, 1883, at 7:00 P.M., as I was observing the sky in the direction of Orion, i.e., toward the south, I saw a luminous point appearing behind Orionis and sliding to Sirius after a double turn as shown on the attached figure. This was not, however, a period of the year with abundant shooting stars. This bolide had the luminosity of a fourth-magnitude star. Its maximum luminosity was estimated by me to correspond to the third magnitude when it was in A, and it had a minimum in B, where it remained stationary for a while. It continued toward Sirius with a brightness corresponding to the fourth magnitude. I lost sight of it as if it had gone behind Sirius and had not reappeared.

The year 1883 was rich in reports; no less than twelve have so far come to our attention. During the summer, at Segeberg, the children and the teacher of an elementary school saw two fiery spheres in the sky with the apparent diameter of the full moon; they traveled side by side, not very fast, on a north-south course. On August 12, in the morning, the astronomer José Bonilla, of Zacatecas Observatory in Mexico, saw and photographed "formations" of circular objects which crossed the disk of the sun on a west-east course. They were separated by regular intervals and were in groups of fifteen to twenty. The author of the report counted 283 such objects. Earlier in the year (April 15 and 25) similar formations had been seen over Marseilles, France. But the reliability of these observations can always be contested: How trained were the authors of these reports? How can we be sure that the alleged objects were not flocks of birds?

In 1885 we have six reports, five of them from *L'As-*

tronomie. Two of these reports are of special interest to us in our attempt to show that the UFO phenomenon is not of recent origin. The first report we will quote here is dated August 22. The time was 8:15 A.M. and the place, Saigon:

> M. Reveillere and Lieutenant Guiberteau have witnessed a very strange meterological phenomenon. Looking toward the south and having in front of them the Southern Cross, these scientists saw a magnificent red object, larger than the planet Venus and having a fairly large lateral motion. Both observers were without instruments. They saw the meteor appear suddenly in the south, and disappear in the southeast. Its elevation was between 15° and 20°. Its motion, practically level with the horizon, was not faster than that of a cloud in an average wind. It took seven or eight minutes for this meteor to travel on an arc equal to about one-third of the celestial sphere, and it disappeared behind a cloud of average opacity. One of the witnesses, M. Guiberteau, thought he saw the meteor above the cirrus clouds, when according to M. Reveillere the meteor lost some of its brightness because of the clouds, and this brightness varied according to the thickness of the cloud. It is difficult to decide what this meteor was.

The second report was made on November 1, 1885, at 9:30 P.M., at Adrianople, Turkey, and reads:

> M. Mavrogordato, of Constantinople, calls our attention to the following strange obsrvations which have been communicated to him.
> (1) On November 1, at 9:30 P.M., there was seen, west of Adrianople, an elongated object giving off a strong luminosity. It seemed to float in the air and its apparent disk was four or five times larger than the full moon. It traveled slowly and cast light on the whole

camp behind the station with a brightness about ten times greater than a large electric bulb.

(2) In the morning of November 2, at dawn, a very luminous flame, first bluish, then greenish, and moving at a height of five to six meters, made a series of turns around the ferryboat pier at Scutari. Its blinding luminosity lighted the street and flooded the inside of the houses with light. The meteor was visible for one minute and a half and finally fell into the sea. No noise was heard when the immersion took place.

Are these two meteors really bolides? One might doubt it. At any rate, these observations are quite interesting (*L'Astronomie*, 1885, and R. Veillith, [22]).

One may think of the phenomenon termed "ball lightning" in connection with the second incident. Ball lightning is a natural, but still largely mysterious, phenomenon. In our opinion, UFO files do contain several very good accounts of objects which fall into this category, and some of the best we have ever read are in the files of the Aerial Phenomena Group of the U.S. Air Force in Dayton, Ohio. It is certainly unfortunate that no physicist with interest in this field has ever studied these reports.* Such an investigation would also reveal that many sightings have been "explained away" as ball lightnings because no intelligent answer could be found, and the specialist would be surprised at some of the reports placed in this category. We have here an old example of the same attitude, from *L'Astronomie* again, dated November 12, 1887, and flatly called "ball lightning":

---

* As a courtesy, several professional scientists, including this writer, have received permission from the interested authorities to study the nonclassified reports. Physicists concerned with the interpretation of ball lightnings could probably obtain information on specific cases through similar channels.

In the North Atlantic Ocean a new case of ball lightning, one of those so strange and still so inexplicable effects, has been observed. On November 12, 1887, at midnight, near Cape Race, a huge ball of fire appeared, *slowly emerging from the ocean* to an altitude of sixteen to seventeen meters. This sphere started moving against the wind and stopped close to the ship from which it was observed. Then it rushed away in the sky and disappeared in the southeast. The whole observation *had lasted five minutes*. [Italics mine—Author.]

In 1893 several observations of disks and "wheels" at sea were made, mainly between Japan and China. In the United States, on December 20, 1893, another huge "wheel" giving off noise appeared; it remained motionless for fifteen minutes before leaving. In Oxford, England, on August 31, 1895, at 8:00 P.M., a disk was seen rising above some trees and disappearing in the east (Dr. J. A. H. Murray) (192). In Chicago, on April 2, 1897, at 2:00 A.M., amazed citizens clambered to the top of a skyscraper to observe an enormous flying object which seemed to have fins at each end and a beacon. On the tenth of the same month the "landing" in Carlinville, Illinois, which we mentioned earlier, was reported. On the fifteenth an object in the shape of a cigar was seen at Benton, Texas, and several other places. It cruised toward the southeast, and was described as "a magnificent sight." The Chicago object, or a similar one, was observed on April 19, at 9:00 P.M., at Sisterville, West Virginia, with flashing colored lights.

But Le Roy, Kansas, is the place we will have to remember. "Last Monday night, about 10:30," said Alexander Hamilton, we were awakened by a noise among the cattle. I arose, thinking that perhaps my bulldog was performing some of his pranks, but upon going to the door saw to my utter astonishment an airship slowly descending upon my cow lot, about forty rods from the house.

Calling my tenant, Gid Heslip, and my son Wall, we seized some axes and ran to the corral. Meanwhile, the ship had been gently descending until it was not more than thirty feet above the ground, and we came within fifty yards of it.

It consisted of a great cigar-shaped portion, possibly three hundred feet long, with a carriage underneath. The carriage was made of glass or some other transparent substance alternating with a narrow strip of some material. It was brilliantly lighted within and everything was plainly visible—it was occupied by six of the strangest beings I ever saw. They were jabbering together, but we could not understand a word they said.

Every part of the vessel which was not transparent was of a dark reddish color. We stood mute with wonder and fright, when some noise attracted their attention and they turned a light directly upon us. Immediately on catching sight of us they turned on some unknown power, and a great turbine wheel, about thirty feet in diameter, which was slowly revolving below the craft began to buzz and the vessel rose lightly as a bird. When about three hundred feet above us it seemed to pause and hover directly over a two-year-old heifer, which was bawling and jumping, apparently fast in the fence. Going to her, we found a cable about a half-inch in thickness made of some red material, fastened in a slip knot around her neck, one end passing up to the vessel, and the heifer tangled in the wire fence. We tried to get it off but could not, so we cut the wire loose and stood in amazement to see the ship, heifer and all, rise slowly, disappearing in the northwest.

We went home, but I was so frightened I could not

sleep. Rising early Tuesday, I started out by horse, hoping to find some trace of my cow. This I failed to do, but coming back in the evening found that Link Thomas, about three or four miles west of Le Roy, had found the hide, legs and head in his field that day. He, thinking someone had butchered a stolen beast, had brought the hide to town for identification, but was greatly mystified in not being able to find any tracks in the soft ground. After identifying the hide by my brand, I went home. But every time I would drop to sleep I would see the cursed thing, with its big lights and hideous people. I don't know whether they are devils or angels, or what; but we all saw them, and my whole family saw the ship, and I don't want any more to do with them.

Hamilton has long been a resident of Kansas and is known all over Woodson, Allen, Coffey and Anderson counties. He was a member of the House of Representatives. He staked his sacred honor upon the truth of his story.

An affidavit follows:

As there are now, always have been and always will be skeptics and unbelievers whenever the truth of anything bordering the improbable is presented, and knowing that some ignorant or suspicious people will doubt the truthfulness of the above statement, now, therefore, we, the undersigned, do hereby make the following affidavit:

That we have known Alexander Hamilton for one to thirty years, and that for the truth and veracity we have never heard his word questioned, and that we do verily believe his statement to be true and correct.

Signed: E. W. Wharton, State Oil Inspector
M. E. Hunt, Sheriff
W. Lauber, Deputy Sheriff

H. H. Winter, Banker
H. S. Johnson, Pharmacist
J. H. Stitcher, ATtorney
Alexander Stewart, Justice of the Peace
F. W. Butler, Druggist
James W. Martin, Registrar of Deeds
and H. C. Rollins, Postmaster

Subscribed and sworn before me this 21st day of April, 1897 (45).

On April 25, 1898, at 9:32 P.M., in Belgrade, a strange meteor was observed which, according to J. Michailovitch, a professor at Belgrade Observatory, remained motionless in the sky for more than six minutes. In Lille, France, a red object was seen motionless for ten minutes on September 4, 1898, then left a few sparks and went away.

OBSERVATIONS MADE BETWEEN 1900 AND 1946

One hundred and seven reports of unidentified flying objects seen in the air, on the ocean or on the ground are known to us for this period. Again, a number of them come from the scientific press. Again, we want to stress the fact that these "old" reports do not lack any of the fantastic characteristics of recent observations, although they were made under very different conditions. We will find extraordinary descriptions, including vertical cigars, landings, kidnappings and even a frightful report of a being eight feet tall who is said to have landed on January 22, 1922! More seriously, the description made at Fatima, Portugal, of a silvery disk which flew through the sky, was seen by seventy thousand witnesses and was photographed as it maneuvered, deserves a place in our résumé of the "flying saucer" *legend* (23, 24, 180).

But we are not free to comment on such incidents; hypotheses are inexpensive, easy to make. One should refrain from offering hypotheses when one is not able to provide at the same time a reliable way of checking them and an objective basis for more advanced investigations. We wish, therefore, to limit ourselves to those reports which can be verified by the investigator; we will comment on them as little as possible in order to keep these data as free from distortion as we can.

Another incident of this period, the explosion in the Siberian Taiga, on June 30, 1908, of some enormous object of an unknown nature, is worthy of mention. According to the *London Daily Express* of May 4, 1959:

> The inhabitants of the Jenissei district of Siberia saw a gigantic ball of fire. Immediately afterwards there was a colossal explosion which devasted a forest area of seventy miles in diameter. The shock waves were registered in England. Scientists looked in vain for traces of meteorite and a crater. Curiously, in the centre of the devastated region only the tops of trees had been snapped off.

The *Sydney Sun*, Australia, quoting from the official Czech trade-union newspaper, *Prace*, stated that the Russian scientist Kazantsev had written in a book called *A Guest from the Universe* that people living near the explosion died of a then-unknown illness with the same symptoms as exposure to atomic radiation and that the explosion had its biggest impact at some distance from its center, exactly like an atomic explosion.

The Legend of "Flying Saucers"

According to an article in (26), a Soviet expedition "discovered a shallow depression about two miles wide in the surface of the earth.... Within the depression were two hundred craters, thirty to one hundred and fifty feet wide and twelve feet deep." The article continues:

> From collected data, Zolotov calculated that the ballistic wave was travelling at a velocity of 1.86 miles per second. Zolotov concludes that so slight an amount of kinetic energy could not have caused the destruction in Tunguska—the explosion must have been the result of the internal chemical or nuclear energy of the body.
>
> Trees between ten and eleven miles from the center of the depression had caught fire and burned as a result of light radiation. Since a living tree can ignite only when sixty to one hundred calories of light energy fall on each square centimeter of tree, Zololov calculated the radiant energy of the explosion of 15^{23}s ergs. At 37 miles from the epicenter, the radiant energy approximated 11^{23} ergs.... These estimates indicated that the radiant energy of the explosion, according to Zolotov, "comprised several tens of percent of the total energy." Additional close correlations among different energy levels of the explosion eliminated the possibility that the blasts was chemical in nature. From further comparison of these energy levels the Russians deduced the temperature of the nuclear explosion at "several tens of millions of degrees."
>
> Zolotov also states: "... one observes an alternation of burned and unburned parts of the area and also an alternation of burned and unburned branches at the top of the same, completely burned tree." He further adds that the combustion of the trees was caused by light radiation and only in those places which were not in the shade of leaves and branches, that is, it was a radiant burn. Such a phenomenon, he points out, is characteristic of only nuclear explosions.

Zolotov further proposes that the trajectory of the Tunguska object was from the southwest toward the northeast. Rather than a regular circle of destruction, the Tunguska area emerges as an elongated area at an angle from the trajectory. The effect of the explosion was obviously not the same in all directions. The asymmetrical shape of the destroyed area has led Zolotov to believe that explosion was somehow contained in an envelope of some other nonexplosive substance.

This incident will be found described in many books on the subject of UFO's, where it is often interpreted as the result of the breakdown of the propulsion system of a "spaceship." Some writers have even suggested that the ship could have been disintegrated by the crew itself to prevent physical samples from falling into the hands of our scientists. It is impossible to conclude that sufficient evidence exists to substantiate this theory. The fact remains, however, that a very extraordinary body collided with our planet in June of 1908 (191).

Incidents such as the Taiga explosion have been plentifully commented upon and are well known. We prefer to focus here upon less known, but equally important, accounts.

On October 28, 1902, at 3:05 A.M., an object was seen by the second officer and two other witnesses aboard the "Fort Salisbury" at 5°31′ S. and 4°42′ W. It was a huge, illuminated object, which sank and disappeared. No ship was reported missing in this part of the ocean. On February 24, 1904, in the Atlantic Ocean, the U.S.S. "Supply" saw three red spheres larger than the sun remain below the clouds for a while, then ascend and disappear. On March 29, 1905, at 10:00 P.M., a vertical luminous tube "like a hot, red-orange iron rod" was reported at Cardiff, Wales. A more humorous object, looking like "a flying pig," was seen at Llangollen, Wales, on September 2 of the same year. A black object with short wings, apparently ten feet long, it seemed to have four legs (27). In December of the same year an object with a beacon was seen in several cities in Massachusetts (including Worcester and Boston). It was a long object with red lights, cruising at a variable speed. There seems to have been a "wave" of reports in May, 1909, in Great Britain; it was perhaps the first wave reported as such. The *Weekly Dispatch* of May 23, 1909, published a list of twenty-two towns "visited" before that period. A light was again seen at Sanford twenty minutes after a similar "light" had been seen in the sky at Southend on May 9, 1909, at 11:00 P.M. We have, of course, no way of determining if the two sightings were of the same "object."

Fort says that

> upon the night of March 23, 1909, at 5.10 o'clock in the morning, two constables, in different parts of the city of Peterborough, had reported having seen an object, carrying a light, moving over the city, with sounds like the sound of a motor. In the *Peterborough Advertiser*, March 27, is published an interview with one of the constables, who described "an object, somewhat oblong and narrow in shape, carrying a powerful light."

The spring of 1909 also yields the first twentieth-century report of "landing," and a description of the operators near their craft. The encounter is said to have taken place on May 18 at 11:00 P.M. at Caerphilly, Wales. The witness, a Mr. Lethbridge, said he had been walking along a road when he saw a large cylindrical object, alongside of which were two men wearing fur coats, who spoke in an excited voice when they saw the witness. Immediately afterward they took off and the object disappeared. This incident is reported in the *Daily Mail* of May 20, 1909, and is discussed by Fort in his book *New Lands* (21). According to Fort himself, a hoax is very probable.

The next month, on June 3, 1909, at 3:00 A.M., men on the Danish steamer "Bintang," cruising in the Malacca Strait, saw a brilliantly lighted wheel under the surface of the ocean. This peculiar object came to the surface and was seen spinning. On the sixteenth of the same month, we find in *L'Astronomie* (22, 28) the following article:

> M. Beljonne, at Phu-Lien Observatory, Tonkin, sends us peculiar bolide observations. The first one, especially remarkable, was made at Dong Hoi, Annam, by M. Delingette, Inspector in the Civil Guard, head of the meteorological station.
>
> At Dong Hoi, on June 16 at 4:10 A.M., a bolide of an elongated shape, truncated at both ends, flew over the city on a west-east course, casting a great luminosity. The witnesses—Hoang Nic, of Dong Hoi; Tran Ninh, of Sa-Dong-Danh; Quyen, of Dong-Duong-Hoi; and Danh Lui, of the same village—who were fishing at sea, reported that the phenomenon lasted from eight to ten minutes, between the time the object appeared and the time it fell into the sea, at about six kilometers from shore.

In the south of the China Sea, on August 12, 1910, at midnight, a bright wheel spining close to the surface was seen from the Dutch ship "Valentijn." At Porto Principal, Peru, in January of 1912, an "aerial ship" was reported at tree height. The same month, in the U.S., a Dr. Harris saw a very large, intensely black object in front of the moon.

Another "wave" seems to have occurred in Great Britain in 1913. The first observation of that year was made on the morning of January 4, 1913, at Dover, England: An unknown flying object was seen moving toward the sea. On January 17 at Cardiff a huge flying object which left a smoke trail was observed. The witnesses were Captain Lindsay, chief constable, and another person. The *London Standard* of January 31 published a list of towns "visited" by UFO's. Among them were Cardiff, Newport and Neath. The wave apparently lasted three weeks.

On February 9 of the same year, between Canada and the Bermudas, five or six groups of flying objects were sighted and were compared, by Professor Chant of Toronto, to an aerial fleet maneuvering. Thirty to thirty-two objects composed this "fleet" (29). The following day, dark objects were seen in Toronto in the afternoon, flying in three groups from west to east, and later returning in disorder. They were too distant for the observers to determine their nature, "but they were not clouds or birds or smoke."

On August 5, 1927, at 9:30 A.M., in Mongolia, Nicolas Roerich and his caravan were watching the flight of an eagle when they observed a huge elongated object speeding through the sky: "We all saw, in a direction from north to south, something big and shiny reflecting the sun, like a huge oval moving at great speed. Crossing our camp, this thing changed in its direction from south to southwest. And we saw how it disappeared in the intense blue sky. We even had time to take our field glasses and saw quite distinctly an oval form with shiny surface, one side of which was brilliant from the sun" (5,191; the date in [5] is probably incorrect). In 1921 in Marseilles the first report of a UFO "kidnapping" known in modern times was made. Unfortunately, we do not know the exact reference of this information, found in the G. Quincy catalogue (11) without any indication of source. We will, however, obviously not consider this report very seriously.

The period of 1915–1925, if not very rich in respect to the number of reports (only eleven observations are known), is characterized by fantastic events. The sighting at Fatima in 1917 (discussed in detail in Chapter 6) is an example; another is this account of an observation made on February 22, 1922, at 5:00 A.M. in Hubbell, Nebraska: A hunter, William C. Lamb, was following mysterious traces when he heard a crackling noise followed by a high-pitched sound and realized that a circular object was flying above his head, masking the stars. The witness allegedly hid behind a tree and saw this object, now brilliantly lighted, land behind a depression. Where he thus lost sight of the disk, he saw a magnificent flying creature that landed like an aircraft and left traces in the snow. It was at least eight feet tall; it came toward the tree where Lamb was hiding, passed by and disappeared. Lamb followed the traces for five miles, then gave up the chase (30).

In 1931, a Mr. Chichester, who was flying above the Tasman Sea from New South Wales to New Zealand in his private plane, saw an object resembling a silver pearl flashing like a bright beacon and going very fast, then losing speed, accelerating again and vanishing. In October, 1935, at Addis Ababa, Ethiopa, a disk was seen motionless in the sky by numerous witnesses, among whom was the French student of Africa, Pierre Ichac. In 1941, a team of mountaineers searching for three missing Alpinists in Switzerland are said to have found traces tending to show that the three men had stopped where some flying object had landed, since three holes in a triangle of thirteen meters were seen in the snow, and their footprints did not continue. The reliability of such a report, of course, is nil. More significant is the observation made on February 26, 1942, aboard the "Tromp," of the Royal Netherlands Navy (31): A large aluminum disk came toward the ship at a very high speed, circled it and left. During the war, many luminous spheres were seen by bomber pilots in Germany and in the whole of western Europe, Scandinavia, Greece and Turkey. Lieutenant E. Schluter, of the 415th U.S. Night Fighter Squadron, met eight to ten balls of red fire flying at a high speed twenty miles north of Strasbourg, France, on November 23, 1944. Lieutenants Henry Giblin and Walter Cleary saw a huge fiery object above their plane on November 27, 1944, at Speyer, Germany. In December, 1944, a Major Leet, a bomber pilot, watched a disk follow the plane's maneuvers at Klagenfurt, Austria, at night. Lieutenants David McFalls and Edward Baker, flying over Haguenau, France, on December 22, 1944, at 6:00 P.M., saw two very bright lights approaching them from the ground. These lights remained behind the aircraft; they appeared to be "under perfect control." But observations of this type are not very conclusive; enormous orange lights can be caused by reflections or even by phenomena of atmospheric distortion, as Dr. Menzel has pointed out. More difficult to interpret in terms of natural phenomena are sightings such as the one made in Kingsport, Tennessee, in 1945 by Charles Hamlet and Edward Cate, who saw an object "in the shape of a chimney." It was a "wonderful" color, and crossed the sky at high speed.

The lights seen at night by pilots during the war have been called "foo-fighters." As we have seen, they were merely balls of light, red or orange, without details or structure. They do not seem to have been detected on radar. Seen at night or during the day, they followed the planes even into the clouds. But these reports have to be considered with caution, for the behavior of the objects is very often that of a distorted image of the aircraft itself or a reflection of some ground object. The wartime conditions, the birth of a new technology involving rockets, electronic guidance and the ever-present fear of "secret weapons" make the sightings of that period difficult to analyze.

After World War II comes a period of UFO history on which we have a formidable amount of data. It seems unrealistic to try to write a single book about them: an encyclopedia would almost be required. We will, however, attempt to organize these data and to show why we should be concerned with the existence of this phenomenon. Before we do, we will briefly review the older reports on a statistical basis.

STATISTICAL ASPECTS OF UFO HISTORY BEFORE THE MODERN PERIOD

If we try to sum up the information found in old reports and to draw general conclusions from them, we could do so along the following lines:

(1) In modern and even in historical times, reports of observations have been made by scientists as well as by the general public concerning flying disks in the sky, objects seen at sea and on the ground. Only in recent times, how-

ever, has the idea of space travel been associated with this type of vision; this is one of the reasons that old reports, interpreted at the time in very different contexts, are not generally recognized as manifestations of the same phenomenon.

(2) Careful study of the best reports made before this century tends to show that:

a) The objects described are similar in appearance to what has been observed since May, 1946.

b) Public emotion over these incidents and the scientific reaction to them since 1946 is an exact duplication of the popular fears of "signs in the sky" in the Middle Ages and of scientific statements made during the eighteenth and nineteenth centuries concerning such unusual events.

(3) Apart from the fact that one country (the United States) has not undertaken official investigation of the modern sightings, and that we tend today to interpret in a technological context (space travel) what was interpreted in a religious context (signs of God's wishes or decisions) in older times, the behavior of the phenomenon appears extremely similar in early and recent reports.

(4) No massive accumulation of observations seems to have occurred before May, 1946, that could be compared with the planetwide "waves" we have experienced since then. However, local "peaks" of observations can be detected when a sufficient amount of data is gathered; these have definitely been recognized as waves by the local populations, at least in 1909 and 1913, when newspapers published lists of reports and fragmentary statistics.

(5) These peaks do not appear to follow a definite, continuous pattern as modern waves do. They are separated by intervals of several years, but we are unable to determine if

the gaps between the main periods of activity are due to a lack of information and bad communication between different parts of the world in those days, or to some real discontinuity in whatever phenomenon underlies the UFO behavior.

(6) The main periods of activity we can delineate on the basis of our present data are:

a) a possible wave in the last six months of 1881, at its peak in December (Spain to Scotland);

b) a definite wave in the last six months of 1883, with observations in Mexico, Puerto Rico, Chile, the U.S. and Great Britain;

c) a possible wave in the last six months of 1885, with significant observations in France, the Middle East and the Far East. These three periods are separated by gaps of total inactivity: not one significant report between December, 1881, and November, 1882; only one in 1882 and one in the first six months of 1883; no significant report during the first six months of 1884; only two in the last six months of that year; and two again in the first six months of 1885. We are unable to find any recognizable pattern in the frequency distribution of UFO reports until 1897.

d) A peak was reached in 1897 over the U.S. Middle West, from Chicago to Kansas City, with reports in Saint Louis and in Ohio, and even some in Texas, Colorado and West Virginia. Then we find the first landing of a classical "flying saucer" with dome, in Carlinville, Illinois—all this in one month, April, 1897, which would deserve attention if for no other case than that of a the butchered cow in Le Roy, Kansas.

e) There is an apparent concentration of sightings in the spring of 1905 and another one in December. It is difficult, however, to conclude that a wave has taken place.

f) We have a recognized wave in May, 1909, over Wales.

g) We have another recognized wave in January–February, 1913, over Great Britain, with a possible extension into Canada.

(7) Between 1914 and 1946 the phenomenon had not completely disappeared, but no pattern can be established, at least from our data, and it seems difficult to believe that any large series of observations could have passed unnoticed; both the efficiency of communications systems and the growing popular interest in science, as well as the concern for aerial flight and the development of aircraft and balloon technology, were such that *all conditions were present for UFO waves to develop fully if they had been mere consequences of misinterpretation, hallucination and newspapers' interest in fantastic stories*. For thirty-two years, however, the sky remained empty of unknown objects. The situation was to change suddenly in the spring of 1946, when the Scandinavian wave developed, as we will see in Chapter 3.

(8) We feel that our documents for the period between 1870 and 1914 are sufficient to justify an attempt to correlate UFO activity with the oppositions of Mars. Correlation of these limited data has so far given negative results, as shown in the following table:

Date of peak (UFO waves)	Closest opposition of Mars	Average difference in months
Dec. 1881	Dec. 1881	0
summer-fall 1883	Feb. 1884	+4

Date of peak (UFO waves)	Closest opposition of Mars	Average difference in months
summer-fall 1885	Mar. 1886	+5
Apr. 1897	Dec. 1896	−4
1905	May 1905	
May 1909	Sept. 1909	+4
Jan.–Feb. 1913	Jan. 1914	+12

One should use extreme caution in interpreting, in any direction, the existence or absence of correlations such as these. It may, or may not, be interesting to remark here that *the "dead" period of UFO activity has been one of the richest in science-fiction stories of all kinds*, and has seen the growing interest of the motion-picture industry in fantastic and "horror" tales which might have resulted in an increasing number of hoaxes and hallucinations, and even in UFO waves, if the "psychological" theory of UFO's were correct. As early as 1916, Otto Ripert's film *Homonculus* was about the creation of an artificial man by a mad scientist. In 1914 and 1920 the German industry produced two films on the subject of the "Golem" (Paul Wegener and Henrik Galeen). In 1924 the film *Orlac's Hands* was made, after a novel by Maurice Renard. In 1926 Fritz Lang created *Metropolis*, and we should not forget that 1920 saw the introduction of the word "robot," with a play by Karel Capek, *Rossum's Universal Robots* (*R.U.R.*). In 1928, Fritz Lang did *The Woman in the Moon* (*Die Frau im Mond*). The first "trip to the moon" had been made by the French pioneer Melies in 1902 (32), and the celebrated series of Frankenstein and John Carter of Mars were created during this period. If UFO sightings are motivated by some mechanism through which the public can release hidden fears and satisfy a need for fantastic or horrifying tales, why did "saucer waves" not coincide with such science-fiction feats as the Orson Welles radio adaptation of *The War of the Worlds* in 1938 or with the happy time of the great comics and their motion-picture versions, such as Flash Gordon (Frederick Stephani, 1936) or *Flash Gordon's Trip to Mars* (1937)?

In our opinion, the theory that the public generates and propagates UFO rumors as a way of releasing psychological tensions is denied by the absence of correlation between important periods of interest in science fiction and peaks of UFO activity.

On the other hand, our analysis of modern reports will show that the idea that individuals "see flying saucers" when they are so motivated or looking for fantastic experiences is denied by the fact that thousands of Scandinavians saw and reported flying disks, flying cigars and even objects on the ground in 1946, and that no one among them suggested that these objects could be of interplanetary origin. We think this tends to prove that the birth, growth and expansion of a UFO wave is an objective phenomenon independent of the conscious or unconscious will of the witnesses, and their reactions to it. Furthermore, we will now see that the permanence of the myth of the "signs in the sky" is even more remarkable when placed within the context of the changing conceptions of life in the universe.

CHAPTER TWO

PROBABILITY OF CONTACT WITH SUPERIOR GALACTIC COMMUNITIES

A PHILOSOPHICAL ISSUE

In recent years there has been a strong reactivation of interest in the question of whether life and intelligence are found throughout the universe. Because of our newly acquired potential for space exploration it becomes increasingly important to evaluate the possibility that natural processes have already brought about the development of intelligent races elsewhere in the universe, including races capable of traveling through space owing to a technology equal or superior to ours. Such races, because of their possible technological superiority to us, might even represent a threat, if not to our existence on this planet (to which we may suppose we should be best adapted), at least to our expeditions to the various worlds of our solar system within the next decades. It is, therefore, important to take a new scientific look at the problem of life in the universe; we will present a brief summary of existing data and considerations about the probability that intelligent races able to communicate with us or to visit our planet do exist.

Probability of Contact with Superior Galactic Communities

The ancient Greek philosophers in the sixth century B.C. considered life to be a property of matter and taught that the world had always been alive. Oparin and Fesenkov (33) remark that that "the panspermic theory" (formulated by Anaxagoras and maintaining that invisible "ethereal germs of life" were dispersed throughout the world, giving rise to all living creatures including man) was further developed by Roman philosophers:

> The doctrine was later adopted by early Christianity and formed part of the teaching of the fathers of the Church. For example, so authoritative a theologian as Saint Augustine taught that the world was filled with hidden germs of life, the invisible, mysterious seeds (*occulta gemina*) of a spiritual principle, which generated the various living creatures from earth, air and water.

The Ptolemaic system postulated that the earth, with its privileged position in the center of the universe, was the only world supporting life. This theory prevailed during the Middle Ages, but the Copernican system, relegating earth to a position equal to that of the other planets revolving around the sun, suggested the possibility that life might have developed on other worlds similar to ours.

Giordano Bruno was the first to express this theory plainly: "There are innumerable suns and innumerable earths, which revolve around their suns, as our seven planets revolve around our sun. . . . These worlds are inhabited by living creatures." After a long incarceration, he died in an *auto-da-fé* in 1600 for this heresy. But the struggle he had initiated continued, and after the Copernican system had gained full recognition Bernard de Fontenelle could publish, in 1686, a book affirming that life existed throughout the universe.

During the eighteenth and nineteenth centuries, due to the lack of observational data, the question remained within the limits of philosophical discussions of the type originated by Fontenelle and little progress was made. The problem of life on other worlds, however, was studied in many of the popular books on astronomy, occasionally giving rise to theories of a perfectly fanciful character. Already Fontenelle had described very amazing inhabitants on the soil of other planets; thus, Mercurians "must be fools because of their excessive vivacity," while on Saturn "the inhabitants are so dull that it takes them a whole day to comprehend and answer a question." The striking contrast between such extrapolations, designed to please an elegant and superficial public, and the serious technical and physical discussions which illustrated the development of the scientific spirit adds a humorous touch to such treatises as the *Lettres sur l' Astronomie* by Albert de Montemont, where we read, concerning the inhabitants of comets:

> We have now to examine the question of the inhabitants that live, according to what is said, on the surface of comets. Without doubt, if they exist, they have been created especially for them. Thus, we can imagine that in order to keep about the same temperature, they reduce their atmosphere when they come close to the sun and that when this atmosphere is later expanded, it surrounds them like a coat to protect them against the rigorous cold, when they go away from the start that vivifies them (46).

However, when he comes to consider the sun, Montemont writes:

> According to Herschel, it is a solid body, surrounded by an atmosphere of fiery clouds that would let us see the dark nucleus when they open slightly. This famous astronomer does not hesitate to believe it is inhabited. But, as remarked by M. Voiron, what organized living beings can we imagine in the midst of this eternal blaze?

Later, in a note, this same writer adds that, according to Herschel, there is a second layer of clouds around the sun that protects the dark globe of the nucleus from the heat and luminosity emitted by the upper layer. "Finally he allowed himself to conclude that the dark globe of the sun could be inhabited by beings similar to ourselves.... But here Herschel's views are purely hypothetical and, as such, do not deserve our attention." And he remarks:

> This idea that the sun is inhabitable seems so extravagant at first sight that in England, in a lawsuit where a man named Eliott was tried for attempted murder of a man named Boydell, the Court was told that M. Eliott had written a letter to the Royal Society of London where he maintained that the sun could be inhabited, this in order to substantiate the idea that M. Eliott was insane. This fact surprised the jury very much, and contributed greatly to the verdict, that was that the crime was understandable, given the state of insanity of the accused (46).

So much for the inhabitants of the sun.
As remarked in (33),

in the nineteenth century and even in the beginning of our own, science had very little factual information concerning the physical nature of the planets and the conditions required for the origination and existence of life. This gave rise to all sorts of speculative and very far-reaching inferences frequently based on very doubtful, uncritically accepted and casual observations.

Such were the assertions by Lowell, tending to present the Martian "canals" as engineering structures designed for the transportation of water from the polar caps to the equator of the planet; although the existence of dark spots selectively appearing in lines on the Martian surface is an observational fact, there is a very large step between the observation of such phenomena and their interpretation as consequences of the activity of intelligent beings, a theory that asks more questions than it solves. We will certainly have to be very careful not to make the same mistake in our interpretation of most UFO reports. There seems to be a natural tendency among some groups to attribute to some sort of intelligence any natural phenomenon they are not yet able to understand. An opposite inclination is found among people who will attribute everything to illusion and the imagination of the observer. These two attitudes simply illustrate once more the Principle of the Least Effort: It is less expensive and much easier to accept any phenomenon we do not understand as either the indication of some unknown, "occult" power, such as a divine or intelligent manifestation, or as a pure hallucination than to undertake objective research. Physics is still full of concepts and theories whose formulation owes much to the early days of science when the first approach was commonly accepted.

It seems surprising that a man like Pickering could have

seriously believed that the moon was inhabited by insects which provoked the observed modifications of some lunar features by their migrations, when one could think of several physical causes explaining the facts.

Some scientists, even today, consider life a primary attribute of matter, as the early Greek philosophers did, and consequently no conditions, even those on the surface of the stars, should exclude its possibility; but this reasoning certainly lacks scientific grounds. The problem we will be considering here is restricted to the probability of the origination of life on planets and their satellites, either in our solar system or in other planetary systems in our part of the galaxy. We will do so under the hypothesis stated by Sagan:

> The production of self-replicating molecular systems is a forced process which is bound to occur because of the physics and chemistry of primitive planetary environments. Such self-replicating systems, situated in a medium filled with replicating precursors, satisfy all the requirements for natural selection and biological evolution (7).

We will, however, work under a different conception of possible intellectual differences between intelligent forms of life; while Sagan seems to have considered only one level of intellectual capacity, we will try to broaden this picture. We will review astronomical evidence of conditions existing in our solar system and try to evaluate the probability of visitation by space travelers presenting the same general type of intelligence we possess, and coming from worlds comparable to ours. For, as unreasonable as it seems to build models of universal intelligence in which only our type of intellect is allowed to prosper, it would be perfectly unjustified to generalize beyond the data of biology and make assumptions concerning intelligence on an infinite scale.

LIFE IN THE SOLAR SYSTEM

In (47) Richardson remarks that "scientists today are exceedingly closemouthed when it comes to admitting the existence of living organisms on other planets." But such an attitude is not based entirely, as some people seem to think, on lack of imagination or pure stubbornness. All scientific evidence seems to point against the idea of indigenous life on the moon in historical times, and the camouflage of a hypothetical "base" on the moon by space travelers would be a very impractical enterprise, even on the part of the moon we cannot see from the earth. The question of the possible uses of such a base founded on the moon by "visitors" (a hypothesis suggested by Sagan) will be discussed later; in our opinion, such a solution would not be optimum for explorers endeavoring to keep our civilization under surveillance without being detected.

Mercury, on one hand, and the planets outside the Asteroid Belt, like Jupiter and Saturn, are not likely to have been conductive to the development of any sort of life. We will not, however, presume that there are sufficient grounds at the present time for us to extend this statement to the satellites of these planets, about which very little is known. For example, Titan (Saturn's sixth satellite), with a diameter of 5,000 kilometers, or 1.5 that of the moon, and a mass double that of our satellite, is likely to have an atmosphere; the possibility, however small, of finding some sort of life on such satellites, even at very low temperatures, cannot be rejected a priori.

Mars and Venus, so appealing to man's imagination, remain today the two main subjects of argument among astronomers and biologists. Very little, however, can be said about conditions on Venus. The remarkable performance of Mariner II has not solved the many difficult questions concerning that planet, which is surrounded by a very dense atmosphere. Never has the soil of Venus been observed, and the discussion of the nature and properties of the elements of its atmosphere is an open field, the subject of many controversies and discoveries to come.

Mars is still very much a mystery. At the closest oppositions, it can be seen with the apparent diameter of a small crater on the moon, and it seems obvious that only space exploration, using automatic probes equipped with special cameras, provides a means of solving the problems posed by that planet to the physicist and the biologist (63). The soil of Mars, however, is observable. Permanent and variable configurations as well as clouds and polar caps covered with hoarfrost can be recognized and mapped. Agreement seems to have been reached concerning the probable density and composition of its atmosphere. Polarimetric studies have provided specialists with reasonable estimates of the chemical nature of the light, red, permanent areas. But the dark, changing areas, often said to have been caused by vegetation or to have allowed its development, are still very much a subject of argument. According to Lederberg and Sagan (48),

... some terrestrial microorganisms survive in purported simulations of the average Martian environment (49, 50). Most would fare poorly, and whether any can proliferate in an accurately simulated environment is less clear. In any event, how well the Martian organisms have learned to cope with the same constraints remains to be seen.

But so little is really known about the existing local physical conditions, which may differ considerably from those predicted by our present "models," that no simple answer can be given to any question about the path life could have followed on that planet.

Meteorites are the only physical evidence we possess on which research of living organisms such as germs or microbes of extraterrestrial origin might be attempted in the laboratory. According to a report by C. Meunir, Pasteur tried to extract viable bacteria from meteorites, but obtained negative results. In 1932, C. Lipman published a report in which he stated that he had obtained microbes identical to the ordinary earthly bacteria, but it seems probable that he had been unable to prevent the penetration of earthly bacteria into his samples during the analysis. By 1834, however, Berzelius had analyzed the Alais meteorite and had found that it contained carbonaceous material.

In 1961 a variety of complex hydrocarbons were found in a meteorite of the same type (Orgueil). The authors of this discovery (B. Nagy, D. Hennessy and W. Meinschein) wrote that "the mass-spectrometric analyses reveal that hydrocarbons in the Orgueil meteorite resemble in many important aspects the hydrocarbons in the products of living beings and sediments on earth. Based on these preliminary studies, the composition of the hydrocarbons in the Orgueil meteorite provides evidence for biogenic activity." According to Mason (51), "the quantities of hydrocarbons in the meteorite indicate that there can be no reasonable doubt that they were present when it entered the earth's atmosphere and are not the result of terrestrial contamination. They are truly extraterrestrial in origin."

Considerable discussion arose on this point when researchers, including Edward Anders of the University of Chicago, pointed out that the compounds may have been formed in nonbiological reactions catalyzed by high-energy radiation in space. But in November, 1961, G. Claus and B. Nagy announced the discovery of "microscopic-sized particles, resembling fossil algae, in relatively large quantities within the Orgueil and Ivuna carbonaceous meteorites." If it can be proved that these particules are not terrestrial contaminants or crystals of organic or inorganic compounds, this finding would be evidence of life in the parent bodies of these meteorities, whether in the solar system or beyond. And even if this conclusion is in doubt, it is still certain that rather complex hydrocarbons and other organic substances have been produced in outer space.

CONTACT WITH OTHER CIVILIZATIONS IN SPACE

The credit goes to Dr. J. E. Lipp for the first scientific investigation of the possibility that extraterrestrial beings are endeavoring to make contact with us, or at least to maintain our civilization under some kind of observation at close range. His work was done for the U.S. Air Force's Project Sign and has only recently been declassified. The

UFO'S IN SPACE

report (52), never made public, concerned itself with the investigation of the unidentified flying objects which had been closely analyzed by the Air Technical Intelligence Center (ATIC) in Dayton. Much of the data in this section is digested from this report.

The problem was well stated by Dr. Lipp when he wrote:

> Conceivably, among the myriads of stellar systems in the Galaxy, one or more races have discovered methods of travel that would be fantastic by our standards. Yet, the larger the volume of space that must be included in order to strengthen this possibility, the lower will be the chance that the race involved would ever find the Earth.... A super-race (unless they occur frequently) would not be likely to stumble over Planet III of Sol, a fifth-magnitude star in the rarefield outskirts of the Galaxy.

In order to evaluate the probable number of such races, Dr. Lipp statistically analyzed neighboring stars, finding twenty-two that can be considered as potentially habitable planets in a sample spherical volume of sixteen light-years' radius. Assuming this volume to be representative, the contents of any reasonable volume of radius larger than five parsecs can be computed.* It is then necessary to make an "educated" guess as to the number of habitable planets. "This guess," adds Dr. Lipp, "will be made with low confidence, since intelligent life may not be randomly distributed at all." If we assume that there is one habitable

---

* If we denote as S the number of eligible stars, as r the radius of the volume considered, in light-years, we have $S = 22\ (r/16)^3$. Note that 1 parsec = 3.26 light-years = 210,000 times the mean distance earth–sun.

planet per eligible star, and if we make the hypothesis that man is average in the spectrum of technical advancement, environmental difficulties, etc., then one-half of the other planets are behind us, while the other half are ahead of us and have achieved various levels of space travel. We can thus imagine that in our sample volume of sixteen light-years' radius there are eleven races of beings who have begun space explorations. The formula giving the number of races exploring space in a spherical volume of radius r larger than sixteen light-years is, therefore: $S = 11\, r/16^3$.

On the basis of these calculations, Dr. Lipp concludes that

> the chance of space-travellers existing at planets attached to neighbouring stars is very much greater than the chance of space-travelling Martians: if the Martians are now visiting us without contact, it can be assumed that they have just recently succeeded in space travel and that our civilization would be practically abreast of theirs. But the chance that Martians, under such widely divergent conditions, would have a civilization resembling our own is extremely small.

This reasoning is based, of course, on the assumption that intelligent life is randomly distributed. A direct consequence of such a hypothesis is that if "unidentified objects" were shown to be of Martian origin, we should expect relations between both planets to have existed in a distant past, possibly before our civilization developed on earth, and a common origin of both races could be sought. For chance alone does not seem to be able to explain that two civilizations so close to each other could independently reach the same state of technological development practically at the same moment. And if the alleged Martians have possessed space travel long before us, then the nonexistence of "contacts" could be explained by postulating that enough knowledge had been accumulated in the past concerning our planet. F. L. Whipple, in (64), carefully considers the possibility of intelligent life on Mars:

> If we have correctly reconstructed the history of Mars, there is little reason to believe that the life processes may not have followed a course similar to terrestrial evolution. With this assumption, three general positions emerge. Intelligent beings may have protected themselves against the excessively slow loss of atmosphere, oxygen and water, by constructing homes and cities with the physical conditions scientifically controlled. As a second possibility, evolution may have developed a being who can withstand the rigors of the Martian climate. Or the race may have perished.

These possibilities have been sufficiently expanded in the pseudoscientific literature to make further amplification superfluous. However, there may exist some interesting restrictions to the anatomy and physiology of a Martian. Rarity of the atmosphere, for example, may require a completely altered respiratory system for warmblood creatures. If the atmospheric pressure is much below the vapor pressure of water at the body temperature of the individual, the process of breathing with our type of lungs becomes impossible. On Mars the critical pressure for a body temperature of 98.8° F occurs when a column of the atmosphere contains one sixth the mass of a similar column on the Earth. For a body temperature of 77° F the critical mass ratio is reduced to about one twelfth, and at 60° F to about one twenty-fourth. These critical values are of the same order as the values estimated for the Martian atmosphere. Accordingly the anatomy and physiology of a Martian may be radically different from ours.

Probability of Contact with Superior Galactic Communities

Dr. Lipp's report was written in 1949, and much progress in the study of the possibility of Martian life has been made since. In (53) F. Salisbury writes:

> Of all the proposals put forth to account for the observed Martian phenomena, the idea of life on Mars seems to be the most tenable.... If in place of struggling lichens we assume a thriving vegetation cover, then it is easy to add other members of the biotic community. If plant-like organisms have solved the problem of growth in the Martian environment so well, one might surely expect to find mobile forms comparable to our animals that feed on plants. And from there it is but one more step (granted, a big one) to intelligent beings. In view of the evidence, we should at least try to keep our minds open so that we could survive the initial shock of encountering them.

The alternate possibility, which, in Dr. Lipp's model, leads to higher probabilities than the system of the "space-traveling Martians," is that of visits by superior galactic communities. It will be discussed in more detail in a NOTE at the end of this volume, where we will see that it is by no means fanciful to estimate that the number of inhabitable systems is about 3 to 5 per cent of the number of stars (S. S. Huang, 1963)—yielding *eight billion inhabitable planetary systems* in our galaxy.

CHAPTER THREE

MODERN UFO REPORTS AND THEIR RELIABILITY

SOURCES OF DOCUMENTATION

To study efficiently an unresearched phenomenon requires time and a combination of techniques utilized by a homogenous team of investigators. A second important problem is data collection.*

Our hypotheses concerning the UFO problem may prove incomplete, or naïve, or wrong. But we feel that if we have only been able to gather a collection of facts which could be employed as the basis of research by other scientists our contribution will have been positive.

In this introduction to the description of modern reports we want to delineate the field of our exploration; the details themselves will be found further in the book, but we feel it necessary to impress upon our reader in advance the *high degree of consistency and reliability of UFO data*. "Noise

---

* Those among our readers who wish to call our attention to published or unpublished reports or to periodicals or reviews from any part of the world dealing with our problem will be most welcome, for our research relies entirely upon a process of data gathering as complete as possible.

level" in UFO reports is undoubtedly very high (by "noise level," we mean that fraction of the reports which are explainable in terms of meteors, aircraft, balloons, artificial satellites, hoaxes or any natural phenomenon or conventional object misinterpreted by the witness). When speaking of UFO data, however, we will always be referring to a subset of these reports which has been filtrated by competent analysts in such a way that all common misinterpretations have been eliminated. To these selected sightings will be attached, during the first step of the analysis, a description in general terms and a reliability index. The handling of the information contained in the report will be described as a process with several stages involving a series of decisions, but the reliability of the operation is kept at a high level throughout this process, as explained and illustrated elsewhere (189, 193).

The first result obtained in this analysis will probably come as a surprise to most "flying saucer" enthusiasts; we are in firm agreement with the previous statistical estimates of the U.S. Air Force concerning the proportion of sightings which can be explained by conventional effects: generally between 70 and 90 per cent.

The files we have developed over the years are the result of the analysis of a number of reports *double in number those in the official files*, on which these previous estimates were based. This is a very large amount of data. Collection of new information from private or official sources does not necessarily result in an increase of the files' volume; in numerous cases, more information results in the elimination of reports which had previously been considered as doubtful or, as the air force would say, as "insufficient information." But we do not classify the reports according to the amount of data they contain; "insufficient data" alone is no ground for elimination. A more detailed discussion of air force methods will show how naïve it is to label as "insufficient information" the very phenomenon you are studying; think of a physicist discontinuing his research because he does not have "sufficient information" about the structure of the atom, or the FBI allowing a criminal to escape because the witness' description of his face is not sufficiently accurate!

When we speak of the sightings we have on file, we repeat that we do not mean the number of observations *made*, or *reported*, or *studied by us*, but only the volume of a selected sample considered of scientific value. We intend to analyze the global and individual features of these accounts to show that *they define a truly unique phenomenon, which cannot be explained by combinations of ordinary effects*. We tend to think that there must exist a common cause that has produced all of these effects. In our opinion, there are reasons to think that this cause may be related to, or a manifestation of, extraterrestrial intelligence.

We have been helped in our data collection problem by several persons, among whom Aime Michel deserves the first mention. We have also found much information in scientific or popular periodicals. We will see that American sightings are generally less interesting than observations made elsewhere in the world, or at least are less important than is generally thought; the UFO phenomenon did not begin in the U.S., with the Kenneth Arnold incident over Mount Rainier in June of 1947. The modern aspect of this activity was first observed in Europe at the end of the war. The first important "wave" which can be accurately traced occurred in Sweden in July-August, 1946, one year before

Arnold allegedly saw a formation of silvery disks from his private airplane in the state of Washington. The most important sightings have been made in Europe, many of them in France in autumn of 1954. The high population density of that area of the world and the small dimensions of the local communities have produced reports of a high reliability; the witnesses are almost always known and the exact location of the object can be pinpointed on the map.

UFO waves are known to have taken place in Russia, Poland, Hungary and other communist countries. Some of the reports involved are quite detailed. Witness this article in *Ogoniok*, No. 11, March, 1958, by Soukhanov (88; see also 87, 89):

> Recently, not far from Moscow and at an altitude of about three thousand meters, a strange object flying at great speed was seen. The witnesses maintained that it had exactly the shape of a disk, of relatively large dimensions. No one was able to say what this disk was, or where it came from. Very fantastic interpretations and hypotheses have been started by this incident. A little later, the disk came down toward the ground with a motion in spiral and started upward again, turned over and, suddenly speeding, disappeared behind a nearby forest.

We have here, incidentally, another example of a type of behavior well known to French researchers: the "dead-leaf" fall or descending spiral motion; we will see several other good cases of the same type.

Australia, New Zealand and New Guinea have been important areas of UFO activity, but the only source comparable with the U.S. or western Europe in sheer numbers of sightings in South America. Some of the "waves" in this region have been very carefully studied by local organizations. The information provided by M. Vogt has been found especially reliable. Olavo Fontes has contributed to the study of the Brazilian reports. In Spain, Antonio Ribera has shown that waves occurred in 1950, and his compatriot Eduardo Buelta has made the first full statistical analysis of the general pattern followed by the successive waves. (Their work will be discussed in detail and the references will be indicated in the Bibliography further in the book.) In Great Britain, the *Flying Saucer Review*, published bimonthly, has opened its columns to all coherent writers interested in this field and has supplied needed clarification.

Scientific publications, although important sources of information on early sightings, treat modern UFO reports with great reserve. As we have pointed out, we do not observe the phenomenon under study, but rather a "sociological image" of it, generated in the minds of other human beings and transmitted through society. Each of the steps involved in this process is affected by distortion and noise. As we will see, however, the "noise" associated with UFO rumors is of a different quality from what we expect generally from popular channels of tradition. We are dealing with a very deep and complex system of stimuli whose study cannot be undertaken without asking fundamental questions concerning our vision of the world as a whole.

A MOMENT OF HISTORY

No survey of the UFO phenomenon has been made by historians or sociologists, although it would seem, from the continual accumulation of sightings since 1946, that we are faced with a problem of sociological significance. In the absence of such studies, no complete documentation is available, and only very few scientists have seen the meaningful reports; the majority of them have been discouraged by the "sensational" interpretation of the facts presented in the newspapers, and by the number of obvious misinterpretations and hoaxes, among which the true phenomenon seems very difficult to find. Intelligent and serious reports, however, do exist; about 10 to 30 per cent of the eight thousand American sightings kept up to date in Dayton by ATIC could be called intriguing, to say the least. It is the opinion of this writer that their accumulation constitutes a true phenomenon in itself, well worth a detailed and extensive scientific study.

Whether or not UFO's were seen, or imagined, during preceding centuries, the Middle Ages or even in Biblical and legendary times remains an open question. Their modern epic seems to have started sometime during World War II, when many pilots reported strange lights apparently under intelligent control. The first great peak of sightings took place after the war, one year before the Mount Rainier incident and the 1947 U.S. wave. This wave reached its maximum by mid-July, 1946, and affected the northern regions of Europe. We will try here to clarify the incidents of that period, from comments that appeared in the French press (94).

UFO'S IN SPACE

The first account we have been able to find comes from the newspaper *Resistance* of July 19, 1946:

> During the last few months the populations of the southern part of Sweden, and those of the northern part, have been somewhat disturbed; from time to time, especially at night, bright meteors, traveling at fantastic speeds, cross their skies. Within fractions of seconds, these bolides appear and disappear, vanishing into the deepness of space with an infernal roaring.

This first description immediately evokes the thought of ordinary meteors, misinterpreted by people still very much under the stress of a terrible war. But *L'Aurore* of July 27 gives more specific details.

> More than five hundred rocket-propelled projectiles are said to have been seen over Sweden since the beginning of July. According to some sources, the projectiles that streak across the Swedish sky look like jet planes, but make less noise than usual aircraft. Others describe them as like "sea gulls without heads." On the map, the projectiles do not show uniform trajectories. They go toward the west as well as the south, which leads to the possibility that they are guided by remote control of some sort. It has been impossible to get hold of any of these "V-1's"; all of them have fallen into the lakes.

We are already far from the meteor explanation; the objects are interpreted by the witnesses as material products of human technology. The reference to the German "V" weapons is very indicative of the psychology prevailing in Europe at that time; at no time during the entire "wave" was a hypothesis of the extraterrestrial origin of the objects made by the witnesses or by the newspapers. It seemed evident to everyone that the observed objects were a new type of aircraft or rocket. It is interesting to remember that this response was also the reaction of many scientists in the United States in the period 1947-1950; the situation, however, soon became more complicated. We read in *L'Etoile*, August 8:

> In an official statement made public on August 6 in Stockholm, General Nils Ahlgreen, chief of the Swedish Air Defense, has announced that some of the objects have been seen at low altitudes, that more than three hundred have been reported between July 9 and July 12, that they maneuvered in half-circles and appeared to come from the south most of the time. One of the objects is said to have fallen into Lake Overkalix, in northern Sweden.

In *Le Monde*, August 9:

> Lieutenant Lennart Nackman, of the Swedish Air Defense, has seen one of the objects as a sphere of fire surrounded by flames of a light yellow. The object was flying at an altitude of about one thousand meters and its speed, despite the height, allowed the eye to follow its course. According to experts, the meteoric hypothesis is absolutely rejected. Thousands of letters reporting the objects have arrived from all over Sweden.

In *Liberation-Soir*, on the same day:

> They generally arrive from the south and do not follow a straight trajectory. Some of them change direction, either slowly or abruptly. The longest trajectory recorded by Swedish observers is one thousand kilome-

ters long, which is three times the range of the German V-rockets. Many of them come from the south, follow the Baltic coast, then curve their path toward northern Russia.

Etoile-Soir, August 14:

> The mystery deepens since it has been impossible to find fragments of the rocket shells recently reported. It has been officially announced in Marieham, capital of the Aaland Islands, midway between Sweden and Finland, that luminous phenomena have been observed there on Sunday night, for the first time.

The same day, in *Paris-Presse*:

> Everyone speaks about it in Stockholm; in the streets, in the restaurants and at home, the only discussion is about the luminous bombs which fly mysteriously over Sweden at low altitude. Popular imagination is stricken. Fantastic descriptions of the phenomenon are circulating. Between July 19 and July 30, three hundred reports have been submitted to military authorities. Others still arrive every day.

To the student of UFO rumors, such reports are familiar; the "meteors" of the first days have become "flying bombs" or "luminous spheres" flying at low altitude, able to change direction, leaving no fragments and exciting popular imagination. Their range is fantastic, compared with the technological state of development at the time. Still, the thoughts of war are so current and so strong that all descriptions are in terms of destructive technology: bombs, shells, rockets. The terminology, however, will slowly change.

La Depeche de Paris, August 17:

> Copenhagen, August 16: According to the Danish press, a new rocket was seen last night by numerous witnesses over Copenhagen.

Le Figaro, on the same day:

> London, August 16: A rocket-like projectile has exploded over the island of Malmoe. A large number of glass windows have been broken.

On the previous day, *Le Monde* had described a similar phenomenon over Finland:

> Helsinki has announced that a flying bomb exploded on Tuesday afternoon over the city of Tammersfors, in western Finland. Witnesses heard a loud explosion, then saw a cloud of smoke in the center of which appeared a luminous phenomenon. Another rocket has been seen over Helsinki on Tuesday night.

Liberation-Soir, August 28:

> The Swedish military authority continues to receive numerous reports about the mysterious projectiles which fly over the country. The following facts have been found:
> (1) There are two kinds of projectiles, those which have a level flight at eight hundred kilometers per hour with a bright light in the rear, and those which fall vertically from a greater height with a superior speed....
> (2) None of these projectiles has exploded on the ground. No one has been wounded and no damage has

been caused. Some of the projectiles may have exploded in the air, but no fragment has been found.

After that date, the situation becomes more confusing, because of the obvious futility of the official explanations (flying bombs, projectiles, rockets), but the facts become more like what we have observed in recent years, i.e., a phenomenon apparently material, commonly interpreted by witnesses as a new type of aircraft, yet displaying maneuvers in contradiction to the technology of the time. Of importance, in our opinion, is the report of landings.

Epoque, August 28:

> Some of the objects are said to change their direction of flight after landing, when they go back toward their place of origin, according to the results of an investigation made by the correspondent of the *Daily Telegraph* in Stockholm.

Another important fact is the extension of the "wave" to other regions of the world:

Epoque, August 29:

> Other objects have been reported from Switzerland and, a few days ago, from Waterford, Ireland. The objects seen in Sweden left a trail of fire similar to the tail of a comet. Others, on the contrary, have a light in front. The American General James Doolittle has just arrived in Stockholm, officially on a business trip for the Shell Company. In reality he is to conduct an investigation along with the Swedish authorities.

L'Aurore, September 4: The article reports that these "extraordinary craft" have been seen more and more frequently over Sweden, Belgium and even France. But more complete information is to be found in *Le Figaro* of September 5:

> More than two thousand ghost-rockets have been reported during the past few months over Sweden. Our English brother, the *Daily Mail*, has instructed its reporter, Alexander Clifford, to conduct an investigation on the subject. We reproduce here the more important part of his conclusions. According to a message from Stockholm sent by the English reporter, scientists are puzzled by the phenomena; in some circles they are attributed to mass hallucination. Others thing they are due only to meteors or luminous balloons used in meteorological experiments. They are the subject of jokes on the music-hall stage, but the Swedish and Danish military staff are taking the matter seriously and have begun an investigation....

Mr. Clifford reports that a fairly large number of the two thousand luminous balloons have been seen by reliable witnesses. These are, he says, the facts on which all of them agree:

(1) The projectiles are in the shape of *cigars*.

(2) Flames are projected out of their tail. The color is orange, but some people have said they were green.

(3) They travel at an altitude of three hundred to one thousand meters.

(4) Their speed is about that of an airplane. Some say a rather slow airplane....

(5) They do not make any noise, except a slight whistling.

Nobody has mentioned wings, but some have said they saw fins, and this is where science comes in to say that the thing is impossible; no wingless projectile could fly so slowly, especially in silence. Mr. Clifford mentions that, during a certain period, these flying bombs seemed to travel from southeast to northwest, but the first ones have been reported last May from the extreme north of Scandinavia and, generally speaking, their lines of travel have slowly shifted toward the south. The more recent of them have been observed over Denmark. The strange thing is that no physical evidence has been found. Where explosions have taken place, researchers and excavations have been made, but nothing has been found.

The reaction to the 1946 Scandinavian wave is typical of what can be expected of political and scientific communities confronted with a new phenomenon and intent upon placing it within known concepts. More generally, we will observe that the features of the UFO phenomenon remain permanent, but the reports made in a certain epoch are written in terms of that particular field of human activity which seems to provide the largest volume for the expansion of power over Nature: mythology for the Greeks, religion until the end of the nineteenth century, technology in our era. At the time of the Scandinavian events, UFO rumors were completely unknown. Since 1915 no important report had been made public. The Fatima phenomenon, which is now claimed by UFO students, was interpreted as purely religious. The reports of "strange lights" seen by pilots during the war ("foo-fighters") were not known to civilians. And no evidence was found that the phenomenon was other than conventional. Only now, with the experience we have accumulated in dealing with the UFO problem, can we observe that no answer has been found, almost twenty years later, to the Swedish incidents, and we can draw an interesting parallel between them and similar events recorded in other countries. Unfortunately, most of the information concerning these early Scandinavian reports lies in stacks of forgotten letters or files of newspaper clippings. Much could be brought to light by extensive study of these documents; on the basis of the data we have seen, there does not seem to have been one single voice suggesting that the "objects" seen in 1946 might have been of interplanetary origin; lack of "sensationalism" has allowed these events to be forgotten, while the systematic exploitation of the American incidents of 1947 had the opposite effect.

THE AMERICAN PERIOD (1947–1952)

The 1947 American scare was triggered by the wide publicity given to the Arnold incident. But scientists in the U.S. immediately had the same reaction as their European colleagues the year before. The explanation, they thought, was obvious. American technology was engaged in a series of revolutionary research projects, especially in the fields of physics and aerodynamics. It is understandable that the idea of interplanetary "visitors" was the furthest thing from their minds; this suggestion was supported only by newsmen interested in selling copy and by a handful of enthusiasts; their arguments were very feeble. For most American scientists, the physical existence of the objects reported could not be denied. They were not astronomical phenomena like meteors, but experimental devices. A few, including the Scandinavians, saw the hand of Moscow behind the mysterious airships. Others, knowing that Russian engineers were then far from capable of developing aircraft of such flexibility and speed, concluded that the objects must be secret experimental devices of American origin. This was the most logical explanation, and the general public accepted it for a very long time, even when reports were received which could not be accounted for under this reasoning.

The original problem—meteors or secret weapons?—has, through the years, slowly evolved. Today, the two theories usually put forth are the "mirage-hallucination-error" theory of Dr. Menzel, and the "extraterrestrial" hypothesis, which explains the "objects" as artificial devices of nonhuman origin. Both involve many speculative elements which cannot be completely tested today by scientific means, and both have inherent weak points, as we will see later.

The idea that the objects were craft of terrestrial (U.S. or Soviet) origin was abandoned when such reliable observers as meteorologists, ballistics experts and pilots described behaviors incompatible with what human physiology could endure in classical propulsion aircraft. Most of these sightings were made in the southwestern U.S. from 1947 to 1952.

1947

When the 1947 wave started, a total of five atomic bomb explosions—Alamogordo (July 16, 1945), Hiroshima (August 6, 1945), Nagasaki, Crossroads A and Crossroads

B—had already taken place. "Of these, the first two were in positions to be seen from Mars, the third was very doubtful (at the edge of Earth's disk in daylight) and the last two were at the wrong side of the earth" (52). At the time of Alamogordo and Hiroshima, Mars was 165,000,000 and 153,000,000 miles away from the earth, respectively.

Hence the suggestion (See Dr. Lipp's report, [52]) that other galactic communities may have kept a long-term routine watch on earth and may have been alarmed by the sight of our A-bombs as evidence that we are warlike and on the threshold of space exploration.

In April of 1947, in Richmond, Virginia, an interesting observation had already been made. A weatherman tracking a balloon with a theodolite saw a disk-shaped object, with a flat bottom and a dome on top, cross his field. On about the eighteenth of May, at sunset, a flat cigar-shaped object crossed the sky very rapidly. In another account, the "cigar" was described as a disk seen at an angle; it was white and sped to the northwest. On May 19, between 12:15 P.M. and 1:15 P.M. at Manitou Springs, Colorado, a silvery object was seen coming from the northeast; it remained motionless for several minutes, then started "dancing"—maneuvering, climbing, diving and finally rising against the wind. These acrobatics are typical behavior, often observed in France and in other parts of the world.

About June 10, 1947, *two weeks before the Arnold sighting*, a UFO wave occurred in Hungary; it could hardly be considered "a psychological flap consecutive to the Arnold incident." Approximately fifty reports were submitted describing "silvery balls" which crossed the sky in full daylight at great speed (30).

On June 14 at 2:00 P.M., at Bakersfield, California, Richard Rankin, a U.S. pilot, saw a "formation" of ten objects flying north; this observation is one of the "unidentified" of that period, still classified under this category in the official files. One might reasonably insist on the similarity of this incident to the Arnold case, for one cannot scientifically discuss UFO reports in individual terms, *but only in terms of classes and behaviors*. Rankin was flying from Chicago to Los Angeles when he saw ten "saucers" in a triangular formation; they seemed to be disks with a diameter of thirty meters, flying at nine hundred kilometers per hour. The dimension—thirty meters—is another constant in UFO descriptions by pilots. It seems to be an invariant of the objects seen in flight, as opposed to the smaller dimensions of the "objects" allegedly witnessed on the ground, which seldom exceeded eight meters.

The Arnold incident took place on June 24, but it is by no means one of the best reports of that period. It happened that Arnold gave his story to newsmen and that the whole country found it across the front pages of their newspapers the following morning. But on June 28, at 2:00 P.M., an air force jet pilot, a Lieutenant Armstrong, flying thirty miles north of Lake Meade, Nevada, saw a formation of five or six white disks at an altitude of six thousand feet. The same day, at 3:45 P.M., M. Beuscher, at Rockfield (sixteen miles northwest of Milwaukee), saw more than seven "disks" above his farm. He described them as blue objects that made no noise, and flew south. According to a news program on the same day, similar objects were seen in Illinois later in the afternoon.

The next day, at 4:45 P.M., seven miles from Clarion, Iowa, a bus driver traveling from Des Moines to Mason

City saw one object followed by four others, then thirteen new objects coming from the opposite direction at an altitude estimated at twelve hundred feet. The shape of these craft was oval, and they looked, said the witness, like inverted plates of a white color. They made the noise of a dynamo and disappeared in the north-northwest.

One morning, early in July of 1947, several white UFO's were seen "flying" in the sky over Cambridge, Massachusetts, "at a fantastic speed, like those low clouds seen before a storm."

On July 3, 1947, at 2:30 P.M., at Harborside, south of Brooksville, Maine, John F. Cole watched a series of objects which gave off a roar; they were in the north and were proceeding northwest at high speed. He estimated their diameter at one hundred feet (thirty meters).

The first two weeks of July seem to have marked the crest of this wave. Several outstanding observations were made during that period, and they show most of the characteristics that were to be observed on later dates. On July 8, 1947, at 9:20 P.M., spherical objects were seen flying against the wind at eight thousand feet, not faster than three hundred miles per hour; the sighting lasted several minutes, and took place at Muroc Air Force Base in California, where earlier the same day two military engineers had watched a metallic disk for ten minutes. The official treatment given this case is not known to this writer. Another classical case is the Twin Falls, Idaho, incident of August 13: A blue "disk" was allegedly seen flying at a very low altitude above a forest, and trees were said to bend below it as under a violent wind.

The 1947 wave lost intensity and subsided at the end of August. We have mentioned here only a very few sightings among the more interesting, but a much larger quantity of reports is known, and these seem to represent only a very small fraction of the sightings that were actually made but were not reported, or were forgotten or lost. The writings of those who, like E. J. Ruppelt, studied this period indicate that a very important series of observations was made, and that repercussions were considerable.

1948

Only isolated incidents were reported prior to the next period of significant activity, which came in the summer of 1948. One of these incidents was the Mantell case, which has been fairly well identified as having been caused by a Skyhook balloon which Mantell tried to chase too high without proper oxygen equipment. Several incidents were, however, reported in January, but we are unable to decide from our data whether or not this sudden burst of observations should be considered significant. On January 9, 1948 (two days after the death of Captain Mantell), at 7:20 P.M., there was seen at Clinton, North Carolina, for thirty-five minutes an object of a type that will be found described in many French reports in 1954 and 1957: a cone-shaped UFO, red with a diffuse green tail, dancing and "fighting" in the sky at an amazing speed. Its brightness was such that its contour could still be discerned even when it was hidden behind some clouds.*

On February 1, another UFO was reported close to the ground at Circleville, Ohio, by Bruce Stevenson. It had a metallic appearance and emitted a tremendous orange light.

---

* This class of objects reappeared over the United States during the summer of 1964.

Other observations of interest were made on February 20 at Boise and Emmett, Idaho. It is difficult to speak in this instance of a "wave," but we do have indications of major UFO activity in the United States at that time. It appears, from our data, that it had vanished by the end of February (30, 11, 95).

In March of 1948 the phenomenon appeared in Italy. On March 23, at Florence, reports were made of disks and spheres leaving trails of smoke as they roared across the sky. Similar accounts were published the next day concerning objects seen under the same conditions between 5:00 P.M. and 6:30 P.M. in Surrey and in Kent, England. Similar phenomena were observed in Birmingham at midnight. In April, the phenomenon returned to the United States. In the afternoon of April 5, Holloman (New Mexico) Air Force Base personnel reported having witnessed an object in the shape of a disk, thirty-five meters in diameter, executing a series of violent turns and maneuvers—it is worth making a note of the dimension of the "disk," as estimated by these competent observers. Another disk was seen the same day displaying similar behavior at Manila; and in Delaware, Ohio, on April 8, there was observed what appears to be the first case of large "luminous cigars" to be found in modern reports; as we will see, a number of outstanding descriptions of this extraordinary and puzzling phenomenon were made later, especially in France in 1954 and in Australia more recently.

Activity subsided after April, 1948, and the only reports that continued to arrive came from Alaska. At this point, it is very difficult to suggest any hypothesis without entering very treacherous ground. By reading the reports that we have, which represent only a small sample of the true activity, one does gain the impression that if the UFO phenomenon has a physical cause this succession of rumors (never before related within one study) is to be linked to a physical effect that traveled across the planet in a few months and left limited traces of its passage. Such a common-sense interpretation cannot be proved and usually should not be trusted. But everything appears as if this was the case. If we tried to interpret the reported activity in terms of machines, we could consider that a single flying object was responsible for all the incidents. This limited activity does not justify the use of the word "wave."

A true wave, however, did occur in July of 1948. (The 1946 Swedish wave and the 1947 American wave also reached their maximums in July.) On July 8 witnesses at Osborn, Ohio, reported a sighting. On the same day, observations were made in several parts of France. On July 17, UFO's were seen around New Mexico. But this period is remembered mainly because of an incident that occurred twenty miles southwest of Montgomery, Alabama, on July 25 at 2:45 A.M. It is often referred to as the "Chiles and Whitted case," after the name of the pilots of an Eastern Airlines' DC-3, from which the object was observed. Described as a thick, torpedo-shaped craft with two rows of lights or "portholes," surrounded by a blue glow and followed by a trail of orange flames, it maneuvered suddenly, as collision with the aircraft seemed imminent, and disappeared. It might be of interest to remark that five days before, a "cigar" with eight lights, having "two decks and no wings," had been observed at The Hague, Holland. The observations were made from the ground, on four occasions. The same type of object was seen at Clark Airfield, on the Philippine Islands, about August 1; the report describes a torpedo-shaped UFO with a double row of lights.

On July 27, 1948, at 8:35 A.M., a scientist at New Mexico University, driving in the streets of Albuquerque, saw distinctly for ten minutes a flat and circular object that seemed to be a metallic disk motionless in the sky. In addition to his scientific training, the witness had had more than two thousand hours of flight as a navy pilot and was, of course, familiar with classical aircraft. This sighting has never been reported officially, and the witness wishes to remain anonymous.

After that date the frequency of sightings decreased in the U.S., but the wave continued to develop elsewhere on the planet. Unfortunately, this activity hit mainly Eastern countries, from which little information can be obtained; this may be the reason the wave appears to have died at the end of July. On August 1, however, as we have already noted, a sighting took place in the Phillipines. The same day, a peak of reports developed in Saigon and, as far as we can tell, in the whole of Southeast Asia. Samy Simon, a French radio-television correspondent, was flying between Hong Kong and Saigon when all crew members and passengers of the plane saw a long, metallic fish-like object reflecting the sunlight. Below it there appeared to be another long, solid object. No flame or smoke was noted. The size was estimated as twice that of a large bomber. Without diminishing speed, the craft made a ninety-degree turn and vanished in the clouds. On August 2, UFO rumors spread to the whole of Indochina with the characteristics of public emotion and masses of reports typical of the classical "flying-saucer wave."

In Moscow during the fall of the same year, similar reports were made, and a few sightings of a new type occurred in the U.S. before the wave died completely. These new incidents were best illustrated by the Gorman case. Gorman was piloting an F-51 aircraft over Fargo, North Dakota, when he saw a light of an estimated diameter of twenty to thirty centimeters. It displayed "remarkable evolutions." This was on October 1, 1948, at 9:00 P.M., and the sighting lasted twenty minutes. The Gorman incident has been commented upon by writers as confirming opposing theories, all with limited success. Twenty-minute ball lightnings would be more surprising to the physicist than flying saucers piloted by vegetable men. The "light" was seen close to the aircraft by control-tower operators and by people in other locations, who viewed it from very different angles and gave consistent descriptions, tending to prove that the phenomenon occupied a definite location in space, unlike a distorted image of a rising star or planet, or a looming effect. But the idea that the light was some kind of "flying saucer" is clearly repulsive. The suggestion made by certain enthusiasts that the object was guided by remote control "of some sort" is inadequate, as it raises more questions than it answers. All we have are several excellent reports by competent pilots and observers, and the recognition of a pattern. A similar incident took place at Andrews Field near the Capital on November 18 at 9:45 P.M. On December 3 a strange "ball of light" of the same type was seen, this time at Fairfield-Suisun Air Force Base in California. The "object" climbed toward a plane against a strong wind and disappeared from view at thirty thousand feet altitude, still rising.

1949

Nineteen hundred and forty-nine is another year that might reveal surprising information to future investigators if they are able to gather more information concerning sightings in Asiatic countries. Between the two excellent American reports of April 24 (Charles Moore) and August 20 (Clyde Tombaugh) a wave may have taken place in Sweden and the U.S.S.R., but it is difficult to support this assumption from our present data. UFO activity that year, at any rate, seems to have begun somewhere in South America in March and developed in the U.S. at the beginning of April. On March 21 the Adams-Anderson incident took place fifteen miles north of Stuttgart, Arkansas, where an object with eight to ten lights (again enthusiastically labeled "portholes" in the specialized journals) was seen traveling north. It was associated with a blinking blue light. On April 6, several incidents occurred at White Sands Proving Grounds in New Mexico. The next day a huge "column of metal" was reported at Des Moines, Iowa; the UFO was seen standing vertically in the sky, surrounded by fiery lights and blue, yellow and purple glows; the witness said that he had never seen anything more dreadful in his entire life.

> The Charles Moore incident is of interest, an air force document notes, because of the high technical qualifications of the observer. Preparing a site for the launching of a large test balloon at White Sands on April 24, 1949, Moore was checking on crosswinds in the valley between two mountain ranges and had launched a small weather balloon, watching it in a theodolite, keeping it on the cross hairs. He had a new man

on the team who wanted experience in tracking balloons. And so Moore turned the theodolite to him, cautioning him to keep it on and not lose it, because Moore did not want to waste a balloon. Shortly after, Moore looked up to check the balloon by unaided eye and thought he saw it moving off to the east. He yelled to the man that he had lost the balloon, but the man said, "No, it is still on the cross wires." Moore looked and confirmed this, and then rapidly switched the theodolite to the strange object, catching it after it had "passed through" the sun. It was elliptical, two or three times as long as it was wide, moving along its major axis, and covered the entire sky from the southwest to the northeast in sixty seconds. Five others saw it and confirmed Moore's sighting. Moore checked his refocus of the theodolite and found it had been focused for infinity. Moore then launched another balloon and tracked it throughout its course of ninety thousand feet. At no level were the winds from the southwest, so a balloon is ruled out (45).

In July, 1949, disks and spheres were reported flying over Sweden and toward the U.S.S.R. The summer was quiet everywhere else, with no special sign of activity in the United States until the Las Cruces, New Mexico, incident of August 20, when the astronomer Clyde Tombaugh, the discoverer of Pluto and a well-known planetary expert, sighted a geometric formation of rectangle-shaped lights. It was lost in the southeast. California, New Mexico and Oklahoma were sources of reports later that year, and a few observations were also made in Europe; they remain vague and ill-defined.

As far as the "American" period is concerned, the most important series of sightings took place from 1950 through

1952. But UFO activity during these three years was by no means limited to North America; we will see that parallel "waves" developed in Spain, North Africa and France, as well as other countries. But the publicity that made the UFO's famous had its origin in the American press during that period.

1950

Nineteen hundred and fifty is a very typical year for UFO activity. A wave developed at the end of February, reached a maximum in the last two weeks of March and decreased in the following months. The United States and Spain shared the more interesting observations, but the Mediterranean Sea—from Italy to Turkey and North Africa as well—was visited by a parallel phenomenon. On March 18 an observation at Farmington, New Mexico, had several thousand witnesses. The phenomenon—another demonstration of "aerial flight"—lasted no less than one hour. The next day, in Texas, a huge "cloud cigar" giving rise to secondary objects was reported.

The Spanish observations of that period have been uncovered and partly analyzed by Ribera; unfortunately, not all the details of these events have yet been published by Spanish researchers. According to another source (96), an interesting sighting was made on April 27, 1950, at 5:30 P.M., twenty-five kilometers from Seville, going in the direction of Malaga. The UFO was a flying disk, described with a fair amount of detail. The observation, lasting twenty seconds, was made by an engineer from Switzerland who was driving toward Malaga with one of his friends:

It was an ellipsoid as could be formed by putting two plates together, or like the body one would obtain by wrapping in one single package planet Saturn and its rings. The material seemed to be the same dull white used by lamp manufacturers. The motion was most irregular. Sometimes it reminded us of that of a plate falling through water.

This observation had another witness, who saw the object from the town of Osuma (eighty-eight kilometers from Seville) after it had departed from the first point. The behavior reported here is again typical; the zig-zag "dead-leaf" motion, which is described by some observers as similar to that of an object falling through water, has been observed on many occasions and in many countries.

In the night of April 27, 1950, an aircraft flying toward Chicago met a thick red disk at two thousand feet altitude just before reaching the South Bend Airport. The entire crew and all of the passengers saw the object flying on edge like a wheel. As soon as the plane turned in the direction of the object, it veered off at 450 miles per hour, went as low as fifteen hundred feet altitude (and was then seen *under* the plane) and finally left at great speed. The "disk" was polished and streamlined, but no detail of structure was visible.

On May 22, 1950, the astronomer Seymour Hess, at Lowell Observatory in Flagstaff, Arizona, saw a metallic disk. On May 29, at 9:20 P.M., twelve kilometers east of Mount Vernon, Captain Willis Sperry, of American Airlines, flying from Washington to Tulsa, observed a bright blue fluorescent light coming toward the aircraft. The "object" then stopped and, as the plane continued, was seen against the moon as a dark silhouette in "the shape of a submarine," without fins or wings. It appeared to be metallic and took off at high speed when the pilots tried to make a turn to pursue it.

1951

To the degree that 1950 was a typical year of activity, 1951 was typically inactive. The largest number of reports made in a two-week period is five (first half of October), but some of these reports are most interesting. UFO activity, it is clear, does not occur only in waves; in addition to the recurrence of large peaks of reports one should consider a constant phenomenon of local "flaps" or isolated sightings such as the following. A flat object of a blinding white color was seen on March 12, 1951, at 4:00 P.M. for fifteen minutes, at Corcelles-Neuchatel in Switzerland (97). The witnesses were Professor Alfred Lombard and his family, and several other persons. The UFO was seen above the lake. It followed a large course across the sky, leaving a white and woolly smoke trail as it progressed with sudden leaps forward. Sometimes it would remain perfectly motionless. After fifteen minutes the object traveled in a half-circle and turned upside-down, appearing as a perfect disk. It then took off vertically, at a fantastic speed, emitting no smoke or noise, and was lost in an instant.

We have already expressed our feelings of puzzlement concerning the interpretation of sightings of UFO's for durations of twenty minutes as "Ball-lightning." Those who are interested in a scientific description of such a twenty-minute ball lightning are invited to such a treat by *L'Astronomie* (98), in which the beautiful object is reported. It was red and remained motionless for a while, then went toward the northeast, then toward the southwest, and at the same time it came closer to the ground. Later it began to ascend again, only to assume a swinging motion, after which it went out of sight. The place was the little town of La Roche-sur-Yon, Vendee, France, and the date was June 15, 1951, at 11:30 P.M. The sky was clear, and the moon and the stars were bright. According to the witness' estimate, the object was spherical and the size of an orange.

On August 25, 1951, at 9:58 P.M., a V-shaped object was seen at Albuquerque, New Mexico, flying from north to south. It was larger than a B-26 and flew at four hundred miles per hour at an altitude of eight hundred to one thousand feet. It was a silvery object with six or eight lights grouped in pairs. On either side of the center, six to eight dark bands could be seen on the wing. No sound was heard. The object definitely reflected the lights of Central Avenue as it flew over the area. There were two witnesses, one of them a security guard at Sandia Base (99). The case has never been solved.

On November 29, 1951, at sunset, close to Highway 5 at Madisonville, Indiana, three duck hunters saw in the sky an object which left a vapor trail; it came lower and stopped just above them. One of the men took his gun and raised it, but the UFO allegedly left at high speed, then turned on one side, and they could see that it was disk-shaped and streamlined. It came lower as if it were going to land, but did not; instead, it took off again. In the setting sun it looked like a white metallic object.

1952

A true worldwide wave occurred in 1952. So many sightings were made all over the planet between April and the end of November that not even the exceptional ones can be completely listed here. Rather than imposing on the reader descriptions of the standard cases, such as the Washington incidents (which can be found in most books on the problem), I will try to select a few lesser-known cases that might also prove of interest.

As early as January, at Gallup, New Mexico, several objects that moved swiftly and occasionally remained in front of the disk of the sun had been seen. On January 30, in Korea, a huge disk that revolved like a large horizontal wheel was observed for several minutes. It radiated an orange light from its whole surface and gave off bluish flames from the edge. On May 10, 1952, at 6:00 P.M., twelve persons in La Roche-sur-Yon saw a flat disk fully lighted; it flew without noise and took off vertically to overtake another UFO seen higher in the sky (100,101). On May 20, 1952, an aerial object was reported at Denham, England, "giving rise to small disks that scattered in all directions."

On June 12, a celebrated sighting was made at Le Bourget Airport in Paris (102). A large number of witnesses saw the "light," including the control-tower operators, pilots in landing aircraft and persons living on the north side of the city.

During the month of July—which marked the maximum of the wave—activity was equally divided between France, North Africa and the United States. On July 6, for instance, two bluish "disks" were seen at Thann in Alsace; a luminous sphere was reported at Bone, Algeria; and another disk was seen at Bou-Hadjar, near Oran, during the night of July 7.

Maximum intensity was reached in the last two weeks of July, and then the wave decreased and fell to a minimum in the second week of September. But even then it did not die completely; a new burst of sightings appeared in European countries. The peak of the wave had been marked by two sensational observations made in Washington above the Capitol and the White House, a restricted-flight area permanently controlled by radar.* The second lobe of the intensity distribution, which took place in the fall, corresponds to another series of sensational sightings, those made during maneuvers of the navy of the North Atlantic Treaty Organization (Operation Mainbrace).

A sighting had already been made in Beine, a French village in the department of Yonne, on September 19. This sighting was described in a scientific journal under the title "suspicious object" (103):

> M. R. Sommer, pilot and aircraft manufacturer, coming back from Beine to Chablis, Yonne, on September 19, writes: "I was driving back in the night, which was dark, without moon or stars. We came out of the village of Beine and drove about five minutes, when we were greatly surprised to realize that a bright, unknown object had appeared in the sky on the left side of the road. It had the shape of an olive and a golden color. Its major axis was vertical. The sighting was indeed fairylike. The phenomenon lasted for five minutes. The minor axis of the object was a little smaller than the

---

* The approved explanation (meteorological return on radar) is not entirely convincing.

apparent diameter of the moon. A few minutes later, I visited the neighboring villages and examined the churches, fearing the apparition might have been caused by illuminations or reflections; but everywhere I found the same absolute calm, and no important light to be seen. The road was deserted."

The next day, three photographs of a flying disk were taken from the aircraft carrier "Franklin Roosevelt" during Operation Mainbrace in the English Channel. The object was flying extremely fast behind the NATO fleet, and the witnesses, obviously, were numerous and competent in identification of flying objects. The same day a number of sightings were made elsewhere in Europe; and the most important military airbase in Denmark saw a flying disk, apparently metallic, at 7:30 P.M. It disappeared in the east.

On September 21, six jet fighters chased a bright spherical object for two minutes. One of the aircraft returning to its base spotted the UFO again and tried without success to reach it. The same day, Morocco was flooded with reports of disks from Tangier to Marrakesh and Casablanca. In the latter case, five thousand persons attending a boxing match saw the object. On September 22, the night shift of a factory in Bayonne, France, watched for twenty minutes the classical "swinging motion" of a UFO. Later that day, an aircraft landing at Titmellil-Casablanca Airfield was passed at a low altitude by a bright object. *Witnesses on the ground simultaneously saw the UFO passing between them and the plane*, an indication that no optical illusion was occurring. On September 24, Operation Mainbrace was the occasion of a third UFO sighting. A jet fighter "meteor" from Topcliffe Air Force Base in Great Britain took off and came close to the UFO, described as a whitish-silvery sphere that revolved around its axis and flew away before further observation could be made.

On September 28, Denmark Sweden and the north of Germany and Poland were flooded with dozens of reports involving spheres, disks and cloud cigars (104). There were thousands of witnesses (105). Other "suspicious objects" were reported in *L'Astronomie* (106). The first "landing" replete with description of "little men" was reported in France about October 15, at La Vigan, Gard.

The most striking events of the end of the 1952 wave were the observations made at Oloron and Gaillac. The Oloron sighting took place about 12:50 P.M. on October 17. The author of the best report is a Mr. Pringent, a teacher, who was accompanied by a number of other witnesses. He describes a white cylindrical object, long and thin, standing at a 45° angle. The object was surrounded by about thirty yellow disks with domes. These disks traveled in pairs and maintained constant distances between them; when they came closer to one another a sort of "electric arc" or discharge would suddenly appear between the two objects. The radar station at Mont-de-Marsan was perturbed by the phenomenon. In addition, the witnesses reported seeing white smoke coming out of the top of the cylinder, while filaments fell to the ground in large amounts. These fibers, sometimes called "angel hair" in UFO terminology, dissolve spontaneously upon touching the ground, as if formed of ionized particles in an unstable state. It has been suggested that cases of "angel hair," often associated with sightings of UFO's, are merely due to the migration of huge clouds of very young spiders; this hypothesis has had little support, especially among biologists.

The Oloron situation was repeated at Gaillac ten days later. Sixteen disks accompanied a "vertical cylinder" or "cloud cigar," then hovered over the town for ten minutes, while the same whitish substance fell from the sky and covered the trees and houses, dissolving rapidly. A few minutes after the Gaillac sighting, a meteorological station at Brives-Charensac sighted a silvery metallic disk that crossed the sky and flew to the southeast. It was followed by another UFO in the shape of a cigar, which remained motionless in the sky for thirty seconds. There were five witnesses.

On October 28 Marc Perrot, an engineer in Paris, saw, while traveling three kilometers from Nemours, an object going toward Fontainebleau. This is related in *L'Astronomie* (109). Later, Africa seemed also to be "visited." At least one significant sighting was made in Bocaranga in French West Africa on November 22 (109).

In Mont-de-Marsan on November 27, 1952, at 6:30 A.M., Paul Bellocq, a contractor-builder, and several other persons witnessed a phenomenon that we will find reenacted in the north of France during the 1954 wave: A luminous object, in the shape of a disk, suddenly seemed to "split" into two parts, while hovering above the witnesses; after it reunited and left at a great speed (111).

The wave subsided in December of 1952, and the very last sighting in this series is extremely intriguing. It is described by D. Keyhoe (112). The crew of a B-29 aircraft flying over the Gulf of Mexico on December 6, 1952, at 5:25 A.M., watched, first on their radar screen and later visually, several formations of blue disks passing the aircraft at a fantastic speed (over five thousand miles per hour), some of them maneuvering to avoid colliding with the bomber. These formations were soon lost to view but could be followed on the radar scope as they converged toward an enormous spot, in the vicinity of which they disappeared as if they had integrated (at least, according to Keyhoe) into a very large machine.

French researchers have suggested that this might be the reverse maneuver of the generation of disks; if we were to hypothesize that UFO's are flying machines, it would be very tempting to follow C. Garreau and Michel in this view—it could even be claimed that what the crew of the B-29 observed was the last maneuver closing that period of UFO activity, as the small craft responsible for limited missions integrated into a large carrier, which was to take them back to their point of origin. To my knowledge, the event has not been commented upon officially or given a scientific treatment.

No sign of UFO activity comparable to what had been observed during the 1950 and 1952 waves can be found in 1953. Several of the best sightings known were, however, made in that period. It is important to recognize that UFO waves are sudden peaks of the *number* of sightings that come as an addition to a constant phenomenon of low intensity, but whose abnormal character can hardly be denied. One of the most remarkable events in the history of American sightings took place on August 6, 1953, when four objects danced, moved rapidly or hovered *for three hours above an air filter center* at Bismarck, North Dakota. In the official files, the special report is several hundred pages long. It contains interviews and accounts made by many witnesses, mainly military personnel and pilots.

The initial incident had taken place at Black Hawk,

South Dakota, where a red object hovered and later sped away on August 5 at 8:05 P.M. It was seen by observers on the ground, tracked by radar and chased by a jet fighter until the pilot had to give up. The object having left toward the north, communication was established with Bismarck, two hundred miles north of Black Hawk. but before individuals in Bismarck saw the object, several civilians quite independently reported seeing it between the two bases in South and North Dakota.

The object was observed at Bismarck at 11:42 P.M. It appeared as a point-source having a general curved course with sudden erratic jumps. It went up and down, turned and deviated from its general course, until it came close to the air filter center. It then hovered and glided slowly in full view of many witnesses who followed its movements from rooftops, making marks to record the exact sequence of maneuvers. The object disappeared between midnight and 1:00 A.M., but three other objects arrived at midnight. A. Globemaster C-154 in the area did not see the four UFO's, but observers on the ground noticed one of the objects suddenly flashing, as if signalling to the aircraft, and two others did the same after a while. Their apparent altitude was of the order of ten thousand feet. They never came close enough for any structure to be discernible, and they went away suddenly after three hours of maneuvering in the clear night.

Ten days later, according to a scientific report (113), two objects were observed close to the ground in Tours, France. On August 23, at noon, a film was taken at Port Moresby, New Guinea—where most amazing events were to take place in 1959—by a witness of very high reliability. The film, an official document, shows a disk coming out of a peculiar "cloud" and making ninety-degree turns. Other sightings of interest were made the same month, for example at Coyote Pass, California, on August 25, and in Vernon, France, on August 31. All of these sightings are interesting, but no "wave" can be detected. And no activity occurred that could be compared with the series we have described above, or with the French wave of 1954.

THE FRENCH PERIOD (1953–1960)

Because of the psychological impact of the French wave of 1954, the patterns observed during that period have become important references in the analysis of UFO behavior, and the various maneuvers observed have been given names of French towns. But the 1954 wave, as well as its successor, covered the entire planet. We have already noted the similarity between French and American observations in the 1950 and 1952 waves. Many of the 1954 descriptions appeared to be truly new and unprecedented when Michel published his important findings, but we will see that the pattern had been set long ago, and that the only peculiarity in the French wave is the amazing number of reports. "Landings," "cloud cigars" and "aerial flights" had already been observed in almost every country on the globe when the period studied by Michel opened; but nobody had paid much attention to the similarities because a particular case was always forgotten before the next one hit the front page.

The French wave of 1954, however, was inescapable. Dozens of reports were made every day in September, October and November, and the phenomenon was so intense, the impact on public opinion so deep, the newspapers' reactions so emotional that scientific reflexes were saturated long before a serious investigation could be organized. As a result, no scientist could risk his reputation by studying openly a phenomenon so emotionally distorted; French scientists remained silent until the wave passed and died. Extensive files were not collected, for the clippings of one single month represented an amazing volume of paper, so that only an efficient organization of experts could have completed the task. By the time the wave died, the problem had been ridiculed; the situation has remained in this state of paralysis ever since.

The name of the little town of Vernon, forty miles northwest of Paris, became associated with a category of sightings after an observation made on August 23; the sighting, which took place at 1:00 A.M., is recognized as the first landmark of importance in the wave.

A Vernon businessman, Bernard Miserey, had just put his car away when, coming out of the garage, he saw a pale light illuminating the town, which had been in complete darkness a little while before. The night was completely clear and the moon was at last quarter, and hence was rising about that time.

Looking at the sky, he saw a huge, silent, motionless, luminous mass, apparently suspended above the bank of the river some three hundred yards away. It could have been compared to a giant cigar standing on end.

"I had been watching this amazing spectacle for a couple of minutes," Mr. Miserey later reported,

> when suddenly from the bottom of the cigar came an object like a horizontal disk, which dropped at first in

free fall, then slowed, and suddenly swayed and dived horizontally across the river toward me, becoming very luminous. For a very short time I could see the disk full-face; it was surrounded by a halo of brilliant light.

A few minutes after it had disappeared behind me, going southwest at a prodigious speed, a similar object came from the cigar and went through the same maneuvers. A third object came, then a fourth. There was then a long interval, and finally a fifth disk detached itself from the cigar, which was still motionless. This last disk dropped much lower than the earlier ones, to the level of the new bridge, where it remained still for an instant, swaying slightly. At that time I could see very clearly its circular form and its red luminosity—more intense at the center, fading out at the edges—and the glowing halo surrounding it. After a few seconds' pause, it wobbled like the first four, and took off like a flash toward the north, where it was lost in the distance as it gained altitude. During this time the luminosity of the cigar had faded, and the gigantic object, which may have been three hundred feet long, had sunk into darkness. The spectacle had lasted about three-quarters of an hour.

The observer was not aware that there were corroborating witnesses. Two policemen making their rounds at 1:00 A.M. had also observed the phenomenon, as had an army engineer southwest of the town. The case was described briefly by a Paris newspaper (114). With the exception of an investigation conducted by Michel, no further study was made of the case.

Three weeks later, on September 14, the phenomenon reoccurred in broad daylight and was observed by hundreds of witnesses in a half-dozen villages 250 miles southwest of Paris. Only one newspaper mentioned it, and only by chance was it investigated, because the story came to Michel's attention. Witnesses were mostly farmers and a few priests and schoolteachers. One witness reports:

> It was about five in the afternoon. Emerging from the thick layer that looked like a storm coming up, we saw a sort of luminous blue-violet mist, of a regular shape something like a cigar or a carrot. Actually, the object came out of the layer of clouds in an almost horizontal position, slightly tilted toward the ground and pointing forward, like a submerging submarine.
>
> This luminous cloud appeared rigid. Whenever it moved, its movements had no connection with the movement of the clouds, and it moved all of a piece, as if it were actually some gigantic machine surrounded by mist. It came down rather fast from the ceiling of clouds to an altitude which we thought was perhaps a half-mile above us. Then it stopped, and the point rose quickly until the object was in a vertical position, where it became motionless.
>
> During this time the dark clouds went on scudding across the sky, dimly lighted from underneath by the violet luminosity of the object. It was an extraordinary sight, and we watched it intently. All over the countryside other farmers had also dropped their tools and were staring up at the sky like us.
>
> All at once white smoke exactly like a vapor trail came from the lower end of the cloud. At first it pointed to the ground but finally rose up to describe around the vertical object an ascending spiral. While the rear of the trail was dissolving in the air and being carried off by the wind, the source of the trail went up to the very top of the vertical object and then started to come down again, turning in the other direction. Only then, after the smoke trail had vanished entirely, could we see the object that was sowing it—a little metallic disk, reflecting in its rapid movements flashes of light from the huge vertical object. The little disk then stopped turning around the luminous cloud and went down toward the

ground again, this time moving away. For quite a few minutes we could see it flying low over the valley, darting here and there at great speed, sometimes speeding up, then stopping for a few seconds, then going on again, flying in every direction between villages that were four miles apart. Finally, when it was almost a mile from the vertical object it made a final dash toward it at headlong speed and disappeared like a shooting star into the lower part, where it had first come out. Perhaps a minute later the carrot leaned over as it began to move, accelerated and disappeared into the clouds in the distance. The whole thing lasted about half an hour (115).

At Amiens, on September 7, at 7:15 A.M.:

> My eyes were caught by a sort of mound, two hundred yards away in a field. It looked something like an unfinished haystack, with an upside-down plate on top.
>
> "That's a queer color for a haystack," I said to Yves, "look at it."
>
> All of a sudden I noticed that the haystack was moving a little, with a slight swing back and forth, like an oscillation. We both rushed toward the mysterious object. When we got close the object took off on a slant, traveled diagonally upward for about fifty feet and then began to go straight up. We watched it for three minutes. The object was about thirty feet in diameter.

We read in *France-Soir*, September 15:

> Three investigators for the air police arrived at Quarouble, Nord, yesterday to interrogate M. Marius Dewilde, the man who saw two "Martians" near his

back-yard gate. They left the village with the assurance that during the night of Friday to Saturday, a mysterious craft had indeed landed, as claimed by M. Dewilde, on the railroad tracks of the line Saint-Armand-Blanc-Misseron, near the railroad crossing No. 79.

Their inquiries seem, in effect, to confirm the statement made by the metal worker. The witness has declared that Friday, about 10:30 P.M., he had seen a machine of an elongated shape, three meters high, six meters long, sitting on the tracks a few meters away from his house. Two entities of human appearance, of very small height and apparently wearing diving suits, could be seen nearby. M. Dewilde walked toward them, but at this moment a beam of greenish light was focused on him from the craft and he found himself paralyzed. When he was able to move again the machine had started to rise and the two entities had disappeared.

The investigators have found no trace of the existence of these entities. The ground, examined meter by meter, does not show traces of footsteps. However, one of the sleepers on the tracks showed traces that could have been made by a machine landing on it. In five places the wood of the sleepers is tapped on a surface of about four square centimeters. These markings have all the same appearance and they lie symmetrically, on one line. Three of them—those in the middle—are separated by an interval of forty-three centimeters. The last two are sixty-seven centimeters away from the preceding ones.

A craft that would land on legs instead of wheels like our own aircraft would not leave other traces, one of the inspectors of the air police has declared.

The narrative made by M. Dewilde is also confirmed by several inhabitants of the region. In Onnaing, a young man called M. Edmond Auverlot and a retired man, M. Hublard, have seen about 10:30 P.M. (the time indicated by M. Dewilde) a reddish light traveling in the sky. The same light has been seen from Vicq by three young men.

The railroad specialists consulted by the investigators in respect to the markings on the wooden ties calculated that the pressure indicated by the prints corresponded to a weight of *thirty tons*. These marks were fresh and sharply cut, showing that the wood of the ties had been subjected at those five points to very heavy pressure. In an examination of the gravel of the roadbed, the policemen found another puzzling fact: At the site of the alleged landing the stones were brittle, as if they had been calcined at high temperature (115). Some blackish traces were also found. Although nothing was determined about the existence of the "operators," it was said in the report that the ground was hard and that the absence of footprints did not disprove the story.

September 18:

> ... An object arrived at high speed over the horizon, stood still several minutes over the town and then disappeared into the zenith.

September 19:

> A circular object appeared suddenly in the north. It was flat, gray, and appeared to be metallic. It slowed, stopped, and remained motionless for about thirty seconds, during which time it swayed back and forth slightly. After a half-minute it went off again in a northwest direction.

September 22:

Under the clouds a huge, luminous ball hung motionless. Reddish and surrounded by a sort of moving smoke, almost luminous. Watched for half an hour. Then suddenly from the lower part of the ball there emerged another, much smaller luminous ball; after a few seconds of free fall it slowed, turned obliquely and disappeared at high speed. A moment later a second ball dropped and went off—and then a third, and a fourth. Just then an airplane appeared in another part of the sky. It seemed on a collision course with the ball. The ball abruptly changed position and rose into the clouds and disappeared.

September 26:

The little dog began to bark and howl miserably. She saw it standing in front of something that looked like a scarecrow. But going closer she saw that the scarecrow was some sort of small diving suit, made of translucent plastic material. Behind the blurred transparency of the helmet, two large eyes were staring out at her. The suit began moving toward her with a kind of quick, waddling gait.

She uttered a cry of terror and took to the fields. Looking back she saw a big metallic object, circular and rather flat, rise behind some nearby trees, move off toward the northeast with considerable speed, gaining altitude as it did so.

Neighbors gathered quickly and at the spot where the object had risen they found a circle, ten or so feet in diameter, where the shrubs had been crushed. Trees at the edge of this imprint had some branches broken and the bark rubbed off, and the wheat in the direction of takeoff was flattened out in radiating lines. The original witness was found in a state of nervous collapse. She was put to bed, where she remained for two days with a high fever.

September 28:

> A tramp locomotive was running on a railway line from Nantes to Vannes. In the marsh close to the tracks a circular, flat machine was in rapid flight just above the ground. Luminous, dark red, tinged with violet. It soon reached the locomotive, flying only a few yards above it. Then it accelerated and disappeared toward the west at a terrific speed. For a few seconds the clouds continued to be illuminated by a violet light. The fireman, bewildered, was trembling so much that his place had to be taken until they reached the station. He had to be helped to his bed and for several days he suffered from nervous shock.

Dr. Allen Hynek, later commenting upon this activity, noted:

> Hundreds of similar reports flooded in. But there was no mechanism whatever to handle them. No scientist would touch this tricky subject, and their official air force team began sorting reports by tossing out the "obviously incredible reports." They latched onto those cases in which they could see a natural explanation, a most human and understandable reaction.

It is October 4 and we are at Poncey. "It was about 8:00 P.M.," Mrs. Fourneret said, "and it had already been dark for some time. About twenty yards from the house, in the meadow, a luminous body was balancing itself lightly in the air, to the right of the plum tree, as if preparing to land. As well as I was able to judge, the object was about three yards in diameter and seemed elongated, horizontal and orange colored. I was beside myself with fright and seized the boy, running with him to Mrs. Bouillier's house, where we closed the door tight."

The neighbors armed themselves, the report continues, and went out to investigate. Nothing was there, but they said they found an area over a yard and a half long, twenty-seven inches wide at one end, twenty at the other, where the ground appeared to have been sucked up. On the fresh soil of this hole, they said, white worms wriggled, and the earth that had been torn out was scattered all around the hole in clods ten or twelve inches across, over a radius of about four yards. On the inner edge of the hole similar clods hung down. The earth had been pulled out in such a way that about halfway down the hole was wider than at ground level.

They reported further that the little roots and rootlets in this fertile soil were intact everywhere on the inner surface of the hole and that not one had been cut, as would have been the case if the excavation had been made in the normal way. At the center of the hole, they said, lay a plant with a long root, still attached by the end of the root to the soil at the bottom of the hole, with all its rootlets exposed to the air, completely undamaged. In short, if we are to accept this report, . . . it looked just as if the mass of earth spread over the surrounding grass had been sucked out by a gigantic vacuum.

During the night of September 26–27, about 2:30 A.M., a bus returning from Vals-les-Bains along Route D-130, in the department of Gard, stopped at Foussignargues to drop off Mrs. Julien and her son Andre. They had turned toward their village of Besseges, about half a mile beyond, when they noticed in the sky to the east a reddish luminous object, encircled by a halo of dimmer light. It seemed to be moving toward the ground. Ten minutes later, Mrs. Roche, living at a place called Revety, went out on her terrace for a breath of air. Her eyes were at once caught by the red light coming from a round luminous object, apparently on the ground beside the road a hundred yards or so away, and lower down. "It was rather like a luminous tomato," she described it later. "Five or six vertical stalks, rather thick, came out of the center of it on top." Mrs. Roche and her husband stood there watching for twenty minutes, not daring to go down and look more closely. As it was cold, they finally left. The object was still there at 3:30. In the morning it had disappeared (45).

It has been suggested that the propulsion of UFO's, if they are machines, has something to do with "anti-gravity" (117). This is a rather inexpensive hypothesis. However, several reports mention observations that could hardly have been simply "imagined," and the hole in the field at Poncey, often quoted by supporters of the "anti-gravity theory," was a reality. In this respect, the following account might also prove of interest.

On October 16, 1954, at Cier-de-Riviere (a small village ten kilometers from Saint Gaudens and seven kilometers from Montrejeau, Haute-Garonne), Guy Puyfourcat, a farmer, was returning from the fields with a mare he held by the rein. Suddenly, the animal seemed to become very frightened. At the same time, a sort of machine with a diameter of five feet, of a gray color and in the shape of a large pan, took off from behind some trees and bushes. It climbed to an altitude of about fifty meters and came toward them. Then, the mare was suddenly drawn up in the air about three meters above the ground and the witness had to release the rein. The mare fell back down like an inert mass and remained motionless for ten minutes. Later, the animal was able to stand up, but would stumble and tremble with fear. The machine had disappeared at a very great speed. The witness himself had not felt anything (116).

In the evening of October 20, Jean Schoubrenner, of Sarrebourg, was driving near the village of Turquenstein when he noticed on the highway ahead of him a luminous body. He slowed down as he approached the object, but, when he was about twenty yards from it, he suddenly felt as if he had been paralyzed. At the same moment his motor stopped and, as the car's momentum carried it forward, a sensation of increasing heat spread through his body. A few seconds later the object flew away and these symptoms disappeared.

We will not supply further examples of sightings from this series, for we are sure that no sample, however large, could give the reader a complete picture of how the wave developed. Michel's second book is probably the best reference in this respect; it discusses about one-fourth of all sightings made during the fall in France. The publication of an extensive catalogue of sightings is, of course, to be desired.

An American wave, although smaller than the French series, had developed somewhat earlier. At the same time, considerable peaks of activity appeared in every country on the globe, as can be seen from frequency distributions where the different countries are shown separately. In January, a peak of reports had already been noted in Australia, where a curious mushroom-shaped object was described on several occasions by highly reliable witnesses (30).

The following year, 1955, was not quiet, as witness the reports made at Kelly, Kentucky; at Cochise, Arizona; at Keflavik Airport in Iceland; at Duluth, Minnesota; and

Cheyenne, Wyoming. An enormous amount of detailed reports is available for the sightings made after 1954; triggered by the formidable impact of the events described above, amateurs and enthusiasts, among whom were several serious students of the phenomenon, organized themselves on a local scale and started to publish some of the information they were able to gather. A few professional scientists also became interested in the UFO problem and began sorting the reports from official or private sources, where hoaxes and errors were obviously present, and compiling limited catalogues. Thanks to this activity, the data are so abundant that we must review the last period summarily. As I write this chapter, I have in front of me three drawers full of index cards covering the period 1955–1964. Each card is a reference to the files in which the sighting is to be found, and each card usually mentions at least two or three different sources available for each case.

UFO waves developed in 1956, 1957 and 1958. The apparent periodicity of two years, discernible in the four preceding peaks of activity, seems to vanish during this period. The sightings continue to follow the patterns established in 1952 and verified with such strength in 1954. Most of the examples we will use in later chapters will be chosen from among these recent documents, for UFO's are still seen and reported today in all parts of the world.

THE UNFINISHED SYMPHONY

UFO activity did not cease after the 1958 wave, the last important and massive series of incidents we have been able to record. We do not yet know all reported sightings of the last three years; publication of descriptions made by witnesses in Argentina in 1962 is only beginning. For other countries, such as Africa and New Zealand, we may have to wait much longer before knowing what has happened in the recent period. In the United States, the delay is generally of a few months only. But it will take weeks before reports made in the summer of 1964 are analyzed and classified, and only then will we know if we are dealing with events of interest to our study, or if baseless local rumors have triggered a series of mistakes, hallucinations and misidentifications.

One hundred and eighty-six observations representative of the UFO phenomenon, according to our criteria, were made in 1959. We count 132 for 1960, 141 for 1961, 163 for 1962. The figures for 1963 will be of the same order of magnitude.

April 18, 1963, at Cherns, England: At 9:00 P.M. a bright orange object was seen, from which fifteen lights detached themselves at intervals.

September 10, 1963: A flat, elliptical object with a metallic appearance remained stationary in the sky over Norland in Halifax at 10:00 P.M.

December 27, 1963: A bright white object landed in a field near Epping, England, at 4:00 P.M. The left side of the object was more brightly illuminated. The UFO was eight feet long, three feet high. It took off horizontally and was hidden to the witness behind an obstacle after thirty yards. The grass had been flattened in a circle. Shallow depressions were found in the ground where the object allegedly had landed.

April 29, 1964, a little after noon: A high-school

teacher and six pupils saw a disk hovering, swaying, sometimes giving the appearance of a flat rim, sometimes an elliptical silhouette.

April 30, 1964: A brown, dome-shaped object hovered above a hill and landed. The observation was made ten miles west of Baker, in California. The UFO landed, leaving a large depression. It was observed by three witnesses for five to six minutes.

The answer to the question these sightings present is certainly not trivial. It can lead the psychologist to elaborate new theories of human motivation. It can lead the physicist to improved models of atmospheric optics. But it could also project us into the fantastic, even though it may not be easy to accept this possibility.

CHAPTER FOUR

THE SCIENTIFIC PROBLEM

When any new and unexplained phenomenon offers itself to our inquiry, the first duty of the investigator is to inform himself, with the most scrupulous accuracy, of all the circumstances, however minute, which accompany it; and if past observation cannot answer all circumstantial inquiries which his understanding may suggest as necessary, he must patiently wait the recurrence of a like phenomenon, and diligently observe. When he shall thus have collected all the circumstances that can be imagined to throw light on its origin, he will then, and not until then, be in a position to justify an inquiry into its cause.

Dionysius Lardner, D.C.L. *Popular Physics*, 1856
(Quoted by Waveney Girvan, [185].)

AN UNUSUAL SCIENTIFIC PUZZLE

The UFO problem appears to be a new type of scientific puzzle in two respects. In the usual procedure of scientific discovery, a specialist is suddenly confronted with a fact or a series of facts which contradict one or more established theories. The new fact is later supported by measurements and experiments within the state of the art; and efforts are made by the scientist to develop theories and experimental devices that will cast light on this new area, until the weak point in the old conception is clearly defined. When this is done, experimental developments take place, with specialists of several disciplines generally taking advantage of the new theory to build unique equipment. But scientists do not commit themselves until all tests have been completed and until they are confident of the precise nature of the new phenomenon. Such an approach cannot be taken in the case of the UFO problem; the analyst is confronted here with two theories, one of which claims that the facts are not "new," that only publicity and exaggeration have made them appear so. The second theory claims that the phenomenon is indeed of an unprecedented nature—not yet recognized and classified by human reason.

This dilemma has been clearly seen by the official investigators. A U.S. Air Force consultant, for example, wrote in 1960:

> This "noisy signal" has been coming at us for the past dozen years at least and occasionally there seems to be a "blip" which rises well above the noise level, as in the case of some of the French sightings; one does indeed wonder whether the time has come to pay some attention to it. The role of the air force in the problem of the UFO in the past dozen years has been in line with its avowed mission, namely that of determining the potential hostility of any action in the air that cannot be immediately explained. Their verdict to date has been that whatever the stimuli for the unknown sightings may be, there is no indication of hostility. And since the great preponderance of the reports are easily explainable as

The Scientific Problem

misidentifications of common objects, it seems almost justifiable to extrapolate a bit and cover the remaining 2 or 3 per cent.... Many of the reports would be most difficult to explain as misidentification. Yet to continue such researches places one on what General Chassin, general air defense coordinator, Allied Air Forces, central Europe, NATO, has called "the difficult path of research that is temporarily in disrepute." He has further stated that "true, the reported sightings include observations of meteorites and balloons, and even lies and dreams. That is why vigorous examination of reports is essential. But after all the examination and screening is finished, we still have a percentage of observations that stubbornly resist every conventional explanation. We can, therefore, categorically say that serious objects have indeed appeared and continue to appear in the sky that surrounds us." His conclusion would be correct if he were dealing with phenomena that occur in any other field of human experience, in law, in medicine, or in the many branches of the sciences. Evidence so well attested would certainly be accepted in court. But it is understandable why it cannot be as yet in the area in which we are dealing. We do need either a breakthrough here—and a breakthrough would consist of one or more sightings that occurred in front of a battery of scientists and their instruments, and which sightings also produced copious amounts of hardware—or we need a very careful and devoted study of the evidence already at hand, even recognizing that the signal-to-noise ratio is extremely low and indeed less than unity. At least, it appears to me that work should be done on testing some of the hypotheses that have been put forward in cases in which numerous witnesses were present and the phenomenon lasted a reasonable length of time (45).

If we let things follow their normal course, therefore, the solution to the mystery might present itself one day or another, when this "breakthrough" might occur in the form of an unusually good sighting; after all, this is how the mystery of meteorites was solved, "when so many stones fell on the little village of L'Aigle in France that the evidence became incontrovertible."

But can we be certain that the apparent nonhostility will persist when this "incontrovertible evidence" is finally at hand?

How do you go about determining whether or not actions possibly planned and executed by nonhuman intelligence are hostile? How do you know if actions that would appear "nonhostile" by our standards are really harmless on a longer scale? In our laboratories, we slowly develop cancer on mice and guinea pigs, all the time keeping the most friendly attitude toward them.

If UFO's are mirages the air force mission is too sophisticated; if they are space travelers, it is inadequate.

THE DANGEROUS PRECAUTIONS

When scientists say that the UFO problem cannot be considered a scientific one because no physical evidence has been found yet, I am tempted to answer that what will happen if physical evidence is found will be anything but science. If there ever was a proper time for research, the time is now. The decisions we will make when physical evidence is finally present will be determined by the level of our knowledge and understanding of the phenomenon, and now is the time to acquire this information. By permitting ridicule to bury the problem and waste our chances of obtaining more accurate, more reliable data from the witnesses, we are not acting as scientists.

Emphasis should be placed on the processing of data already known, not solely on "physical evidence." If the "objects" are craft developed by an advanced technical civilization, their "operators" have probably possessed space travel for a very long time, and the sampling of our planet had in all likelihood not been planned before all problems of hardware reliability had been solved; this is precisely what we ourselves are planning to do with our own space problems. It is not very realistic for us to wait for a "flying saucer" suddenly to fall apart in our back yard.

It would indeed be very dangerous to take too many precautions when confronted with a problem of this importance and to refuse to study it before physical samples are collected. Because the possibility of an extraterrestrial origin of the UFO's is considered too "emotional" to be allowed into a scientific discussion, one has to break the barrier and say in plain words what the specialist's jargon would not permit. This is a new occasion for us to wonder if logicians do not restrict a little too much our area of responsibility when they ask us to disregard our emotions and block our imaginations to the bare facts, and to see everything through a microscope with the mind of a machine.

As a specialist in date processing I have exactly the opposite view: The logical, unemotional part of my work is performed excellently, much better than I could perform it, by computers whose lack of imagination cannot be questioned. I feel perfectly justified in asking questions and interpreting answers with that part of my brain that makes me different from the machine—my imagination and my emotional mind. By so doing, I claim I stay on a safe scientific ground, and that only scientists who continue to ignore modern techniques and tools should make up for it by lowering their human brain to the level of unemotional reasoning.

THE NEED FOR A NEW SYSTEM OF ANALYSIS

Science has always chosen the subjects of its own investigations; new facts generally have been discovered in the course of scientific experiments and, by definition, study was undertaken within the state of the art. Our logic and our philosophy of science are adapted to this particular process. When it is not followed, when events occur from the outside, scientists react as emotional human beings, not as well-trained specialists. Other areas of human activity, such as philosophy or theology, are in a position to undertake a study of the phenomenon, but science must remain silent. The Fatima vision, for example, could be interpreted by theologians and philosophers; similarly, C. G. Jung could discuss the UFO problem long before the scientist could adapt his methods of investigation to the phenomenon, for new concepts had to be defined and solid psychological barriers broken.

When scientists are thus confronted with the totally unexpected, their normal reaction is labeling the unknown instead of studying it. A monstrous animal always looks less terrible when it has a name, preferably Latin. From the label, scientists can jump to conclusions, all the time keeping as far away from the monster as possible, later searching for some aspect of the phenomenon which will fit their models computed a priori. Of course, they can prove their

The Scientific Problem

point very well by this process, and the whole argument seems very reasonable and objective; any new phenomenon has aspects that, when isolated from the whole monstrous body, "look like" already known and classified effects.

This point is excellently illustrated by meteorites and "flying saucers"; certainly, we have not chosen to be confronted with these objects, and similarly no farmer has ever chosen to have a stone fall from the heavens through the roof of his barn. Whatever the state of the art, the phenomenon is here, and so is the hole in the roof. If the cause of the manifestation is natural, one day the expansion of science will absorb it; if I drop my pencil now, and watch it fall to the floor, I am performing an experiment which is only accurately described—but poorly explained—by science. I am, however, confident that some day physicists will master this amazing effect. On the other hand, when we are confronted with a manifestation of seemingly intelligent origin, the problem is much more complex. Because we ourselves are reasoning animals, we feel compelled to try to understand it. As a consequence we are tempted to interpret it in a subjective fashion; the risk involved is much greater than in the case of natural events.

Since the concepts that would allow us to grasp the phenomenon in its entirety may not have been formed yet, or may lie beyond the potentiality of the consciousness which is characteristic of the present state of the human brain, we have a tendency to start from plausible solutions and work backward. But this is no longer science:

> It is not in the spirit of science for an investigator either to do a sloppy job or to, a priori, jump to a conclusion. He may be dead right, but in science conclu-

sions are not arrived at by jumping; they are arrived at by a careful step-by-step analysis (45).

Our problem, therefore, is clear: We must analyze the evidence already gathered, in such a way that we neither presuppose nor pre-exclude any possible conclusion. And this is not at all what previous investigators seem to have done.

THE HARVARD SYNDROME

Very uncommon indeed are astronomers who consider with excitement the possibility of life and intelligence in the universe. They seem to have practical reasons for being afraid of discoveries in this field, but there is, in addition, a psychological barrier that prevents them from conceiving of extraterrestrial life. They cannot replace in their imaginations the huge cosmic cemetery for celestial bodies which they describe in their books with a world of life and thought. In this respect I like to remember the wonderful words of the Astronomer Royal (the highest astronomical position in Great Britain): "Space travel is utter bilge." This was, mind you, in 1957, a little before October.

Another reason astronomers tend to dislike this subject is a direct consequence of their education. Nine astronomers out of ten started as young students in astronomy, went through high school and college with the idea of becoming what they are now, considered only astronomical matters at college and have jumped directly from their doctoral dissertation into research and teaching without indulging themselves in any romantic affair with earthly matters. This results in many a disaster when they are later faced with decisions involving business matters, industry contracts or computer programming. It also results in their complete inability to survive if they must live in a different environment; they are therefore careful not to risk their astronomical positions.

Some astronomers have, however, understood the UFO problem and have studied it seriously, even if they have until now neglected to send the result of their discussions to the *Astrophysical Journal*. These researchers have carefully studied many UFO reports and have analyzed them according to the techniques with which they are familiar. Our own results, obtained in the light of different techniques, seem to indicate that the present prevailing attitude is too limited, that there is more to be found in this phenomenon than is claimed, because the samples of data they study are too small and the techniques they employ too narrow. In this book, we oppose a certain method of analysis, *namely, the system which distorts a set of unknown phenomena until it is recognizable by ordinary standards*. This process is the normal interpretation scheme employed by science in its investigations. But manifestations of extraterrestrial intelligence, if they occur, will filter through this type of analysis without being detected because they will always show aspects which can fall under ordinary classifications, thus allowing the skeptic to claim that the observed phenomenon can be explained as a combination of ordinary effects, "seen under peculiar circumstances."

When only individual cases are taken into consideration, this approach, which is illustrated in Dr. Menzel's work and, more generally, in the U.S. Air Force's investigations, is quite correct. But this type of study is insufficient in cases involving new concepts to be extracted through research; investigation of individual cases should be combined here with general analysis. Today's official attitude is an illustration not of extremely careful scientific research as claimed but of this chronic weakness of the human mind excellently termed by Professor Remy Chauvin the Syndrome of Resistance to the Future.

SPECIALISTS AND ANALYSTS

"Dammit, which of them is a poor fellow to believe?"

"Both of them, as long as they simply put their facts down on the table. But neither of them, if they ignore each other and start to piece the whole puzzle together on their own. That's the strength of pure research," I said.

"And that's its greatest weakness," said my Aku-Aku. "In order to penetrate ever further down into their subjects, the host of specialists narrow their fields and dig down deeper and deeper till they can't see each other from hole to hole. But the treasures their toil brings to light they place on the ground above. A different kind of specialist should be sitting there, the only one still missing. He would not go down any hole, but would stay on top and piece all the different facts together."

"A job for an Aku-Aku," I said.

"No, a job for a scientist," retorted my Aku-Aku. "But we can give him a hint or two."

Thor Heyerdahl, *Aku-Aku*

A number of specialists have studied the reports of UFO observations and have "put their facts on the table." But no

The Scientific Problem

one has yet been called to gather their results and attempt to gain access to the general behavior of the phenomenon. As a matter of fact, one could even say that the "specialist" approach has represented an attempt to deny the reality of the UFO phenomenon and that the spirit followed in this approach has been very antagonistic, in practice, to the idea that the reports could lead to the definition of a consistent pattern.

UFO reports have never been analyzed as manifestations of a global effect; the very existence of "waves" of sightings is ignored, or simply denied, by officials in charge of the investigations. The reports are analyzed one at a time, with an amount of energy directly proportional to the publicity they have received in specialized "enthusiast" reviews or in the press, radio and television. *A side effect of this process is that the most interesting reports are completely unknown to the public and to civilian scientists who might, otherwise, have a very different attitude toward the subject.* The more widely discussed cases, such as Washington in 1952, are rather poor and, in our files, would be considered second-rate.

Abominable selection effects have been introduced and work of very unequal quality has been done on the various reports. The typical period is that of Captain Ruppelt, who was in charge of the UFO problem during the 1952 wave.* It was during the 1952 wave that the official pattern for handling and classifying reports seems to have been set up by Ruppelt, who surrounded his office with a series of

---

* Captain Ruppelt died in 1960. The field of UFO research is now old enough that other eminent pioneers are no longer alive. C. G. Jung died in the summer of 1961. Wilbert B. Smith, a Canadian researcher, died on December 27, 1962, and Waveney Girvan (author of *Flying Saucers and Common Sense* and editor of the British *Flying Saucer Review*) died on October 22, 1964.

specialists—an astrophysicist, a psychologist and so forth. He himself made the selection among incoming reports, automatically eliminating accounts of "landings" (and throwing them into the trash can, he writes in his book [118]) and submitting to his consultants only those few reports which he thought could be best explained in the light of their specialties. The astronomer, for example, saw only cases of probable meteors and mirages, and had no access to the remainder of the files.

Once again I am purposely avoiding discussing this process in scientific terms, *for science had nothing to do with the official motivations at that time*. I shall, on the contrary, try to expose and dramatize the enormous contradictions of this methodology by taking an imaginary example.

Let my reader suppose that a fleet of atomic bombers of the Strategic Air Command suddenly finds itself projected backward in time. It is now rushing through the European sky in the time of the empire of Charlemagne, in A.D. 800. Thousands of farmers, soldiers, monks and officials watch it and hear it. The news reaches the Emperor, and a committee of specialists is appointed to solve the mystery. This committee includes: *a*) an erudite in Greek manuscripts; *b*) the Astrologer of the Palace; *c*) the Archbishop of Paris; *d*) two theologians; *e*) the Physician of the Court; *f*) the Chief of the Royal Cavalry; and *g*) the Emperor's jester.

Each committee member is given only those reports that fall under his jurisdiction. Of course, people of very different backgrounds have seen the objects, some at night, some during the day. Since none of them has ever witnessed anything of the kind before, they will describe their vision in ordinary terms, and they are very likely to differ

The Scientific Problem

in their interpretations because they are not all familiar with the same usual objects. Undoubtedly, most of the daytime witnesses will say they have seen a flying crucifix, and heard the cries of Jesus jolting the horizon. These reports will be given to the Archbishop and, since they may contain information of very high value to the Church, and could even shake its very foundations, they are not communicated to the other members of the committee, especially to the physician, the astrologer and the jester.

At night, many farmers and shepherds have seen strange lights dashing through the sky. These reports are completely uninteresting to all except the astrologer, who locks himself in his obervatory to study them in peace.

By that time the Greek erudite has read all of Herodotus and Plato again and comes up with a couple of suggestions: He points out that nothing similar has been reported by these authors, and remarks that the human soul is often affected by strange dreams and visions. Noting a possible new interpretation of an obscure mythological point, he goes back to the library and is never heard of again.

The Physician of the Court is given a hundred reports made by farmers, who describe enormous birds flying in clusters through the sky, accompanied by strange noise and wind. But this does not fool him, and he explains at once these facts, which may appear "strange" only to vulgar, uneducated people, by the yearly migration of some species of birds, which apparently falls earlier this season. The gracious animals have probably taken advantage, he says, of the strong winds generated by a storm—whence the noise. But, of course, uneducated farmers see supernatural phenomena everywhere! The doctors, fortunately, know better.

The Chief of the Royal Cavalry is very angry because he has not yet been consulted. He must agree that the objects do not represent a threat to the welfare of the empire, since it is obvious that they do not carry spears, bows or arrows. He will open a file, however, to keep the record of what is done and classify the observations. But in order to do any serious research on these documents he would need part of the money reserved for the Department of the Royal Ships, and the Great Admiral will never let him do that. Exit the Chief of the Royal Cavalry.

By that time, the Emperor's daughter has fallen deeply in love with a handsome prince, and the people are very busy filing income tax reports, so that nobody speaks of flying crucifixes any more. The general opinion at the Court is that it is not in the interest of the Crown to favor the spreading of rumors, and the less said about it publicly the better.

A nice little old fellow had reported a very strange vision. He said he was working in his field when he suddenly heard a most unusual noise, and saw a huge flying cross rushing from behind a cloud, surrounded with smoke and fire, and falling into the ocean at some distance from the coast. A few minutes later a large white flower appeared in the sky with the shape of a human being dangling below it, as if at the end of a string.

The strange entity landed on top of a big tree in the forest and disappeared. Ten minutes later, as the farmer was still trying to figure out the meaning of his vision, and was pondering whether he should tell it to the priest, a very tall man in green clothes with peculiar hoses hanging around his neck, an insignia on his overcoat and a black tube in his right hand came toward him from the forest and said a few incomprehensible words. Realizing he was not understood, he left and did not return.

The author of this fantastic tale was asked many questions; since he never touched a bottle of wine, he was declared mad in the seventh degree and possessed by the Devil. Therefore, he was neatly and promptly hanged the same week.

The astrologer published a monograph in Latin concerning the interpretation of moving lights. His general conclusion from the sightings he had studied was that the next summer would not be quite so dry as the last one and that the Emperor would have six grandchildren, all male. As a token of royal gratitude for this good news he was promoted and given two pounds of gold.

The Church did not release any general statement at that time, but a considerable number of sermons were made throughout the land concerning the necessity of believing in the Old Texts and being careful in the interpretation of miracles, since the Devil often plays tricks with the imagination of the honest citizen.

But the people were unhappy and still in a state of shock after the strange visions. The Jester of the Court fortunately had an inspiration and wrote a ballad saying that the whole thing had been a good joke and that it was ridiculous to look at the skies to discover strange signs when the land of France was so full of pretty girls. The ballad soon became very popular. Everybody laughed and danced for three days and three nights, and many children were born less than a year later.

This little tale, I claim, bears a striking resemblance to the official process for handling UFO reports: The main piece in the mechanism is missing. A different kind of specialist should be sitting there. The missing man is the analyst.

During the last decades, on the basis of scientific, technical and industrial experience, and under the pressure of wartime necessity and the requirements of private enterprise, a body of techniques has emerged which encompasses operations research, decision-making large-scale data processing, information theory and control analysis. These new techniques, disciplines and sciences have been employed to classify human activity, technical processes and natural events in sets and classes and to generalize the finding of specialists into global approaches and general descriptions. In the last twenty years, they have found application in every field of human activity. Some of the techniques thus developed could find immediate application in UFO research.

The analyst would demand access to *all the facts*. He would completely ignore the labels used by official authorities—"good report," "bad report," "unreliable," "insufficient"—because they reflect subjective, nonscientific verdicts. He would introduce his own system of classification without bothering to state first that the phenomenon must belong to this or that field of research, because there is no such thing as a "field of research," and research itself is only a part of human activity that has not been defined in scientific terms. He has learned that, although specialists sometimes use different techniques, tricks or know-hows and like to think of their work as an entity separated from the rest of the universe by golden barriers, there are wide bands of similarity across these little cells through which can be gained almost immediate access to any of these disciplines. He will not bother to ask for permission to

The Scientific Problem

contradict accepted theories, because he is a researcher and any researcher must be conscious of the possibly novel nature of the phenomenon he may suddenly be confronted with. Nor will he apologize for including in his research so-called "fantastic" reports, for "fantastic" can only be defined with respect to a local system of reference; he will try to work in a scale where he knows no other constraint than the relative laws of human reasoning and the limits of his own imagination. Human limitations of memory and capacity to process huge masses of data without forgetting or making mistakes are no problem with the advent of computers; the UFO problem is made for the analyst. But he has never been asked to study it.

If an analyst were given the opportunity to study the UFO problem his first demand would be that one or two mathematicians be added to the team of specialists. If new phenomena are present in the set of patterns that constitutes the UFO problem, there is a possibility that these phenomena may lie outside the scope of any one of the specialties recognized today by science, and still be discernible to the mathematical mind. At least, the abstract structure of these behaviors may fall under some mathematical category or may be approached by mathematical descriptions when all other specialists have come to the limits of their competence.

I will not endeavor to prove that specialists have indeed come to the limits of their competence in their attempts to see through the blackness of the UFO mystery; this is obvious, since after twenty years of investigation we are still at the point where Ruppelt was when he set up his "committee of specialists."

It is a fascinating experience to review the old arguments used against the pioneers of astronomy—Copernicus, Kepler, Galileo—and to realize that the mental processes that today oppose the hypothesis of extraterrestrial intelligence are precisely those we like to suppose were abolished four centuries ago. In this respect, it is of interest to remark, in the light of official interpretation of UFO's as reflections, mirages, distortion through haze layers, etc., that some early Greek philosophers believed that the sun and the stars did not have substance or permanence; they were thought to be

> ". . . hazy effluvia that rose from the earth and caught fire. Stars are consumed at dawn; in the evening new exhalations form new ones. Similarly, a new Sun is born each morning, constituted of accumulated sparkles. The moon is a compressed cloud, that takes one month to dissolve; later a new cloud is formed. Above the different regions of the Earth we see different moons and suns: all are nebulous illusions" (quoted in [120]).

Such a position was very tenable. It solved the problem much more completely than any of the systems astronomers painstakingly elaborated later. There is, however, a part of the human mind that rebels against this negative approach to the interpretation of reality.

Theories tending to deny the reality of physical phenomena are seen recurring in cosmology each time dogma is shaken by new observational material. In order not to destroy mental contraptions called theories—which the scientist knows are born only in his imagination and stay alive only by constant investments from his imagination—the scientist claims that physical facts themselves are in his imagination; there is something fascinating indeed in the spectacle of the human mind denying entrance to the kingdom of material existence to facts that do not fit into theoretical models.

On November 11, 1572, Tycho Brahe, while walking outside his observatory before dinner, became aware of the existence of a new star brighter than Venus, close to the constellation of Cassiopeia. This discovery of the first nova since the birth of Christ was in complete contradiction to the astronomical doctrine of the time. The contemporary view was that all changes, all effects involving modification, birth or death could only take place in the vulgar part of the universe, in the immediate environment of the earth. On the contrary, the eighth sphere, the sphere of the fixed stars, remained unchanged since the creation of the world.

The reality of the phenomenon could not be denied, but a number of ingenious theories were invented to prove that the new object was not a star. Some explained that it was a comet formed by the condensation of the vapors of sin and set to fire by divine anger (120). It produced a sort of poisonous dust that fell on the people's heads and generated all sorts of evil things such as "bad weather, pestilence and Frenchmen." Most astronomers described the new object as a comet which has no tail and moved very slowly. Tycho Brahe's answer to these acrobats—*O coecos coeli spectatores*! (Blind spectators of the Sky!)—could find applications today.

No less an astronomer than Galileo occasionally made the same mistake. Because comets did not fit into his model, he denied their reality as material objects. He decided they had to be optical illusions like aurorae or sun dogs; they were provoked by a reflection of the hazes from the earth "that rise in the sky higher than the moon."

Material existence, however, should obviously be tested. In the case of UFO's, the recognition of this property is so crucial that one has indeed to be very careful. The official approach is satisfactory if the data are representative of the phenomenon one wants to study, and if criteria exist which limit the possible complexity of the final "explanation." In his book (121), Dr. Menzel works from a selected sample of UFO reports and does not limit the potential complexity of his system. But very few of the cases he studies would be thought worthy of consideration in an objective system of analysis where weights are distributed according to well-defined criteria, and not according to the amount of publicity the case has received in "enthusiast" circles obviously unconcerned with scientific analysis. Thus we find ourselves confronted again with this selection effect of official* and private secrecy on good reports and exaggerated publicity on average or frankly bad reports. A classical example is the Lubbock case, highly acclaimed in the ranks of the "believers."

We would like to confront those scientists who are opposed to the theory of the material existence of the UFO's with sightings like Vernon, Poncey, Ponthierry, Foussignargues, Quarouble in France or Levelland, Texas and Lock Raven, Maryland. The same omission is deplored in their analysis of the difficult problem of "landings." No serious investigator has ever been very worried by the claims of the "contactees"† (see Chapter 5). But the reli-

---

* Regarding the so-called "official secrecy," we shall point out, however, that because the cases are not individually publicized does not mean that they are secret.

† The word "contactee" applies to persons who claim to have received knowledge of the nature and origin of the "flying saucers" from the operators of the craft themselves. Most of them, like George Adamski (formerly head of a mystical cult known as the Royal Order of Tibet), add that they have actually traveled in "flying saucers."

able reports of objects seen on or close to the ground are ignored by the present official analyses, and nothing is done to satisfy our curiosity concerning such excellent accounts as those given by Gachignard in Marignane or Marius Dewilde in Quarouble. The books written by leading scientists opposing the material reality of the UFO phenomenon contain many comments on physical effects that take place in the atmosphere and natural phenomena that could puzzle untrained persons and, granted, are commonly misidentified in the enthusiast journals. But they do not give one new piece of information to the competent investigator.

REQUIREMENTS FOR AN OBJECTIVE ANALYSIS OF UFO REPORTS

How can we approach the problem so that we will be certain that most simple natural and conventional effects are rejected from our analysis at an early stage and that no feasible solution (however fantastic, in a natural or artificial sense) has escaped because of selection effects?

We certainly cannot do it if we begin with the idea that UFO's *must* be natural, and sort them as they arrive as our good friend Charlemagne did. We have to be much more careful and refuse to work from selected samples. We must patiently gather objective information from all sources; officials and amateurs, enthusiasts and crackpots or cultists have the right to send us their views.

We will then make a series of general comments and statements regarding the purpose of our investigation. We could, for example, open our research by stating that we are not interested in proving the existence or nonexistence of "flying saucers," which is not in itself a scientific problem, but in finding the motivation behind the observed generation of reports by the public concerning celestial objects. By so doing, we will have defined a problem much more simple than the one astronomers such as Dr. Menzel, the U.S. Air Force's consultants or the groups of enthusiasts are trying to attack, and we can reasonably hope to solve it within a few years.

We would not start from known effects and try to fill the hole in the roof with them. We would be concerned with one single effect: *Reports are indeed generated*. They are observable and can be printed and sent through the normal channels of communication between researchers; they are indeed pieces of scientific data. To get more information on the cases is a matter of phone calls.

From this basis, we would work by successive deductions, hoping to define objectively the characteristics of the phenomenon's cause, and later to identify it through constant reference, not to isolated cases, but to consistent classes, permanent entities, invariable patterns. Only then will we be able to define a UFO. Until our work reaches this point, we will simply remark that in the 1963 edition of the *Encyclopaedia Britannica*, Dr. Hyneck's definition has found its place—between the headings "Unicorn" and "Unified Field Theory"!

RELIABILITY OF THE SOURCES OF INFORMATION

In addition to reports found in the official records we have studied a number of other sources of documentation, which

The Scientific Problem

may be classified mainly into the categories of published and unpublished information. Their reliability, of course, is variable. Homogeneity and consistency can be achieved only by reduction to a common basis in a rigidly defined system of classification. And it remains impossible to eliminate completely the influence of the spirit of each nation; descriptions made by French witnesses are in general more detailed than those made by Americans, while the terms used to describe the same thing in Japan or Great Britain will be very different. Clearly, it would be a mistake to put the emphasis on the specific terms used by the witnesses. A typical example in this respect is that of the "cigar," which may turn out to be either an "egg" or a "disk." And we will have to ask questions that are independent of the witness' character and background. Defining categories according to the reported *size* of the object would lead to considerable confusion; the average American witness compares the apparent dimension of Venus or Jupiter to that of "a baseball at arm's length."* This should not be viewed as an indication of the unreliability of the report, or as a "basis of contradiction" which would eliminate the case, as some official investigators assume. This particular piece of information should simply be ignored or, if apparently reliable, taken into account with a weight relative to all the other characters in the report.

It is always possible, even in the presence of such natural mistakes (which are expected and should not come as a surprise to the researcher), to define an approach that will minimize the risks of misclassification; information from

---

* We have even found an object as big as "a star at arm's length." But let my reader, if he laughs at these mistakes, see how much of his TV screen is covered (when watching from a usual distance) by an ordinary stamp held at arm's length.

very different sources, even if very disparate, can still be formed into a general catalogue by the process we shall describe later.

One should be very careful when using books as sources of information, for the psychology or personality of an author (and also the fact that he is trying to use these accounts to prove something or to make the reader grasp a certain point) will always generate distortion effects. This is why we have tried, both in this book and in other publications on the subject, to put the emphasis on classes and behaviors rather than on individual cases.

Quite a large number of volumes have already been written on the subject and those we have found intelligible are listed in the Bibliography at the end of this volume. A person who would like to become familiar with the problem could, however, find most of the scientific material, in addition to a large number of specific examples, in the books of the serious students of the phenomenon who have avoided the pitfalls of "loose thinking" and resisted the temptation of fantasy:*

(1) C. G. Jung, *A Modern Myth*
(2) E. Ruppelt, *The Report on Unidentified Flying Objects*
(3) Aime Michel, *The Truth about Flying Saucers*

---

* A poll made in 1958 by a UFO journal, *Saucers*, among U.S. amateurs disclosed that Ruppelt and Keyhoe tied for first place as "Best author of UFO material" (28 per cent each), followed by Aime Michel (18 per cent). At the question, "Which of the following has most harmed UFO research?" 59 per cent answered "Official censorship and ridicule," 27 per cent "Fantastic claims by some contactees," 9 per cent "Public apathy and conformity" and 5 per cent "Press apathy." The "Best book on UFO's" was *The Report on Unidentified Flying Objects* (Ruppelt, 32 per cent). Michel's two books tied for third place, with Keyhoe's *Flying Saucers from Outer Space* (9 per cent) behind Miller's *Flying Saucers: Fact or Fiction* (14 per cent).

(4) Aime Michel, *Flying Saucers and the Straight Line Mystery*
(5) D. Menzel, *The World of Flying Saucers*

In addition, the general background will be provided by the following popular books:

(1) Charles Fort, *The Book of the Damned*
(2) D. Keyhoe, *Flying Saucers are Real*
(3) C. Lorenzen, *The Great Flying Saucer Hoax*
(4) NICAP, *UFO Evidence*

We have already mentioned the scientific journals as a source of documentation. Of course, there is a definite drop after 1947, when banning of UFO reports became general. However, some astronomical publications, especially those put together by amateurs, continue to report "peculiar" meteors and "ball lightning" so strange they deserve a card in our UFO file.

Researchers who want to study the 1954 French wave should consult newspaper collections as Michel did, and as we did to corroborate some of Michel's findings. But let them be prepared to be confronted with an enormous quantity of work! Most of the good reports have become collector's items, and the early documents that circulated as private communications, such as the Quincy catalogue, cannot be found today.

Between the periods of mass publicity one cannot gain information concerning the sightings through the large newspapers and must therefore turn to the local press, a very difficult task if one does not receive help from local correspondents. Another solution would be for local UFO groups to collect information in their areas and send it without distortion or comment to a data-processing center, where the general file would be kept. But everybody prefers to keep jealousy his own documents and most of the information never comes to light. One could also subscribe to a news-clipping service, but this would require a fairly good organization set up by data-processing experts, because of the volume of material involved; the U.S. Air Force tried to do that at a certain period *but had to give it up because they received too much information*!

Unpublished information is superabundant and would seem almost limitless to a naïve researcher who would start a systematic review of all stacks of letters or clippings kept by enthusiasts throughout the world, or would obtain permission from local police or large newspapers to consult their archives. Michel received so much information that he was unable to read and classify all of it. Most of the old documents contained in his files have since been clarified (which is how the forgotten 1946 wave was rediscovered) and a thorough analysis of the remainder of his files, begun four years ago, is still in progress. Such work can be conducted with efficiency and relative speed only within the frame of a general system of classification and with the aid of indexes and catalogues, and even this preliminary work will represent years of activity for a group of experienced researchers.

Rumors and unreported personal experiences are still the largest reservoir of information. They are quite variable in quality; many astronomers,* pilots and official person-

---

* In 1959, a restricted newsletter from the Smithsonian Astrophysical Observatory had this to say on the subject of "popular comments on UFO's": "It is exceedingly undesirable to become associated with these 'sightings' or the persons originating them. . . . on no account should any indication be given to others that a discussion even remotely concerned with UFO's is taking place.

nel would fiercely deny having seen anything like a disk in the sky. Some will admit, in private, having seen peculiar objects, but will never report them officially, not because they feel they do not have evidence to support their account, but because they are afraid of the consequences; pilots are not supposed to see things, and astronomers are not supposed to spread superstitious rumors—not to mention the fact that in some countries "spreading rumors" is a crime punishable by two weeks in jail.

Through personal association with interested astronomers and scientists we were in a favorable position to discover how different their private attitudes are from their official standpoints, and we could often gain access to otherwise "reserved" information. An unfortunate consequence is that we would be in difficulty if we were asked to cite the exact reference or source of some of this information. In France, for example, no official record has been kept of the observations. A special bureau of the army seems to have existed when public emotion was at a maximum, but the useful part of its files contains only a few reports made by meteorologists in Sahara and control-tower operators, in addition to naïve considerations about meteors taken from some encyclopedia. The Italian Air Force once issued a vague statement concerning its files, which contained, in their own words, only very limited information on objects seen flying on the eastern coast of their country in 1954.

Considerable private activity has developed and is being maintained in Europe. Although no unifying force exists, this activity is not always wasted. Interested scientists search for new facts and their findings are often of high quality.

One should always, however, check completely the original source, for UFO data are generally transmitted burdened by superstition and falsehoods. Through extremely careful analysis of the original facts one can generally find the truth. But a very intimate understanding of the people and of local conditions is required for such research.

THE SEARCH FOR INVARIANTS

We have not yet defined the UFO phenomenon. We have to do so in such a way that a scientific study will be permissible, and this implies not trying to define "flying saucers," for the events connected with their alleged apparition are not observable at will or reproducible under the guarantees of official science. We will propose the following definition:

Manifestations of the UFO phenomenon are to be found among reports of the perception of a visual image, commonly interpreted by the witness as that of a material flying object, which possesses either or both of the following properties: a) an appearance which, to the witness, is unusual; b) a behavior which, to the witness, is unusual.

UFO phenomena are thus subject to scientific study (since the *reports* are observable by official scientists), whereas the alleged "object" escapes rational analysis. In addition to this definition, we will make the following statement:

Manifestations of the UFO phenomenon occur as the

result of physical causes that can be described in terms of natural laws.

UFO's may therefore be mirages, meteors or interplanetary vehicles, but not mystical entities escaping rational analysis. This may seem a superfluous precaution to the scientific reader, but it will be seen that the student of the UFO problem needs a statement of this sort to claim the right to analyze some of the cases he is bound to meet in his investigating.

In the following, we will call a "UFO event" the generation of an unusual image by a physical cause, and we will call a "UFO sighting" the perception of this image by a witness. The report of this perception is the phenomenon the scientist observes.

In the present chapter we will try to give as clear an outline as possible of the method we have used in our own investigation of the UFO phenomenon. The basic strategy is to accept all reports and to deal with classes, not with individual cases, in the first (classification-codification) and the second (analysis of behavior) steps of the process. The third step will be an attempt at interpretation in physical terms, in which we will evaluate the results already obtained and will allow ourselves to consider specific points present in a few well-defined sightings. Only in this third step will the door be open to speculation and hypothesis.

Confronted with masses of letters, clippings and documents, how are we to proceed to organize a "hierarchy of reliability" among the reports? How may we classify this information in such a way that our work will indeed result in clarification and will be objective, a necessary condition for other researchers to be able to use our data and to criticize them meaningfully?

This can only be done through a long process of pattern-analysis. The first steps in this process are elementary. Whoever the witness, whatever his background, occupation or drinking habits, we possess at least two objective pieces of information concerning him: the place of the sighting and the date. This is our most natural access to the case: its coordinates in space and time.

Obvious as this seems, many "Ufologists," officials and amateurs who claim they are doing "scientific research," neglect this point; even such specialized journals as the *UFO Investigator* or the *APRO Bulletin*, published in the United States (see p. 117), not to mention publications of less importance, print numerous descriptions of UFO sightings but do not bother, in many instances, to mention the date or the place. In books by UFO enthusiasts one finds quite often the irritating situation of knowing the exact day, hour and minute when the author received a very important call from the Pentagon concerning a certain sighting, and we are given all the details of the call, and we know that the author was getting ready for breakfast and had already put butter on his toast when the phone started ringing, but we remain totally ignorant of the date and place of the sensational sighting. Some official reports will indicate carefully the name, address and military status of the witness, but not the place of the observation.

A third piece of information contained in the report is a description—the witness claims he has seen something either in the sky or on the ground. His claim is real, but the object of his claim may be a hoax or an illusion. We must not, therefore, classify mainly according to such factors as the dimension, the shape or the course of the object, but according to its behavior, which is an integrated impression of very high stability. And this should again be in terms so general that mistakes made by the observer, or failure of his memory concerning the apparent diameter or elevation of the phenomenon, will not affect this classification to a large degree.

CRITICISM OF THE OFFICIAL CLASSIFICATION SYSTEM

The interested services have never, to our knowledge, tried to codify the sightings for the purpose of research since the days of *Special Report 14*.* A classification system has, however, been introduced to help in the tedious task of keeping the official records in order. This is a perfectly sound thing to do, as long as one does not try to use this classification as a basis for statistical or any other kind of analysis. And even the findings of *Special Report 14* are, in the view of this writer, as void of scientific interest as the work of the mathematician who tried to evaluate the probability that the sun will rise tomorrow.

Like a computing machine, a statistical procedure never creates information, but only transforms it. A statistical result is only the expression, under a new and possibly more readable form, of the information present in the data, i.e., translated through the code. The analyst, if working with a reliable classification system developed with this

---

* Project Blue Book *Special Report No. 14 was declassified* by the U.S. Air Force in 1955. It was mainly concerned with elementary statistical analysis of sightings of the early period.

particular application in mind, is able to extract from the data entities that were already present, but not perceptible, in the original material.

We would agree with the statement that at least 50 per cent of the reports that we have studied (and, in some cases, as many as 80 or 90 per cent) cannot be considered as representative of the UFO phenomenon. But the term "unidentified" has no meaning; as a specialist in this field, this writer denies categorically any significance to the claim that "only so many percent" of the sightings contained in the official files are unidentified under the present system of reference. No scientist could accept such a statement any more than he could accept the idea that a rabbit has suddenly disappeared into a magician's hat, even if the magician says so.

The official system consists in attaching to each UFO report one of the following labels:

(1) Was balloon
(2) Probable balloon
(3) Possible balloon
(4) Was aircraft
(5) Probable aircraft
(6) Possible aircraft
(7) Was astronomical
(8) Probable astronomical
(9) Possible astronomical
(10) Other
(11) Unknown
(12) Unidentified
(13) Insufficient data

Categories 1, 4, and 7 are supposed to contain only those reports which have been shown to refer to a conventional object, when this object has really been identified, not only as a balloon (or an aircraft, etc.) but as a specified balloon, aircraft, etc. For example, a witness calls the sheriff's office to report seeing a sphere in the sky. Policemen go out, observe the sphere and, by calling the local airport, determine that the origin of the sighting is a balloon tracked at that very moment by the local station. This is a true identification. Similarly, a so-called "strange light" photographed at night is shown to fit exactly the trajectory of an artificial satellite. Such reports obviously have no place in a study of UFO's.

In categories 2, 5 and 8 are found reports of objects that displayed a behavior so similar to that expected from a conventional object that no reason exists to believe that this particular object was other than conventional. To give an extreme example, I cannot prove that my grocer is not a Venusian in disguise, but on the other hand I have no reason to believe that he is other than human as long as his appearance and behavior are human. We will often find ourselves in agreement with the official conclusion and ignore most of these reports.

Even if disagreement sometimes exists concerning the "probable" categories, it is never very considerable. Real disagreement begins when it comes to the "possible." For this is a human, not a scientific, notion and there is no control over the amount of complexity one is allowed to accept to make up these imaginary "possibilities." The analyses of UFO reports published recently by certain professional astronomers are an illustration of this type of situation. The discussion is purely "literary" and no weight can be attached to either interpretation. It is as void of real meaning as the nineteenth-century dispute about "mystical" properties of the Empty Set. The percentage of rejection through this category is a function of the imagination of the man who happens to be in charge of the project at the time; the result is disconcerting.

The limit of astonishment is reached when it comes to the "insufficient information" category. We read in Thor Heyerdahl's extraordinary book *Aku-Aku* the following remark: "How far would the F.B.I. get if they only collected fingerprints without trying to catch the thief?" The category "insufficient data" has been defined in a way that would have delighted a Jesuit of the good old days. A report is said to give insufficient information when there is reason to believe that had the investigator possessed more information on the case he would have classified it in one of the conventional categories. The amusing point is that some of the reports stamped "insufficient" contain a full page of fine print with all possible details. But you can always assume that the missing information would have contained details such that it would have become clear to the investigator that the cause of the sightings was conventional. This is anything but science.

We must limit ourselves here to a few of these contradictions, for this is not an accusation against official commissions obviously not qualified in this type of analysis. What worries us is that the scientists' judgment against the reality of UFO's has been based on such nonscientific evaluations made under no general plan of research and in conditions one must criticize. The expensive *Special Report 14*, for example, was made for ATIC by a private consulting firm whose name is kept secret, not because of the results or contents of the investigation, but because this company did not want its name attached to a study of "flying saucers." What sort of science is this, when the authors of a scientific report that will be used for years as an authoritative reference do not want their names to be mentioned because they fear the ridicule attached to the problem could affect their business?

The classification system is very poor for another reason. A "possible aircraft" could very well *also* be a "possible balloon," and I do not see how one could prove that the description of a ball of light seen very far away in the western sky is Venus rather than a balloon when no accurate position is given; *all these categories overlap* and the classification is purely arbitrary. In addition, "astronomical" can refer to a misinterpretation of Venus, Mars or Jupiter, as well as to a meteor. An analysis based on divisions of such poor homogeneity is not likely to lead to satisfactory results when the testing of hypotheses is attempted.

We are left with three categories into which we can put reports that, from the point of view of the UFO student, are interesting. They are "other," "unknown" and "unidentified." This is not very appealing.

THE MYTH OF "UNIDENTIFIED" OBJECTS

What does "unidentified" mean? Take the Vernon sightings as described by Michel in his second book or as we described it in Chapter 3. In the official classification the Vernon cigar would be "unidentified." But is it really?

Identification is realized when a certain event or object

is recognized by human intelligence as belonging to a class. What this class is is irrelevant. The incident that took place in Vernon may seem strange or fantastic by our present standards, but this is a lay reaction, not a scientific one. Its fantastic character should not prevent the student of the phenomenon from recognizing the same pattern already seen at work in Poncey, Montlevic, Oloron, Gaillac, as well as in Dallas, Trenton or in the Gulf of Mexico. This consistent behavior is typical of a *set of events*, which may or may not later be found to be of material nature but do have in common the same *properties*.

As soon as consistency in the report is such that class properties can be defined, *we can speak of identification*; as far as I am concerned, the Vernon report is perfectly indentifiable as a member of a specific class of behavior. The fact that I do not at present know the exact nature of the cause of the report is not of primary importance at this stage of analysis—the exact nature of UFO's is precisely what I am trying to find. Similarly, a nuclear physicist knows a pion from an ordinary meson when he sees one, but he does not know what they are.

I cannot think of anything more treacherous than this label "unidentified." Anything you have never found on your way before starts as unidentified. When my prehistoric ancestor saw a mammoth for the first time, it was in his view a perfect URO (Unidentified Running Object). Of course, this was only a small percentage of all the animals he could recognize in the jungle. However, I do thank Heaven he was a better logician than our official researchers, and did something about it before identification was complete!

We can also have the opposite situation: A report classi-

The Scientific Problem

fied as "unidentified" by official investigators may be of no interest to the analyst concerned with the UFO phenomenon. For example, on January 26, 1955, at 6:15 P.M., a black smoke trail was seen at Lakeland, Florida, for an unknown duration. The trail of black smoke made a large circle, an explosion took place and the object was observed falling. This is called "unidentified" because the investigator has been unable to find the exact cause of the phenomenon. But the behavior described is so similar to that of a missile out of control that we should not include this in a UFO file, even with very low weight.

On January 9, 1956, twenty miles southwest of Chanute Air Force Base in Illinois, a light whose color changed from red to green to white was seen at approximately two thousand feet; this is classified "insufficient data for evaluation." But it would seem that we have from this limited account a quantity of information concerning not the object itself, perhaps, but the conditions under which the observation was made. We know that the witness saw only a light changing color; it would not be very realistic to hope that more information could be gathered concerning this "light" if it was flying at that altitude. We know that an aircraft, as well as several other physical causes, could produce the same appearance. This is a type of sighting from which we simply *cannot* obtain more. Even knowing the exact distance, the azimuth and elevation of the object would not help us. We have to make a decision: either reject the case, or include it with an extremely low weight.

Consider the following case, also classified "insufficient information": in Anita, Iowa, on June 15, 1955, a cigar-shaped object with a blue and white glowing color and a red exhaust was observed. The object appeared to be five hundred to one thousand feet above the ground, and the observer noted a soft hissing sound. Even if additional information would be welcome, it seems to us that one could already start doing something more with this sighting than putting it into the same category as the preceding one. And we wonder what their reason was for not making it an "unknown."

All these categories may be of help as far as the administrative routine is concerned, and they certainly could be maintained. But they cannot help in an analysis of the UFO problem. The two operations—maintaining a file of reports in accordance with official regulations, and doing research on the information contained in the reports—should be very clearly separated, and separate codes should be used.

BASIS OF A SCIENTIFIC CLASSIFICATION

We will not try to define a "scientific classification" with reference to the "administrative classification," but will rather start from a completely different point of view, which has apparently never been presented before. *We will forget about all identified reports and we will neglect all those involving objects similar in behavior to conventional objects as they would usually appear.*

When this elimination is made (and it could be made objectively, by reference to a computer program, for example, thus eliminating problems of "personal choice") we are left with a set of reports which we call manifestations of the UFO phenomenon. The existence of such manifestations is an empirical fact, not an as-

The Scientific Problem

sumption. It is the set of all these manifestations that is the object of our study. This criterion completes the general definition given on page 132.

We want to determine if all these reports can be explained as conventional objects and phenomena seen under unusual circumstances, or if a fraction of them does correspond to some effect still unknown to science. We want to distribute them between "disjoint sets"; i.e., we want to define classes that do not overlap, as the official categories do, and we want to define them as simply as possible. We can remark that there are not many sorts of UFO's, even if the witnesses use very different words or expressions to define them. Their behavior is bound to fall under one, and only one, among the five categories that follow (122):

I. They can be seen (or imagined, or perceived) as objects situated on the ground or close to the ground (at tree height).

II. They can display the behavior observed at Vernon or, more generally, appear as huge cylindrical forms surrounded by cloudlike formations, often vertical. The latter behavior defines a subclass II-A, when descriptions of actual generation of secondary objects are called II-B.

III. They can be described as aerial forms hovering in the atmosphere, or following a path interrupted by a stationary point; a precise point will be defined on the ground from this discontinuity.

IV. They can be seen as objects crossing the sky without such interruption or discontinuity.

V. They can be distant objects seen as lights.

Experience has shown that clarity is increased when three to five categories are defined within each group. We will thus speak of a report of Type II-B, III-D, etc.* The reliability attached to each category is obviously variable. We will describe now the approach that is followed when problems arise in the use of this classification system.

COMMENTS ON VARIOUS TYPES OF UFO REPORTS

Each of the categories defined above is closed on itself and contains consistent reports that can be significantly compared. From a comparison of objects *of the same class* one can now try to extract global information. The gap between any two of these classes is so considerable that there is little chance of misclassification, even if the code is used by an untrained person, except for extreme cases when greater experience is needed. In general, only classification within Type II will require a great deal of familiarity with the problem and considerable attention. These events are rare and remarkable, but sometimes treacherous. Only in twenty or thirty good cases is there no possibility of mistake. Some of the average reports of this category should be analyzed in the light of Dr. Menzel's approach, in which one puts the emphasis on the very strange behavior that extreme cases of mirages and other natural phenomena can present. We will give two examples of cases where the author has until now been unable to reach a definitive verdict, although he has classified both reports under Type II-B:

On July 9, 1686, at 1:30 A.M., at Leipzig, the German

---

* This system is completely described in (189).

astronomer Gottfried Kirch reported that he saw a burning globe with a trail that appeared 8.5° from Aquarius and remained motionless for more than seven minutes. Its apparent diameter was one-half that of the moon, and it gave so much light that one could read with no other source of illumination. It vanished gradually at the same place. The object pointed downward at an angle and left two small globes that were visible only with a telescope.

The second observation is described in (5) in the following terms:

> A startling cosmic body appeared over the Terrace of Windsor Castle on August 18, 1783. It was watched by Tiberius Cavallo, F.R.S. He called it "a most extraordinary meteor." He wrote: "Northeast of the Terrace, in clear sky and warm weather, I saw appear suddenly an oblong cloud nearly parallel to the horizon. Below the cloud was seen a luminous body. It soon became a roundish body, brightly lit up and almost stationary. It was about 9:25 P.M. This strange ball at first appeared bluish and faint, but its light increased, and it soon began to move. At first, it ascended above the horizon, obliquely toward the east. Then it changed its direction and moved parallel to the horizon. It vanished in the southeast. I saw it for half a minute, and the light it gave out was prodigious. It lit up every object on the face of the country. It changed shape to oblong, acquired a tail, and seemed to split up into two bodies of small size. About two minutes later came a rumble like an explosion.

The first of these sightings carries in our files a weight relegated to incidents we feel could have natural causes, and the second one, a weight indicating that we are almost positive it is not a UFO phenomenon, but an extreme case of a meteor. These two examples will give our reader an idea of how we define the "boundaries" of our classification.

Type I will be discussed later; the reports in this category are those where objects are said to have been seen on the ground or close to the ground. But we will clarify immediately some points that concern the subclass, in which we find reports of "objects described close to the ground, and said to have displayed interest in, or followed, a moving terrestrial object as a train, a car or a motorcycle." Many natural situations can be expected to cause emotional witnesses to report that they have been followed by a strange light. The moon is very often the origin of the scare, especially when the witness travels on a winding road at night; under the influence of fear he will become unable to realize clearly the turns he makes, and will say that the mysterious object was sometimes to his left and sometimes to his right, thus proving to him that it could not have been the moon. Stars or planets seen through haze layers, or headlight reflections, will sometimes do the trick. But one should not disregard this type of observation on the basis of these understandable errors.

As we have said above, Type II-B is sometimes critical. Enthusiast publications speak of "a huge mother-ship with small objects" in the case of a bright meteor breaking into fragments! A necessary condition for a sighting to be entered under Type II is a duration of at least several minutes, not seconds. And one should remember that the really good events of this category have lasted between a half hour and several hours. The extreme case is the Wyalong-Toompang incident in Australia, described in (123), that took place in June, 1961:

The Scientific Problem

"We were making lambs in Toompang. Near the lunch hour we heard what we thought was a jet. I looked up for the jet and saw an eagle-hawk, high in the sky. I was taking a bit of interest in the eagle-hawk when we heard another sound, as if the jet were overhead again. But I still could not see a jet.

"Then I saw this round object. It looked like a silver star, and seemed to be over Wyalong, it was so high up and so far away. It was stationary. I said to the others—there were seven of us—'Get a load of this.' One man is short-sighted. Another who is could not pick up the object. But four others did, and watched it off and on for over an hour, possibly two hours. I saw one object leave the first object and go to the left, and later two objects go to the right, then come back. One of the other men said he saw two objects go to the left. I would not know about that, we were working, marking lambs, and we were not able to keep an eye on it all the time.

"The objects I saw leaving the stationary object seemed round. But when the one I saw leave it on the left came overhead as it went towards Young I could see it seemed to be V-shaped. I do not know what I saw, but I know that when the objects left the stationary object on the right-hand side they went out to the side and then went straight up fast. The one that passed overhead towards Young was really trevelling."

A second man backed this up. He said he could not say that any of the objects were V-shaped. They all appeared to him to be round, shimmering slightly in the sun. At times the silver sheen winked a little on the small objects as they were leaving or returning to the main object. They left slowly, then went out at high speed, circled and returned, slowing down as they approached the big stationary object. Then they seemed to land on it or go into it because they disappeared when they reached it.

Three or four at a time watched an object leave the

big object commenting about where it was going and what it was doing. This man said he had told the others that "somebody should phone some authority about it." But a combination of being four or five miles from a phone, of having work to do, and of risking scorn decided them against this. However, the man did get a pair of dark glasses out of the glove box of his vehicle; "The glasses made it easier still to watch the things." Mr. Neville Sheanan, a Toompang employee, said he was the one who saw the objects repeatedly. Mr. Sheanan, who gave permission for his name to be used, said the large object seemed to him to be round, with a dome on it. The small objects which left it seemed flattened.

"We watched them when we sat down to lunch," he said. "About two o'clock the sun moved around in that direction and we could not see the things any more against the strong light." All the men were interviewed separately. Their stories agreed in substance, with just enough discrepancy to testify to the truth of their stories. Dr. Gascoyne, of Mount Stromlo Observatory, said he could not hazard a guess about what the explanation might be. He asked for a copy of the report. A meterologist at the weather bureau said that no equipment used by the Bureau would behave in this way.

It should be clearly understood that under no circumstances will point-sources alone be classified under the first four groups. Without this precaution, Type III would be crowded with misinterpretations of Venus and Type IV would be flooded with artificial satellites. All reports in types I through IV should be relative to extended objects seen at a distance such that a certain amount of detail could be presented (as in the above example) without the aid of binoculars or telescopes.

Even with these precautions, we cannot claim that Type IV is absolutely free of misinterpretations of aircraft seen under such peculiar circumstances that our elimination system has failed to reject them. But Type III should be practically free of balloons, if one has been careful not to admit cases when the motion of the alleged object did not show definite extremes.

Type V is open to wide discussion, since we reach here the frontiers of our domain. But we feel that if the UFO phenomenon is original in nature and still unknown to our intelligence, a certain proportion of the total information lies in this category and we should take certain chances, it being understood that we will compensate for that accordingly by attaching a low weight to this category.

THE MYTH OF ABSOLUTE RELIABILITY

In the case of Vernon, Michel has remarked that under different circumstances the report made by the two policemen would have been judged sufficiently reliable to send a man to jail or to the guillotine. However, since the event had to do with an unusual phenomenon and not with a thief or criminal, the report was treated lightly and forgotten by all but Michel's readers. *Thus the present official system uses a reliability factor when it tends to show that a report is poor, but it does not use it when it tends to show that a report is significant.* When the witnesses are numerous and, according to all investigators, reliable, what happens to the report? Is the attention of the public called to it? Are astronomers and other scientists shown the facts? No—the report silently goes with the others, wearing the label "unidentified" or "unknown." During the same week enough misinterpretations of Venus are sent to the official services so that the figures show a reassuring 5 per cent unexplained. This is not the way percentages should be calculated. How many misinterpretations you receive is insignificant; misinterpretations are not what you are studying.

Like our courts of justice, official commissions seem to direct their attention only to the "bad guys." I wish a good guy were shown to the public from time to time, so that everybody could see what he looks like.

PROPOSED REORGANIZATION OF UFO RESEARCH

It has been suggested that the U.S. Air Force turn over its UFO files either to an agency dealing more directly with scientific investigations or to a group of civilian scientists. Our appraisal of both proposals is very pessimistic. Keeping so enormous an amount of data both up-to-date and reasonably organized is routine work which must be conducted with great attention and care; we feel that the air force has done a good job in this respect, a job smaller groups could not possibly have done successfully. A group of civilian scientists, especially, would certainly have failed, for a number of reasons, to provide the absolute consistency necessary in such an analysis. This lack of rigorous consistency also makes the efforts of nonscientific amateur groups almost worthless.

In addition, the air force group has, under the present system, acquired experience in dealing with this particular problem which is without parallel. Turning the files over to another group would be a waste of energy and possibly a source of error; this field requires a great deal of experience and persons unfamiliar with the very delicate problems involved would certainly be led to irreparable mistakes.

It is true, however, that something is missing in the present structure. No serious, large-scale scientific work can be done under today's conditions, because the system is built entirely on the assumption that UFO's can be identified without exception as conventional items if each case is sufficiently investigated; that there are pseudo-UFO's which exist at different stages of the identification scale, but there is no absolute UFO and, therefore, no UFO-phenomenon; under this approach there is simply addition, superimposition of mistakes and conventional effects. The lack of scientific value in this system is becoming increasingly apparent. But this deficiency could easily be eliminated; instead of calling upon individual scientists as assistants or consultants with no real power and no funds to test their own scientific ideas about the problem, the Aerial Phenomena Group should work in liaison with a *permanent research bureau which would be given the task of analyzing the UFO problem as a whole*.

In the system we propose, the air force would retain its files and its methods of classification, investigation and evaluation. The scientific group would be a team of from six to ten civilian researchers competent in their various fields and already familiar with the field of UFO research, who would volunteer to conduct independent studies. They would be given permanent access to the nonclassified cases kept up-to-date by the Dayton group and would have sufficient funds to cover telephone calls, travel expenses and such things as laboratory equipment or computer time.

UFO'S IN SPACE

They would have the ability (which the air force does not have) to examine foreign reports as scientific data, and to meet serious foreign researchers for consultation. Such a team would conduct, on a global scale, an analysis of the reports which would be of interest in more than one respect.

It has been suggested, especially by members of the amateur group of NICAP, that a congressional hearing on UFO's should be held to examine the "evidence" that UFO's exist and are "space-vehicles under intelligent control." The air force files are said to contain such evidence, which is at present (according to the NICAP Director) kept from the public. There is little ground to support such a claim and NICAP representatives would realize that plainly during the first hours of such a congressional debate. Although it could be the occasion of an interesting scientific confrontation, only confusion and probably further ridicule would result from it in the long run. Not one of the seven hundred cases presented in NICAP's recently published report *The UFO Evidence* could, in the view of this writer, stand the test of an extensive scientific discussion. An experienced opponent of UFO's, such as Professor Menzel, would certainly be able to show that some doubt exists in each case, simply because no UFO report has yet been investigated as such by scientists working within the framework of a general analysis. NICAP's cases would be interesting elements in such a research, but the "evidence" they contain, if real, is still to be extracted through a long and careful scientific analysis of the type illustrated in this book. Taken individually, the best report does not prove anything.

What is required here, therefore, is not a change in offi-

The Scientific Problem

cial policy or a sensational disclosure of the fact that "we are visited!" but a careful, quiet and necessarily slow series of analyses on the material already on hand and on reports to come. Such a study, if made in liaison with the Aerial Phenomena Group of Dayton, and oriented toward the investigation of the nature of UFO's as a phenomenon rather than toward their individual "explanation," could possibly produce (after three or four years of work) material worthy of congressional attention, and by-products that would be of interest to several branches of science.

CHAPTER FIVE

FLYING SAUCERS AND HUMAN REASON

THE SCIENTIST'S EMOTIONAL REACTION TO UFO'S

We do not presume here to be adding anything to the psychological description of the UFO problem made with such authority by the late Professor Jung. But we feel some of our documents should be treated as psychological data, and this includes certain phases of report generation as well as the scientist's reaction to the reports.

As we have seen earlier, men of science react to UFO reports in a very peculiar fashion. They go so far as neglecting to conform with the basic rules of scientific honesty when confronted with this problem, and they allow themselves to act as they never would in the presence of a more "classical" mystery. On the contrary, anxiety has been released on perfectly innocuous projects like certain programs sponsored by professional astronomers, in which one would record the radio signals coming from nearby stars and look for possible strings of pulses or "messages" of intelligent origin (Project Ozma). All this points to one conclusion: The scientist's reaction to the problem has never been anything but emotional. In this line of thinking, it is justifiable to assume that other civilizations are sending radio signals through space because radio waves are a good vehicle of information and because space travel between planetary systems is inconceivable. Both assumptions are extrapolations of conditions existing on earth today. They neglect entirely the fact that our idea of space travel as well as our idea of information exchange are very closely related to present physical conceptions.

It has been repeatedly affirmed by scientific authorities that what constitutes a scientific subject is not its nature but the way it is treated. Therefore the scientist, on one hand, has every right to study the UFO problem and, on the other, has no right to take into account the public reaction and emotion or the official concern over this question, or the ridicule that may be attached to it, once he has perceived its importance.

Unfortunately, this is only theory. In practice, men of science are not confronted with Nature alone. Besides this common mother, they have families, friends, students and bosses. Their work is defined within a certain structure and their own careers as professionals depend, in large measure, upon the subjects they choose to investigate, the degree of success they meet in these investigations and their attitudes toward accepted theories. This is today the main limitation to the free expansion of fundamental research. Similarly, only half-hearted attempts have been made to investigate the process of scientific discovery and to define what is to be called a scientific problem and who is going to determine the amount of energy required to solve each problem in a certain amount of time. A constant source of wonder and amazement to me is the realization that specialists in the study of Mars, whose number on our whole planet does not exceed seven or eight, have never been able to get together, plan their experiments in common and pool their results. They are working today with obsolete equipment and ideas as isolated artisans, with no highly qualified technical help, on what could become in a few years one of the most important problems facing our civilization.

We reach here the crucial point of the UFO problem, with the realization of the fact that scientific structure is heavily hampered by emotional aspects and is still relying for its development on random processes rather than rational acquisition of knowledge. The UFO problem lies well within the capability of modern research. But official attention is denied it for purely emotional reasons that have nothing to do with science.

SOCIETY'S REACTION TO UFO'S

Perhaps we should now generalize and ask if the reaction recorded at the sociological level does not follow the same general contours. The leading communities in our world—the west European, the North American, the Russian—have always chosen their ways of doing things and have always been limited or helped in their ambitions by the same well-known enemies or friends. Irruption of representatives of other societies, possibly organized in higher levels of jurisdiction on a galactic scale, possibly depending upon types of relations unknown to our planet, would be a psychological infringement as well as a legal violation.

We should even proceed a step further, and ask if mankind as a whole, led by the proud communities we have mentioned, would not react to such "visitation," if evidenced by physical proof, with deep shock. Civilization could be hurt by this experience like a self-conscious virgin brutally confronted with unknown forces, unwilling to accept them within her limited universe.

This brings to mind a conversation between H. G. Wells and Lenin in 1920 which the former related to Krassine (186):

> "I said to Lenin that the development of human technology might some day change the world situation. The Marxist conception itself would then become meaningless. Lenin looked at me and he said:
> 'You are right. I understood this myself when I read your novel *The Time Machine*. All human conceptions are on the scale of our planet. They are based on the pretension that the technical potential, although it will develop, will never exceed the "terrestrial limit."
> '*If we succeed in establishing interplanetary communications, all our philosophical, moral and social views will have to be revised*. In this case, the technical potential, become limitless, would impose the end of the role of violence as a means and method of progress....'"

Think how deeply we are still supposed to be attached to the land in which we were born, and in which our parents were born, although we receive, through education, multiple evidence that our fathers were not wiser, or better scientists, or better warriors than the father of the guy across the river. We can even go out in the open at night and see artificial satellites circling this tiny planet of ours in a matter of minutes; indeed, if all the peoples of the earth had not brought something of their genius, from the Chinese to the Greek, the Khmer, the Russian and the Briton, this light would not be in the sky. But we remain attached to a little piece of land between two lines of mountains, where our emotional roots are sealed. And if this is so, what feeling must we have for our planet! For earth is indeed all we have. If other communities are able to travel to us and land here, then we are at the mercy of their intelligence and of their feelings toward us as a civilization—and both may be entirely foreign to anything we have known before.

ENTHUSIASM AND UFO GROUPS

A complete list of UFO groups throughout the world would have several hundred entries, and a list of the regular publications on the subject would be impressive. This gives an idea of the degree of enthusiasm generated in the public by the possibility of a visitation by other civilizations.

One may well wonder whether amateurism is a characteristic of superficial or futile minds or, on the contrary, indicative of man's desire for personal participation in important events, and the proof that passion for research does not necessarily coincide with payment for it. The recent history of astronomy has shown that amateurs, because they have not been bound by traditional views, have often come up with more than interesting suggestions. At the same time, their work is less reliable than the output of a team of professional researchers who have access to large collections of documents and modern equipment.

Flying Saucers and Human Reason

The UFO mystery, because of its appeal to human imagination, provides an opportunity for persons who live a generally dull life to bring a touch of extraterrestrial horror into their existence. UFO "investigation" has thus become a popular hobby. Clubs and groups have developed, mainly since 1952, apparently in every part of the world. The curve of activity of these groups has been closely related to the density of UFO events. Their only positive contribution has been the publication of sightings, but very few of the groups, unfortunately, have devoted their attention to this point. The others have found much more fun in publishing foggy "theories" concerning anti-gravity, the fourth dimension and the hair of Venusian dogs, or in letting the world know of the details of their editor's private life.

A very few UFO groups have risen above this generally hideous level, and have left some imprint on the literature of the subject. The *Flying Saucer Review* of Great Britain, established in 1954, is the only periodical a student of UFO problems must consult regularly.* Although its attitude regarding "contactees" and its discrimination between meteors and "true UFO's" have not always been clear, the *Review* was (until the death of Waveney Girvan in October, 1964) the official journal of UFO controversy and has been honored by articles by Professor Menzel himself.

A number of groups have organized in Great Britain independent of the *Review*. The British UFO Research Association (BUFORA) early in 1964 united the British UFO Association and the London UFO Research Organization. Both bodies previously issued regular publications, and BUFORA now publishes a quarterly journal.

---

* *The Flying Saucer Review* is edited bimonthly and published by Flying Saucer Service, Ltd., 72–78 Fleet Street, London E. C. 4, England.

UFO'S IN SPACE

In Italy, the few groups of enthusiasts we know of are not worthy of mention; their only activity is merging one into the other every two or three years.

In Spain, Antonio Ribera and Eduardo Buelta founded in Barcelona the Centro de Estudios Interplanetarios in 1958. The group published a bulletin, of which we have regrettably seen only one number, which contained excellent statistical analyses of the frequency distribution of sightings on a planetary scale. Unfortunately, as much as the Italian groups have a tendency to merge, Spanish groups have a tendency to split, and it is difficult to evaluate what amount of real work is being done at the present time in Spain.

In Argentina, CODOVNI (Comision Observadora de Objetos Voladores no Identificados) has done serious work on analysis of the local sightings and has regularly published reports. In France, CIEO (Commission Internationale d'Enquetes Ouranos) started publishing a review and maintained it for some time, but too often neglected significant information and turned to pseudoscience and backyard nuclear physics. It preserved in UFO literature, however, excellent investigations into the important 1957 cases. A new group, called GEPA (Groupe d'Etudes des Phenomenes Aeriens), was founded at the end of 1962 but unfortunately started on a similar path. It is not easy to determine if this lack of success comes from incompetent management or absence of public concern.

Australia is a more interesting country in this respect. Although irregularly published, the *Australian Flying Saucer Review* has generally maintained a good level and an original presentation. Its main appeal is the large amount of practical information it has given concerning sightings made in the area. It was originally edited under the aegis of the UFO Association of Australia, which amalgamated several groups in September, 1960.* Similar groups exist in all countries where the UFO problem is commented upon and is the object of public concern at times. The numerous UFO groups in the United States have proved low in quality, although it is the only country where an educational institution, Ohio Northern University, has undertaken a study of "flying saucer" reports (1960).

Two large organizations exist in the U.S. One is NICAP† (National Investigation Committee on Aerial Phenomena), a very official-appearing group founded by Major Keyhoe, and the other is APRO (Aerial Phenomena Research Organization) of Tucson. It seems that NICAP's main concern is to obtain official recognition of the existence of "flying saucers" by the U.S. Congress, while APRO claims it is more seriously dedicated to investigation and research, and has gone to some effort to present reports of sightings made abroad, as well as articles by foreign contributors. The progress made since 1952, however, seems microscopic, even when one reads the well-documented report *UFO Evidence*, published by NICAP in 1964; this activity obviously misses the point, since it is not seen that the UFO problem is basically a problem of methodology, and a very difficult scientific question that

---

* It is now available from the Victorian Flying Saucer Research Society, P.O. Box 43, Moorabbin, Victoria, Australia.
† NICAP, 1536 Connecticut Avenue, N.W., Washington, D.C. APRO, 4145 E. Desert Place, Tucson, Arizona.

cannot be solved by political or military authorities. Although they often use the names of scientists said to "approve" of their actions, apparently none of these groups has obtained practical assistance in their daily work from competent professional researchers, but their publications are at best acceptable documentaries. But this is already much better than what most UFO groups produce.

In our view, the reason for the apparent failure of the American groups to present intelligent assistance to the official services is that their leaders are unfamiliar with sightings made in other parts of the world and make no effort to learn, when only a planetary picture can cast light on the American cases. The attitude seems to be the same in official circles, but this is more easily understandable, since under the specific *mission* they have no authority to investigate incidents in foreign countries.

For a very small but active number of UFO cultists in America, however, the only real problem is to "sell flying saucers," as one would sell hot dogs or ice cream. What does it matter if the sightings are invented, if the photographs are faked, if the trip to Venus is imaginary? What does it matter if the serious reader, deceived two or three times, decides on the basis of this mockery that UFO's are a joke? The "easy buck" is the sole motivation for their "research" activity. Sometimes the tale is told with real talent. Sometimes it is rather sad and disgusting. But the dream remains:

> O the poor lover of chimerical lands!
> Shall we put into iron, or cast into the sea
> This drunken sailor, inventor of Americas?

Baudelaire asked. No; let them dream. Maybe they will balance the conservative part of the scientific mind that always looks behind.

THE WITNESSES' REACTION AFTER A SIGHTING

Every possible step seems to have been taken to prevent ideas or feelings favorable to the existence of UFO's from finding their way into official and educated circles. This process has clearly developed unconsciously. For example, when official authorities decided to obtain a scientific evaluation of the problem, they selected scientists who were entirely ignorant of it; it would have been simple, and interesting, to have arranged a meeting of Tombaugh, Hess, Moore and other well-known scientists who saw and reported UFO's. But this would probably have contradicted the official view that "astronomers do not see flying saucers," one of the arguments often presented to a misinformed public.

Witnesses of UFO's are generally characterized by their silence. As if they had experienced a very bad or revolting dream, they talk only reluctantly about it, both because some of them remain nonbelievers and are shocked by their seeing something which does not agree with their reason, and because they suddenly find themselves on the other side of the fence; newsmen come, ask them questions and print imaginary tales concerning them. They can feel, even in their immediate family, a modification of the atmosphere about them. Human relations are affected and their whole world changes almost imperceptibly.

Those who write to military authorities give in their letters evidence of deep concern and high reliability. In a typical report, a New York physiotherapist wrote:

> During World War II, I was a pilot in the U.S. Air Force and all my flying experience was within the Continental limits of the United States. In all that time I never once, night or day, observed anything unusual in the skies. Now, at age 43, I have observed phenomena which are beyond my comprehension, and which tax my sense of reasoning and credulity.

Many others express interest in the problem in general, following their experience, and ask for more information.

The inadequacy of the official questionnaire sent to those who ask for it in their letters is evidenced by a comparison between the original letter and the answers given by the same witness to such specific questions as elevation, size and direction, which break the consistency of the report into series of points sometimes irrelevant to the main problem, or points that cannot be answered with precision by an average person without covering the whole incident. This is not the proper place to discuss in detail how the questionnaire could be revised, for the whole data-gathering system should be improved. The point applies even more to unofficial questionnaires sent by groups of enthusiasts. We would advocate the replacement of such forms by a single sheet on which the witness would write his own description of what he saw, with space reserved for the coding system and a series of ten to twenty clear, specific questions requiring information on points which are not usually covered by the original description made by the witness. Such a form would be completed in a much shorter time, and could give the author of the report more confidence in the amount of attention the case will be given later by the investigators, a personal contact thus being established. However, we would certainly recommend keeping the detailed forms for cases in which the investigators interview the witness directly.

Clearly, I cannot speak here with the authority a team of psychologists could after careful analysis of a sample of typical letters. But it is my experience that from such descriptions, spontaneously made by the witnesses, the cause of their concern is generally recognizable when it is a conventional object such as a meteor, an aircraft, a star, a balloon, a kite or a unique luminous effect seen under conditions not extremely peculiar, even when the authors of these descriptions show signs of deep emotion or excitement as a result of their experience. This seems to be an indication in favor of the high reliability of most UFO reports.

Thanks to the efforts of Veillith and Michel we are able to present here a document which we think of remarkable interest in this respect. This case would be automatically dismissed by a commission of military investigators, or by any committee of scientific officials; the documents consist of two letters from the witness to a French student of UFO's who wrote to this person after seeing a brief account of the sighting in a local newspaper. The observation took place at dusk. The witness was alone, and is known to have been a mental patient under treatment. A detailed study of the account, however, shows a remarkable stability in the characteristics of the behavior described, and the reader will notice that all the basic criteria of our Type II are met very clearly. It is our opinion that the witness has indeed observed a UFO phenomenon behaving exactly as in the Vernon case, and has given an account of it fantastically distorted by her mental disability. Here is the first letter:

> At my house it has passed a flying saucer which formed into a very bright cigar towards its behavior of spindle very luminous of a very beautiful brilliance, leaving behind a smoke trail more than three meters as it comes closer to the house the smoke was better less the cigar formed three cordons very close the one in the middle flattened, a little lower has stopped the cordon to the right withdrawing and small balls like O to detach themselves and to disappear one after the other in the sky. In spite of my curiosity I was unable to wait for the end of this phenomenon, the cold forced me to go inside—Good luck.

Puzzled by this description—which could seem to point simply to a misinterpreted smoke trail left by a jet, for example—the investigator asked for more details regarding duration, shape, weather, conditions, time of day, exact movements. He received the following answer:

> You know the time for the month of October it was the evening almost at night fall the weather neither overcast nor clear the craft come from the direction of———straight on. The craft was a little in the shape of a cigar but which formed three tight ribbons or cordons if you want. The craft not flying very high coming straight crosses the roof of my habitation I said what a pity if it had been earlier in the evening I would have been able to make out certainly what was going on inside the craft but a brilliant craft which seemed to my

eyes all made of diamond the nose in the shape of an aircraft but half longer than having passed my habitation by four to five meters making a slight deviation toward the east at this moment it stops a little the ribbon in the middle detaches itself from the other two, from the one in the middle detach themselves very fast several little balls O—crossing the right ribbon goes higher and go back into the sky then the three ribbons unite the craft starts again weakening and coming back lower straight on then I saw the nose which dived to go and land not much farther away in spite of my desire to see it land very close this was impossible to me the cold had forced me to go back into my house the stars lit the sky it was freezing the distance from my house to towards the landing three minutes the time I observed the phenomenon twenty minutes if not thirty a policeman had asked me if I had not been afraid when it had passed over my roof I had answered oh no it was too pretty.

DREAM AND HOAX AS EMOTIONAL EXPRESSIONS

Jung has given numerous examples of dreams in which the shape of the saucer, the mandala or the cigar were present, and were associated with unearthly feelings such as absence of weight. The very elusiveness of some UFO apparitions suggested to him that an interesting link was to be found between their observation and certain fundamental needs in the subconscious part of the mind. "What I have always thought as the most beautiful thing in a theatre," writes Baudelaire, "during my childhood and even now, is the chandelier, a beautiful luminous object, crystalline, complicated, circular and symmetrical." This fascination of a poet's soul for the circular, luminous object is indicative of the existence of complex mental mechanisms which may be linked with UFO observations. Unlimited space and unlimited power are associated with the vision of a UFO. Marvelous speed, blinding light, silence are characteristic of a class of objects that seem to lend themselves most easily to interpretation in terms of psychological entities. And the old appeal of the mystery can be felt again in these stories where science fiction seems to flourish and take life.

Our domain reaches here the border of these carefully concealed areas where the full complexity of the human mind appears among unwonted creations of the brain. Theodore Flournoy, a professor of psychology at Geneva University in Switzerland, published in 1900 his observations on the alleged travels through space performed by the medium Helen Smith (135). The book contains a dictionary for translating Martian into French. More recent examples of similar claims, especially those that developed after the American waves of 1950–52, show less ingenuity.

An emotional climax is reached when the dream is artificially forced into reality, when the witness becomes an actor, the maker of the mystery, when a hoax is performed and presented as a true manifestation of unknown forces. it is interesting to remark that when Leo Taxil, setting the stage for the series of enormous hoaxes that shook both the religious and the atheistic worlds in the last decade of the nineteenth century (136), described a meeting between Thomas Vaughan and the Devil, he used terms similar to those found in many "contact" stories:

> During a summer night, according to Philalethes' narrative, as he was walking in the moonlight, the

moon, which he saw through the branches of trees in the forest, suddenly seemed to come nearer and appeared to glide like a blinding and penetrating light. Little by little, the lunar crescent, that kept coming closer, took the appearance of a sort of curved couch, luminous, floating through space, and coming, coming towards the Earth.... The legend also states that the ship-bed landed in a clearing and that the brush caught fire all around, without being consumed; many little devils, similar to seven- or eight-year-old children, came out of the ground, their arms full of flowers....

In many cases, hoaxes have been perpetrated as mere jokes, not as serious attempts to gain official recognition. This has been the general case in France and in most European countries. In the New World, however, more credit is usually given to the individual and one thus has a better opportunity to find a public ready to believe in the fantastic. "Contact" stories have emerged into life on this basis. We read in (137) the following story:

> Gabriel Green, a bright and youthful Johnny-come-lately to the candidate game, is right in step with the space age. Mr. Green was not running for the presidency in 1960 to promote a noble cause, or for publicity, or because the Bible told him to. He was a candidate because (says Gabe) one night, while he was sitting in the living room of his California home, there was a knock at the door. And on the front steps there stood what looked like an earthman. But the "man" introduced himself as a visitor from a planet of Alpha Centauri, a nearby star. The visitor said: "We want you to run for President of the United States." Gabe said yes, without hesitation.
> This celestial ambassador never did explain why he

and his fellow Alpha Centaurians wanted Gabriel Green to become President, but that did not stop Gabe from entering the race. Possibly, the folks from Alpha Centauri wanted as America's Chief Executive a man who was concerned with the problems of outer space. And wasn't Gabriel Green president of the Amalgamated Flying Saucers Club of America, Inc.? Surely, he had the interest of the entire universe at heart, Alpha Centauri included.

Green claimed to have received many phone calls from other inhabitants of the distant star and also said that alongside the Alpha Centauri females "Earth women just don't compare."

The investigator of the UFO phenomenon is rarely concerned with such reports of contacts, which follow an easily recognizable pattern, and no confusion is possible unless information is very fragmentary. I was once criticized by the editor of a specialized review (138) for not including "Venusians" of the type described by the "contactees" in a survey of entities reported to have been associated with Type I sightings.

> It would seem that consistency has a measure of scientific approval [read the article], but this is not allowed as a virtue when the long line of contactees from Adamski to Siragusa come to beg for admittance. Certainly these stories are very similar and have much more in common than exists between any of the groups in Vallee's type-I list.

Indeed, consistency is always a virtue, but it does not necessarily result in what the author of the text called "approval"; it can also result in rejection, when all criteria of imagination and fraud are met by these "consistent" stories. A consistent thief is not an honest man, although it is much easier to find consistent thieves than consistent honest men. But I do not think anyone has ever been seriously worried by childish descriptions of space conditions copied from newspapers' comics or stories whose author is said to have landed on Venus or on the mysterious planet Clarion, permanently hidden by the moon! The pieces of "physical evidence" presented to support such accounts—a few blurred photographs and a reproduction of a design taken from the sole of a Venusian shoe—are so poor that we start to doubt if the author's imagination is so bright after all, for only very naïve persons can believe that any credence will be attached to photographs so evidently faked that the positive image itself is already a confession of crime!

But credence is a very relative notion for the authors of these little space operas. The mention of their names is all they hope for, and they find the fulfilment of their dreams in the worship of them by their fanatics.

An astronomer has given a description of these characters:

> Long years of experience with people who come to the observatory, or write in about their stories... have taught me how a typical fraud... chooses his words and phrases. Among other things, he cannot conduct a rational discussion, but resorts to constant repetition. He will not listen to the other person and cannot answer questions rationally or intelligently.... Scarce wonder that the whole subject—which undoubtedly has some scientific pay-dirt in it—is so easily tossed aside by responsible people. At a convention [of "flying saucer" fanatics] one could buy a book entitled *My Saturnian*

Lover, photographs of saucers, the moon seen from an approaching saucer, moon scenery, and could buy a record of Saturnian music. And, if they stayed late enough, the conventioneers would see mysterious blue lights at play and observe a balloon-shaped saucer that rose opportunely from behind the barn. . . .

No joke could stay alive long enough to cause so much disturbance, however, if deeper feelings were not associated with these "experiences." In (139) Norkin writes about one of the "contactees":

> He had been taken up in a balloon-shaped spacecraft to a great height above the earth and then given the opportunity to view it from that height. The incident happened on the night of July 23, 1952, from the dry bed of the Los Angeles river, where it borders Los Angeles and Glendale. It was a beautiful sight, but Orfeo said he wept unashamedly. The realization came that underneath that surface beauty was a sick humanity suffering from untold misery. He didn't want to come back but was told he had to because it was now his mission to tell the people the truth—about life in outer space. Just like those who were advanced had come from other planets to help us, so those who were contacted here should help their fellow men with the information that had been revealed. As proof that his experience was real, a scar was imprinted on the skin of his chest below the heart. It was the mark of the hydrogen atom, of which everything in the universe is ultimately formed.

This is a very common theme in this sort of story, and such accounts appear to be a way for certain souls to release their anguish in the face of modern scientific changes, their fear of war and atomic cataclysm and their inability to adapt to the present rhythm of life. These experiences are indeed consistent; they are nothing but the ever-repeated story of the humble man suddenly chosen by Providence to fulfil a terribly important mission, to be entrusted with amazing secrets and become the master of supernatural powers.

This is also a convenient subjective way to criticize modern life and to release personal resentments. In (140) another contactee gives this information on his "visitors":

> She said: "We are visiting regularly on your earth, and enjoy it very much." She added: "We enjoy your laughing mirth," which she said was new to them. That they had expected that people with all our problems and troubles would not be able to joke and laugh. That on Clarion they liked a good joke and loved to laugh.
>
> She also made the statement that they were never in a rush up there on Clarion, and they always wondered why everything on earth appeared to be rushing or in a hurry to be finished. She said it was a similar sight all over the earth, people rushing madly in all directions.

METAPHYSICAL UFO'S

I had quite a shock once when I happened to come across a booklet entitled *Flying Saucers and Space Men, A Scientific and Metaphysical Dissertation in Interplanetary Travelling*, by Dr. John H. Manas, Ph.D., N.D., Psy.D., Ms.D., D.T.D., B.Sc., D. Hum., M.H., and Founder-President, Pythagorean Society (141).

Until then I had divided my attention between professional scientists, who generally thought that life was possible elsewhere in the universe but did not believe that other communities could travel to us and, therefore, did not want to consider the possibility of UFO's being material objects; and the people who, on the opposite side, accepted enthusiastically the existence of "flying saucers" without reservation, saying that "they had no proof, but they had evidence." I had no idea that a third category existed, made up of strong believers in the existence of "flying saucers," but firmly opposed to their spatial origin, and even to their physical reality. I was thus quite unprepared when I read in Dr. Manas' book:

> There is another very important reason against the physical existence of "space ships." Suppose that a certain soul or a spiritual entity from Venus or from Mars wants to pay us a visit. Is it necessary for it to travel in a "space-ship"? Cannot the soul travel in its astral or etheric body or vehicle?

I wonder what Pythagoras would have answered to that. Dr. Manas later makes the following statement:

> It is a well-known fact to all metaphysicians and occultists that even a clear and strong thought can be projected and be sent many thousands of miles away and be materialized at its place of destination, and under proper conditions, to be seen by men. All these phenomena are not mysteries or miracles.... This *is* the truth about UFO, commonly known as "flying saucers," space ships and space men, disrobed of all superstition, ignorance, emotionalism and human weakness, which is the lot of young human souls.

It would seem, therefore, that earthbound "entities" or spirits produce images of "flying saucers." Being a "young human soul," characterized by the weakness enumerated by Dr. Manas, and many others, this writer is obviously incompetent to comment on the theory. However, he finds it interesting that ardent spiritualists are seen taking against the material existence of UFO's the same extreme positions as ardent "materialists."

We could extend this chapter into an entire book without ever reaching the limits of the extraordinary, and not even the limits of fraud or lunacy. But these few pages may have been sufficient to give our reader a clear image of what the human mind can produce when it does not work within the boundaries set up by rationalism, and denies the necessity of control. Our problem is not original in this respect; similar fancies have been found in all branches of science.

One point, however, is very clear in the present case: When one has heard the messages of all "contactees," listened to the tales, read the stories, traveled to Saturn and back in the arms of a nine-legged octopus and shared the evening dinner of a friendly average Venusian family, one comes back to this detestable planet and finds the UFO mystery unsolved. Theories are often like the good servant of the play, who talks with the irritated father while his lovely daughter escapes with a musician. We have watched Dr. Menzel's mirages and listened to Adamski's harpsichord; we have seen Captain Aura Rhanes returning to Clarion and have touched a hair of a 185-pound Venusian dog; we have also observed meteors and the rising moon. Now we would like to come back to our problem and find out what it is reliable witnesses have seen; for the Vernon cigar was not a cloud, the hole in the field in Poncey was not of a metaphysical essence. Officer Zamora had not heard the noise of a spiritual motor, and it was not a meteor that lifted Hamilton's cow in April, 1897. Someone once asked, if angels are pure spirits, why do they eat and make love? We might add, speaking of modern legends appearing under our own eyes: If spacemen are thought images, why should they butcher a cow and drop her head in the desert?

Beliefs and theories; imagination and dream and pretension; tormented human souls, trying to reach for their small infinite, fancy they catch a star. In a forest of theories, each man climbs his own tree. He reigns on his branch and directs insults at the mockingbird. Undisturbed, lines of facts stretch across the horizon with patience. But night falls on the scene, and men go to sleep. In this night they remain, unidentified in their relative universe. A hand from Heaven reaches down into their dreams, and they wonder.

CHAPTER SIX

TYPICAL PHASES OF UFO BEHAVIOR

THE GENERAL TYPE I EVENT

Whether they actually correspond to the "landing" of a machine or only to a misinterpretation or hallucination, Type I events are of interest to us because they allow a deeper analysis of the mechanism through which individuals are led to write a UFO report.

If average imagination is sufficient for a witness to interpret the rising moon or the planet Venus as a "spacecraft," it requires much more for a citizen to fabricate completely a long and consistent story like the Quarouble or Foussignargues episodes. This is evidenced by cases of the Adamski type, and by "contact" stories in general, credible or half-credible when first narrated, which become more and more complicated and inconsistent as details are added.

Most Type I reports, on the contrary, are simple and very clear: Individuals of varying age, occupation and reliability rush to the police, write under oath perfectly unbelievable stories and are never heard of again. The typical witness generally states in his report that he was performing a quite ordinary task when the sighting took place. He was not out in the fields looking for a UFO because he had just read a book about it. He had not rushed into the desert in answer to a "telepathic" message. He was coming back to his farm or riding a bicycle. Most of the witnesses state that they did not believe in "flying saucers." Some of them stay unconvinced, but feel they must report what they have seen, even if they do not understand it.

On October 14, 1954, at 6:15 P.M., Jose Casella, working at Antibes, was riding his bicycle through the town of Biot, in the Maritime Alps, when he suddenly found in front of him on the road a massive, oval aluminum-like object. He applied the brakes; simultaneously, the object took off without noise, at a very great speed. It was shaped like an egg, perfectly smooth and bright. Five to six meters long and a little over one meter in height, it left no trace. Several inhabitants of Biot made independent reports that confirmed the reality of Casella's experience. Descriptions of the incident can be found in the French newspapers of October 17 (*France-Soir, La Croix, Paris-Presse*, etc.).

On October 21, 1954, in the department of Charente, a man from Cherbonnieres was driving his car toward Pouzou. With him was his three-year-old son. Suddenly he felt pricklings all over his body, similar to electric discharges; this painful feeling became more intense as the car kept going. Soon the child started to cry and, as the car proceeded, the engine died and so did the headlights. At the same time the witness noticed a bright, glowing red color changing to orange, soon becoming of a blinding intensity. For a few seconds he saw an object hovering; it disappeared soon afterward. He was then able to start his engine again.

In *L'Astronomie*, in 1954, we find the following account:

> Suspicious object. M. G. Mouillon, engineer at Genelard, Saone-et-Loire, has observed, on October 14 at 8:50 P.M. between Ciry-le-Noble and Montceau-les-Mines, an enormous object surrounded with a green flame quickly falling to the ground over an area of about 10° in elevation. The object itself certainly had an apparent diameter of several degrees, maybe as much as five degrees. No noise was heard.

This observation is quite interesting in the light of the series of events that took place in the same area that very day, and which were summarized by Michel in his second book, from which we extract the following:

> M. B., living in Montceau-les-Mines, was riding a motorcycle on the road from St.-Romain-sous-Gourdon to Brosses-Tillots, also in Saone-et-Loire. Suddenly without apparent reason his motor stopped and could not be started again. He got off, and a bright light burst out about fifty yards in front of him, revealing a circular object that looked, he said, "like a plate turned upside down."
>
> M. B. looked at the sight in amazement, then in fear, and decided to turn back, walking and pushing his motorcycle. But when he reached the point where his motor had stopped, it started up again. . . . (115).

A few minutes later, Andre Cognard, who lives at Ciry-le-Noble, was driving toward his town, coming from Gueugnon:

"All at once," said M. Cognard, "at the top of a slope I found myself face to face, so to speak, with a sort of disk of such brilliance that it blinded me, like a lighthouse beam. I had to stop. The object flew over me slightly to my right at a low altitude and continued its route westward, where it remained visible for several minutes before disappearing in the distance."

Both incidents above occurred "at nightfall." At about 7:30 P.M., two inhabitants of Gueugnon, Messrs. Jeannet and Garnier, were driving on road D-25 from Clessy toward Gueugnon. They were crossing a wooded area called Chazey Wood when a sort of reddish glow flew over their car at high speed:

"All at once the motor stopped and we had no lights. After a few seconds, when the light shed by the ball had gone out in the distance on our left, the headlights came on. I pushed the starter, and the motor began to turn over again."

This series of events took place in a very narrow patch of a few kilometers. The identity of the witnesses is known. They reported their experiences independently. One of them was published by a scientific journal unknown to Michel, who did not use it in his description of the sightings of October 14. The impression made by this series of reports is, as Michel remarks, inescapable: An uncommon activity, associated with the presence of a brilliant disk-shaped object, took place in this area. This object was very close to the ground, and it remained on the spot for at least an hour.

One might have the impression one is reading some

kind of ghost story when confronted with such accounts, or one might think that the whole thing is only a dream; the reader will awake and find himself again in a rational world, where only cars and bicycles use the roads and where only farmers and their familiar, reassuring equipment are to be seen in the countryside. However, these reports do exist. We have even found several of them in the scientific press. They are still unexplained and "unidentified."

France has no monopoly on this type of activity. However, early American reports of Type I—those made in the years 1946 to 1952—are difficult to find. Such sightings were not, in general, reported to authorities, and practically no civilian activity was seriously organized to gather information on the cases. As a result, only a few incidents, like the case of Desvergers, a Florida scoutmaster who claimed he was burned by a "saucer," or another sighting made at Flatwood, West Virginia (in which monsters were described by apparently reliable witnesses, but no evidence was produced), were publicized, when a large number of sightings of interest would have deserved equal attention. In addition, we should remember that numerous reports turned in to the U.S. Air Force concerning "landings" before 1952 seem to have been thrown into the trash can as "obviously unbelievable," especially when they contained descriptions of "operators." This made it very easy to claim later that too little information was present to investigate these events. The official handling of these cases fortunately seems to have improved.

As an example of a sighting that should have been investigated thoroughly we will call the reader's attention to the observation reported by B. Stevenson of Circleville,

Ohio, on February 1, 1948. He saw a metallic disk hovering above a farm. It had, he said, a diameter of sixty feet and was ten to twelve feet thick at the center; it gave off a blinding orange light from its central part.

In the fall of 1949, at night, D. Bushnell, a plant superintendent at the Southwestern Porcelain Steel Corporation, was driving with his wife near Tulsa, Oklahoma, when an object dived from the sky toward the road in front of the car, then disappeared (described by Keyhoe in [142]).

In December of 1950, another observation of interest was made by American personnel aboard a U.S. ship in Korean waters. They saw two objects in the sky, followed by trails of white smoke. Both objects fell into the sea at very high speed; two columns of water rose up to thirty meters in the air (cf. *Aviation News*, February 18, 1951 [143]).

More information becomes available after 1952, when the UFO problem assumed its new look and when public opinion became seriously concerned. Although the reliability of the report is unknown, we feel we should mention here the Oscar Linke incident of July 11, 1952, as an introduction to the next American sightings. The event took place at Hasselbach, Germany, in a forest a few miles from the frontier between the American and Russian zones. The witness, accompanied by his eleven-year-old daughter, allegedly saw two men in shiny coveralls standing by a large disk, eight meters in diameter, that took off when the witness was heard approaching.

On July 29, 1952, a man "as white as a sheet" entered the Enid, Oklahoma, police station. He said his name was Sid Eubank and told Sergeant Vern Bennell his impression that a "flying saucer" had tried to kidnap him. He was driving, he said, on Highway 81 between Bison and Waukomis, before dawn, when a large flying disk dived toward him, followed by such a shock wave that the air pressure threw the car off the road. The object remained above the car for a while, then departed at high speed toward the west (144). In August several memorable (if not reliable) incidents took place, including the Desvergers monster and the alleged kidnapping of Tom Brooke, in the same part of Florida. On August 31, H. Long, of Kutstown, Pennsylvania, said he saw a disk land fifty feet from the road, and he made a sketch of it. This entire period has been excellently described by Captain Ruppelt in his book (118).

Since 1955 the material concerning American "landings" has been abundant. On August 1, 1955, at 9:00 P.M., a Mr. Sheneman, coming from Willoughby, Ohio, got out of his car at Chardon Road with his wife and two children when he saw a circular object with a red light coming down rapidly and hovering above the ground. Two beams of light appeared on the object and several openings allegedly became visible. The witness started running toward their house. The object hovered two hundred feet above the ground; it had a diameter of one hundred feet and a dome on top, which was illuminated with a white light.

In the first days of November, 1955, a similar object was seen by an officer in a police car at Williston, Florida; according to Keyhoe (142) the witness felt his arms and legs paralyzed and his clothes hot.

After this date more reports are found in the official files. Some of them are quite interesting. They provide a good basis for contradiction of the accepted theory that "landing" reports are all unreliable and therefore cannot be studied scientifically. On April 6, 1956, at McKinney,

Texas, a silvery object reportedly landed in a field one hundred meters from the two witnesses, who stopped their car and got out; the object then took off at very high speed. On June 6, 1956, at 5:30 A.M., an object was seen one hundred feet above the ground at Banning, California. The witness stopped his car, watched the object slowly cross the road one hundred yards from him, turn to the left, then come back to cross the road again behind the car and disappear.

On September 2, 1956, at 4:30 A.M., the night watchman of the Dayton (Ohio) Country Club saw an oval object, eight to ten feet thick, hovering five or six feet above the ground. It came slowly toward the witness, lighting the area in a radius of five to six meters. However, this sighting cannot be ranked among the best, for the night was very dark and the object gave only a weak light; it might have been a balloon, although the shape (like two saucers glued together by the edge) is peculiar. A more valid case, by our standards, is the incident that took place in South Dakota, on Highway 34, on November 25 of the same year. Two policemen patrolling the highway saw an object hovering on the side of the road. It had the shape of an egg and gave off a red glow sufficient to light the highway. It took off rapidly and the witnesses chased it, but remained one mile behind it throughout the six-mile chase. The object made no noise. Several photographs were taken, one of which shows an egg-shaped object, three times larger than the moon, with a projection at one end, also visible on the film. The witnesses were Don Kelm and Jack Peters of the South Dakota Highway Patrol (145). Two nights before, a civilian pilot flying over Aberdeen, Maryland, reported he was passed by a rocket-shaped object that went down toward the ground. It was seen in flight for five minutes. Later, witnesses saw a red glow like a fire on the ground where the object seemed to have landed.

On November 6, 1957, at 9:00 P.M., near Lake Baskatong, one hundred miles north of Ottawa, Jacques Jacobson and three other witnesses saw a bright sphere much larger than the moon hovering above a hill two or three miles away from them. This incident is described by A. Mebane in his addition to the American version of Michel's second book (115). From the bottom and the top of the sphere spread cones of light so bright that the trees and the clouds were illuminated. No structure was visible through binoculars. The radio was blacked out. One of the witnesses was an electronics engineer and tried a short-wave receiver he had, but all wavelengths were blocked except one, where a very strong signal was perceived. It was rapidly modulated like Morse code, but it was not Morse code. Fifteen minutes later the sphere took off and the radio worked again.

On April 19, 1957, at 11:52 A.M., two metal disks were seen entering the Pacific Ocean at 31°15′N. and 143°30′E. A violent turbulence followed their immersion. The witnesses were Japanese fisherman on board the "Kitsukawara Maru." The point in question is among the deepest in the Pacific Ocean (more than ten thousand meters deep).

On November 2, before midnight, Pedro Saucedo and Jose Salav were driving a truck on Highway 116 in Texas when they saw what they described as a bluish-green torpedo-shaped machine 150 to 200 feet long which remained close to the ground for two or three minutes, then ascended, its color changing to red. The headlights of the truck were off and the motor had died.

OBSERVATIONS OF THE NIGHT OF OCTOBER 14, 1954, IN FRANCE

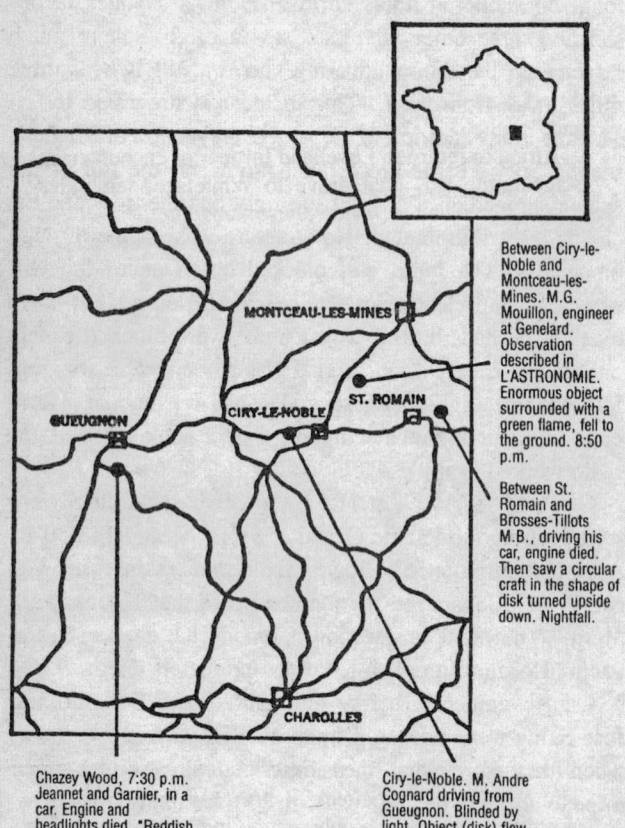

Between Ciry-le-Noble and Montceau-les-Mines. M.G. Mouillon, engineer at Genelard. Observation described in L'ASTRONOMIE. Enormous object surrounded with a green flame, fell to the ground. 8:50 p.m.

Between St. Romain and Brosses-Tillots M.B., driving his car, engine died. Then saw a circular craft in the shape of disk turned upside down. Nightfall.

Chazey Wood, 7:30 p.m. Jeannet and Garnier, in a car. Engine and headlights died. "Reddish fireball."

Ciry-le-Noble. M. Andre Cognard driving from Gueugnon. Blinded by light. Object (disk) flew over his car. Nightfall.

Typical Phases of UFO Behavior

"We first saw a flash of light in the field to our right, and we didn't think much about it—then it rose up out of the field and started toward us, picking up speed. When it got nearer, the lights of my truck went out and the motor died. I jumped out and hit the deck as the thing passed directly over the truck with a great sound and a rush of wind. It sounded like thunder, and my truck rocked from the blast. I felt a lot of heat. Then I got up and watched it go out of sight toward Levelland."

Afraid to return to Levelland for fear of encountering it again, the two men drove to Whiteface, ten miles west of Levelland . . . where they phoned in their report. Although Saucedo sounded terrified, the officer on duty did not at that time take the report seriously.

But an hour later the police got another telephone report. Jim Wheeler, about four miles east of Levelland, had seen a blazing two hundred-foot egg-shaped object sitting on the road ahead of him. At the same time, his car lights went out and his motor died. The object rose and disappeared. A few minutes later came a call from Witharral, ten miles north-northeast of Levelland. Jose Alvarez reported that his lights and motor had gone dead as he drove near a bright, egg-shaped object on the road. At 12:15 A.M., Frank Williams of Kermit, Texas, reported a similar encounter in the same area (45).

According to Mebane in (115), and corroborated by the study of the official reports:

After a few such calls, police cars and firemen were on the roads looking for the object; county sheriff Weir Clem himself saw "a streak of neon-red light crossing the highway less than a quarter of a mile ahead, that lit the whole pavement in front of us for about two seconds."

While officials were investigating, the police headquarters received another call from James Long, who reported that 1:15 A.M. he had been driving on a farm road five miles northwest of Levelland when he came upon a 200-foot long, egg-shaped mass that glowed like a neon sign. His engine coughed and died, and his lights went out.

As he got out and approached the object, which was less than a hundred yards away, it suddenly took off straight upwards. After the object was gone, his engine started easily.

A Texas freshman was approaching Levelland at 12:05 A.M. when he noticed his amperemeter jump to discharge and back—then his motor quit as if it were out of gas—and the lights went out. He got out and looked under the hood but could find nothing wrong. Turning around he saw on the road ahead an egg-shaped object with a flattened bottom—like a loaf of bread and glowing not as bright as neon. No portholes or propellers were visible. Frightened, Wright got back into his car and tried to start it, but without success. After a few minutes, the egg rose almost straight up, veered slightly to the north and disappeared from view in a "split instant." After it was gone, the car started normally.

Here it may be interesting to point out, in addition to these sightings in the immediate vicinity of Levelland, the following:

a) A "blue" UFO had been reported at 11:20 P.M. by two operators of the control tower at Amarillo Airport (142).

b) Three miles west of Canadian, Texas, civilian and military sources reported the landing of an object in the shape of a submarine, two or three times larger than a car and eight feet high. Close to this machine someone was standing and a flash of light was directed toward the witnesses (official files).

c) A large object with a blue light was seen at Midland, Texas, the same day (142).

d) Odis Echols, owner of Radio Station KCLV, saw a yellow object traveling at high speed at 8:00 P.M. at Clovis, New Mexico (142).

e) The next day a UFO was seen flying over Deming, New Mexico, and three other *landings* took place, one at Abilene, Texas (Dyess Air Force Base, Sergeant Jack Waddell), and two at White Sands Stallion Site in New Mexico (army patrol) at 3:00 A.M. and 8:00 P.M. (142, 146, 147).

The official fairy tale concerning the Levelland case is that the "sensational" interpretation of the sightings by the press triggered the series of reports now known as the 1957 wave. It is difficult to apply this theory to the incident that took place in Seoul on November 6, 1957, when military personnel saw (according to Keyhoe) a white, luminous object hovering above the ground that went out suddenly and disappeared "like a bulb turned off." On November 9, at 1:00 A.M., a man driving a car near Lake City, Missouri, reported that his motor had died as an elongated object appeared, hovering fifty feet above the ground. Everything returned to normal when the object left, as in the Levelland incidents and in many cases in France.

In November of 1957, in the Nevada desert between Tonopah and Las Vegas, a U.S. soldier driving a car saw four disks on the ground. He reportedly observed them for twenty minutes, but they took off with a humming sound almost unbearable when he approached them closely.

On April 24, 1964, Officer L. Zamora saw a bright object which landed on four legs two miles out of Socorro,

New Mexico. It has been argued, and even categorically stated, that the Socorro object was not interplanetary, but very probably one of the experimental devices recently developed by the U.S. for the exploration of the moon and planets. it is true that modern technology has now reached a point where machines built by man could almost display the behavior attributed to UFO's in most average reports. However, the analysis of older reports is not affected by this reasoning, and it is difficult to believe that Canada, for instance, could build in 1959 an object that would behave like the machine described in Socorro by Officer Zamora. But this is precisely what one could be tempted to say after reading the following report.

The sighting took place near Grassy Plains, 360 miles north of Vancouver, on April 29, 1959. Alex Gillis and Jerry Monkam, the witnesses, fearing ridicule, reported the event one month later. What they had seen was an object in the shape of an egg, about fourteen feet long, which had landed on the road. The upper part radiated a bright light. After a few minutes the object took off silently. This brings to mind a number of other reports of egg-shaped objects seen in flight or on the ground before this date, too numerous to be quoted here in full detail, but very often of fair reliability.

About October 5, 1959, a young girl riding a horse near the Canadian town of Glenora was frightened by an object hovering above her and illuminating the ground with a brilliant light. She rushed back home and called her father, who observed with her an orange object producing a noise so high and loud they felt pain in their ears (149).

During the night of September 19–20, 1961, at about midnight, Mr. and Mrs. Barnley Hill, of Portsmouth, New

Hampshire, were traveling on U.S. Highway 3 in that state when they saw a large object flying across the sky. Using binoculars, they were able to see a string of lights that seemed to be on a line around the edge of a disk. The whole thing seemed to be revolving. About five miles from Woodstock, it came down in front of the car and hovered at twenty-five to thirty meters above the ground. The witnesses then saw two red lights, before the object took off again (150). On September 15, 1962, at Oradell, New Jersey, two bright disks were seen hovering above a water reservoir. They were surrounded by a bright glow (151).

Observations of such "landings," or Type I reports of all kinds, have been made in all parts of the world. In addition to the few American cases we have just mentioned, we should make a note of the following accounts:

On October 26, 1951, in Australia, at 4:00 A.M., the engineer of a transcontinental train on the east-west line was surprised to see the track brilliantly illuminated by an object that came close to the train, seemed to examine it closely and even gave the impression it was going to land in the desert, but took off and disappeared. On October 12, 1952, in the evening, Jim MacKay and Jim Robinson were in Sunshine Road, a Melbourne suburb, when they heard a swishing sound and saw a red and blue disk coming toward them. They took cover while the "saucer" sped above them at low altitude and vanished.

In LeVigan, France, on October 15, 1952, at 7:10 P.M., a brilliantly illuminated yellow cigar-shaped object was seen, with two figures wearing helmets standing nearby. The craft was allegedly thirty meters long, six meters high. It was surrounded by a sort of haze at both ends.

On July 31, 1953, at 7:00 P.M., on a road near railroad

tracks at Wolin, Poland, a metallic object sixty-five feet in diameter came down at high speed and landed. There were seven witnesses, five Poles and two Germans. The center of the object was closed and spherical. The disk itself was flat, with circular openings.

On August 16, 1953, at 8:30 P.M., an observation was made in France which was related in the scientific press, a new indication of the fact that UFO reports, even when they involve objects on the ground or very close to the ground, are not easy to dismiss:

> M. Claude Pastier of Tours, in Indre-et-Loire, relates with numerous and accurate details the apparition over Tours, on Sunday, August 16, at about 8:30 P.M., of two circular machines flying very low with a "resonant and hard" sound which did not bear resemblance to that of any known craft. The motion was very slow, absolutely rectilinear, and both machines moved in a perfectly similar manner, as if mechanically connected. (*L'Astronomie*, 1953.)

In March of 1959, on the coast of Poland near Kolobrzeg, Polish soldiers saw the sea suddenly become agitated. A triangular object, each side measuring about four meters, came out of the water and started to fly in circles over the barracks, then sped away and vanished.

In an earlier publication (152), we have presented statistics concerning the distribution in time of Type I sightings. These statistics were based on 211 cases of alleged landings when the time of day was known. From these statistics, we estimated that about 50 per cent of Type I events, if independent of human imagination, were not observed because they would occur mostly during the night hours. We also estimated that the total number of "landings" that must have occurred on our planet—of which, under these conditions, approximately half were seen and reported—would be in the neighborhood of 700. But this figure took no account of the events that could have taken place in desert areas, or in countries from which we receive but little information. This evaluation would certainly have to be revised now and set in the neighborhood of 1,000 "events" since 1946.

THE "OPERATORS"

In some of the reports mentioned above, we have already found cases in which the authors of the accounts state that, in the vicinity of the objects they interpret as machines, they saw entities of human form, often called "pilots" in the subsequent treatment of the sightings by the press. Another popular term for these entities is the familiar name "Martians."

If we confine ourselves to a study of the statistical aspect of the question, which we have every right to do, and if we try to reduce our study of the lists and files to rough figures, we find that more than 150 such "Martians" have been described in UFO reports all over the world, this figure being broken down as follows: about 20 before 1954; 100 during the 1954 "wave"; more than 40 since. Obviously, cultist claims and hoaxes of the usual "Venusian" type have all been eliminated from this list.

Are these sightings coherent, and what are the characteristics most often attributed to their "entities" by the authors of such reports? What do we obtain if we seek to extract the chief features from these accounts? Let us hurry to claim that "little green men," which everybody seems so fond of, have never been described in reality. "It is a curious fact," remarks I. Davis, "that it seems impossible to discover the exact origin of the word 'green' with saucer-occupant reports. Where and when the expression 'little green men' was first used, by whom, why or in connection with what case, has not yet been determined." Our own efforts to clarify this point have proved equally vain. If we gather all reports that seem to present some guarantee of reliability, and if we try to extract from them a coherent interpretation, we have to divide the alleged occupants into two groups. On one hand, we find descriptions of men (more than fifty have been described in about twenty cases) similar to us in height and behavior; on the other hand, many accounts speak of "dwarfs" measuring between three and four feet in height. The agreement on this small stature is unanimous. According to M. Carrouges, who made a special investigation of the French cases (155):

> There would seem to exist two kinds of "pilots," at three points of view:
> (1) small pilots one meter or 1.20 meters tall and pilots of human height;
> (2) pilots wearing "diver's suits" and pilots wearing ordinary clothes, with the face visible;
> (3) pilots speaking in a manner which is incomprehensible and pilots speaking a language easily understandable.

However, on the basis of our own documents—apparently more extensive than Carrouges'—the third point should be disregarded; alleged reports of contact with

French-, Russian- or German-speaking entities have always been extremely suspect. The first two points, we must admit, constitute a correct statement of the characters described in the reports. There is a definite correlation between the "dwarf" and the "diving suit," whether the latter is heavy equipment as in the Quarouble, Orchamps or Premanon episodes, or a light silver suit as in Fontenay, Hennezis, Erbray, Lugrin, Saint-Ambroix or Kelly.

UFO erudities will reserve in their classification a place for the "hairy dwarfs" which were described in France on six occasions. These are stories built on little ground, whereas the two categories seen previously can be reasonably substantiated. The best description of a "hairy dwarf," cited here only for its picturesque character, was made by Starovski in Erchin. It is frightfully specific. The witness, a miner, was allegedly confronted with a midget, three feet, six inches tall, with a large head, wearing a brown skullcap forming a fillet a few inches or so above the eyes. These were protruding, with a very small iris, and were slit. Long hair fell down from under the skullcap onto the shoulders. The nose was flat, and the lips thick and red. A strange detail; the witness did not describe any UFO. But his story happens to be typical of a small category of reports, in which similar "entities" are described close to their "machines."

Another category, which is slowly becoming classical among enthusiasts, can also be considered only with suspicion, not only because the authors of these reports may have been mistaken as to what they saw, but because they may not have seen anything at all. In at least two cases, giants have been described in connection with UFO sightings. But one case was a recognized hoax, and the other

OBSERVATIONS OF NOVEMBER 2, 1957, IN TEXAS

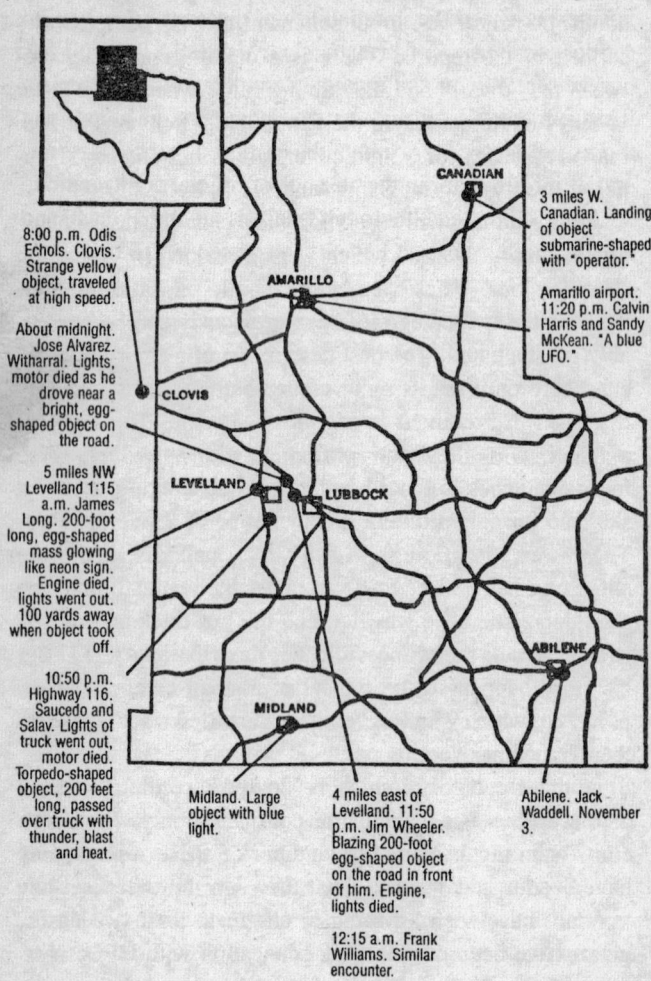

one was extremely vague. Similar reports, however, seem too have originated more recently in South America; we have experienced the unreliability of these reports when no serious local group of investigators such as CODOVNI has checked into them; as far as we know they did not confirm these rumors, which may have originated anywhere along the line of newspapers and enthusiast groups that carry this sort of information, in the absence of official confirmation.

After a new and thorough analysis of the French and American files of Type I events, we stated in (162):

> As a consequence of this improvement and clarification of the files, the category of the giants," already very dubious, can be completely disregarded now, as a product of pure imagination. And the "Erchin" entity (a dwarf with no diver's suit) should be considered with renewed caution. In our opinion, the investigation about the "entities" associated with Type I sightings narrows now into the more simple problem of checking only two categories of reports: the descriptions of men of the "Chaleix" type and the descriptions of "dwarfs with divers' suits." Obviously, the discussion about the real meaning of these incidents in connection with the UFO phenomenon remains open.

Descriptions of "pilots" or "occupants" being commonly observed in connection with UFO reports, some writers argue that the discussion on the "purpose of the landings" is inescapable: Why would an interplanetary craft land for a few minutes in Mrs. Brown's back yard to take off as soon as somebody comes into view? On the basis of such reports, these writers think they can realistically make the assumption that our planet is indeed visited by another community using circular craft, but that direct contact is systematically avoided. We will discuss later the reasons they have imagined that could motivate such a decision to be taken by the "visitors." As far as we, as analysts, are concerned, their present questions cannot be answered and their hypotheses are beyond the reach of our current data.

We do notice, however, that only in two cases have visitors been described that remained in full view for a considerable length of time. One is the 1959 New Guinea episode, in a country that has one of the poorest communications systems on the planet; the other is the puzzling 1955 Kelly-Hopkinsville case, whose link with our problem is not clear, if real; again, the event occurred in a region poorly supplied with official centers.

The few cases when direct contact with men is said to have been made (i.e., gestures from a distance of a few meters) were associated with deserted areas or, at least, very retrograde regions of France, Great Britain, Italy, the United States and South America.

The large majority of other Type I events were of very short duration and took place far from highly populated areas. Landings made in populated areas were of extremely short duration, and landings of long duration made in moderately populated areas, like the Foussignargues episode, were never associated with the appearance of the "operators" themselves.

THE JUNE 1959 NEW GUINEA EPISODE

This is one of the great classics in UFO history. It is, however, known to few persons, although it has a perfectly official character and has remained unidentified after a number of investigations. The main witness, Rev. William Booth Gill, is an ordained priest of the Church of England and a graduate of Brisbane University. He was accompanied, mind you, by thirty-seven other witnesses when the sighting occurred and the narratives are extremely consistent and clearly reliable.

Mr. Gill had been on the staff of the Anglican Mission in Papua for thirteen years when the event took place. He had been working mainly on the northeastern coast of Papua, in the Goodenough Bay area, about ninety miles from Samarai, and his main interest had been educational work (161). He states very clearly, in an interview with Australian reporters, that before the sightings he thought UFO's were "a figment of imagination, or some electrical phenomenon." The interview continues as follows:

> "The first sighting occurred over Waimera about twenty-five miles from us. It was observed by Dr. Ken Houston at a place called Waimera, near Tagora, and that was late November of last year. At Boianai itself, where I am working, the first recorded incident was on the night of Sunday, the 21st of June. My own observations began on the 26th of June and extended over a number of days."

We have here the indication of repeated sightings taking place, once again, over a small area. This is a new example to be added to similar concentrations of UFO activity, like the Charente area in France in 1952, the Haute-Loire area in 1954, or the northern regions of France at another period within the same wave. The states of New Jersey, Illinois and Michigan have known similar "flaps" in recent

UFO'S IN SPACE

years, and the series of incidents over Texas and the Southwest in November of 1957 is memorable. But nothing similar to the New Guinea episodes was ever reported there.

Mr. Gill states that he came out of the dining room on June 26 at 6:45 P.M., after dinner and

> "casually glanced at the sky with the purpose, I suppose, of seeing Venus. Well, I saw Venus but I also saw this sparkling object which was to me peculiar because it sparkled, and because it was very, very bright.... The whole thing was most extraordinary. The fact that we saw what appeared to be human beings on it, I think, is the important thing. It is certainly the important and exciting thing to us. They were not noticeable at first. The object came down at about, I should say, 400 feet, maybe 450 feet, perhaps less, maybe 300 feet. It is very difficult to judge at that time of night and, not having experience in measuring elevation, it is purely guesswork, but as we watched it men came out from this object, and appeared on the top of it on what seemed to be a deck on top of the huge disk. There were four men in all, occasionally two, then one, then three, then four—we noted the various times that men appeared, and then one, two and three appeared and one and two, and then numbers one, three, four and two and so on. And then later all those witnesses who are quite sure that our records were right... signed their names as witnesses of what we assume was human activity or beings of some sort on the object itself.
>
> "Another peculiar thing about it was this shaft of blue light which emanated from what happened to be the centre of the deck. They would bend forward and appear to manipulate something on the deck, and then straighten themselves up occasionally, would turn around in our direction, but on the whole they were interested in something on the deck. Then from time to time—this blue light—rather like a thin spotlight

emanated skywards to stay on for a second or two, and then switch off. I recorded the times that we saw that blue light come on and off—for the rest of the night. After all that activity it ascended and remained very high.

"The craft looked like a disk with smaller round superstructures, then again on top of that another kind of superstructure—round rather like the bridge on a boat. Underneath it had four legs in pairs pointing downward diagonally. These appeared to be fixed, not retractable, and looked the same on the two nights—rather like tripods. On the second night the pencil beam came on again for a few seconds, twice in succession."

Mr. Gill, after stating that he was a poor mathematician, said that the dimensions of the object seemed to him to be about thirty-five or forty feet at the base and perhaps twenty feet at the top.

At the question: "Did you try to establish contact with the pilots of the craft?" he answered:

"We did. As one of the men seemed to lean over as though over a rail and look down on us, I waved one hand overhead and the figure did the same as though a skipper on a boat waving to someone on a wharf. I could not see the rail but he seemed to lean over something with arms over it. We could see him from just below waist up. Ananias, the teacher, waved both hands overhead and the two outside figures waved back with two arms over heads. Then Ananias and I both waved arms and all four figures seemed to wave back—no doubt that movement made by arms was answered by the figures."

"What was the reaction of the natives at signal?"

"Surprised and delighted. Small mission boys called out—everyone beckoned to invite the beings down but no audible responses.... No expressions discernible on the faces of the men—rather like players on a football field at night."

"We understand you tried to signal the beings with a torchlight?"

"Yes, we flashed the light and the object swung like a pendulum, presumably in recognition. When we flashed the torchlight towards it, it hovered, and came quite close towards the ground... and we actually thought it was going to land but it did not. We were all very disappointed about that."

A strip of motion-picture film of ninety-four frames was taken at Port Moresby on August 23, 1953, by T. C. Drury, deputy-director of the Civilian Aviation Department in New Guinea. It showed a disk shaped object in flight, making ninety-degree maneuvers, after coming out of a peculiar cloud. This is a sign that the area of Port Moresby was indeed repeatedly the source of important reports. According to the former Minister for Air, the man who took the film was a "reliable, credible person." The film has been studied by the Intelligence of the Royal Australian Air Force and was also examined by experts of the United States Air Force, according to (163).

FATIMA: THE MIRACULOUS UFO

If we were to restrict ourselves to the sightings already mentioned, and were content with statistical analyses, we could continue to regard our problem as a purely scientific question, even after realizing that several hundred witnesses, of average or fair reliability, have described "entities" in connection with their experiences. After all, the alleged operators never did show signs of hostility. If we attach credence to most of the reports in question, it seems that they were careful not to be approached at close range by human witnesses and, in the case we have just seen, they even showed some contempt in the face of human enthusiasm. But we have never found an indication that any aspect of their activity, if real, could constitute an effort to interfere with human problems; even if they did come to this planet—as enthusiasts claim—they left no trace and did no harm.

This has been a characteristic of most UFO sightings since 1946. But some UFO students have become aware of the fact that older events suggest different interpretations, and they consider with increasing interest reports that were, in older times, simply classed as miraculous by theological authorities. In the view of these writers, there is no better example than the Fatima episode.

"Fifty years ago," writes Ribera in (23),

> Portugal was a very backward country and the strange happenings which took place in that remote corner of it, among illiterate peasants, were apt to receive a religious explanation, more so in times of superstition, such as existed in the Portugese countryside in 1917. Those happenings were currently interpreted as an apparition of the Holy Virgin, but two thousand years ago they could have been interpreted as the coming of the gods upon the Earth.

"Fatima is inescapable," writes G. Inglefield in (160).

> There is no possible doubt that something occurred there; it is by far the best authenticated "miracle" of the

twentieth or, for that matter, of any century, and it was seen by at least 70,000 witnesses. You may find photographs in G. Renault's *Fatima, Esperance du Monde* of their perplexity as spectators watch the phenomenon.

There are articles in contemporary newspapers and there are people alive today who were there. Lucia herself, now in a Spanish convent, is still with us.

The crowd that stood in a field at Fatima, a small village in the district of Leiria, some sixty-two miles north of Lisbon, on October 13, 1917, was waiting there for a miracle, because three children had been assured such an event would take place after a number of meetings with an "entity" that came from the sky in a globe of light. The witnesses were three shepherds: Lucia, aged ten, and her cousins Francisco Marto and Jacinto Marto, aged nine and seven. Today, Fatima is one of the most celebrated places of pilgrimage in the entire world. The Roman Catholic Church has authenticated the miracle. The Basilica each year receives thousands of believers who come to pray to the Holy Virgin. And, as remarked by Paul Misraki, "sick persons are cured and sensational conversions take place."

"These children's sightings," writes Ribera,

> would today be included among the contact claims, for contact they were: in all the six instances reported (from May 13 to October 13) the children met a "celestial being" in the Corva da Iria, an enormous creek, roughly circular in shape, which lies at 2.5 kilometers from Fatima. In that place, while the three children were collecting their sheep about noon, they saw a flash in the heaven. Some minutes later, a white, bright figure appeared near a small oak tree. Now we must bear in mind the general law quoted above; how could a space being have looked to ignorant, illiterate children

Typical Phases of UFO Behavior

from a Catholic country of fifty years ago? As the Holy Virgin, naturally. As they later said, "The wonderful lady looked young. Her dress, white as snow and tied to her neck by a gold band, wholly covered her body. A white cloak, with a golden edge, covered her head.

The strange dialogue between the Holy Virgin and the children began. "Remember," continues Ribera, "the white explorer who presents himself to backward natives as 'the great white god' in order to win their reverence and to convey to them some simple ideas and truths."

A second and a third contact occurred, at exactly one-month intervals, June 13 and July 13. Many clergymen were hostile to the story; some local authorities suggested that the children were tempted by the Devil, and emotion was such that they were even put into jail for several days! But on the third sighting the entity announced that a great miracle would be performed in October in order to convince everybody. A variety of other episodes took place. The fifth meeting was on September 13. There were a number of witnesses, and they could see the "sphere of light" used by the entity to come to the place of the meeting. According to the very words of the Reverand General Vicar of Leiria, who was one of the witnesses, the lady came in an "aeroplane of light," an "immense globe, flying westwards, at moderate speed. It irradiated a very bright light." Some other witnesses saw a white being coming out of the globe, which several minutes later took off, disappearing in the direction of the sun.

The last episode was the miracle itself. It was seen by seventy thousand persons, among whom were pious individuals and atheists, clergymen and reporters from a socialist newspaper. As promised, it happened on October 13

Case	Date	Hour	Location	Witnesses	Weight	Type
1	June 27, 1959	8:00 P.M.	Danville, Va			B(4)
2	July 5, 1959	7:00 P.M.	New Albany, Miss.			A
3	July 21, 1959	10:30 P.M.	Broken Hill, N.S.W., Austr.	dozens		B(5)
4	July 21, 1959	9:30 P.M.	Henderson, N.Y.			A
5	July 28, 1959	2:10 P.M.	Corpus Christi, Tex.		—	A
6	Oct. 4, 1960	6:10 p.m.	Cressy, Tasmania	Numerous	+	B(5)
7	May 31, 1961	12:00 NOON	Toompang, Wyalong, N.S.W., Austr.	Numerous	+	B(X)
8	July 7, 1961	11:00 P.M.	Beulah, Michigan	6		B(4)
9	July 25, 1961	night	Palatka, Fla.			B(X)
10	Aug. 7, 1961		Heaton Moor, Stockport, Eng.			B(X)
11	May 26, 1962	11:45 P.M.	Westfield, Mass.	7	+	A
12	Feb. 23, 1963	9:45 P.M.	Highcliff, Eng.	1		B(2)
13	Apr. 11, 1964	6:30 P.M.	Homer, N.Y.	4	+	B(2)

A blank in the weight column indicates average reliability. An equal sign (−) indicates that a conventional explanation can be proposed to explain the observed phenomenon, although with difficulty. A plus sign (+) indicates that according to our system of evaluation this sighting is typical of the UFO phenomenon. Type A corresponds to accounts where only "cloud cigars," generally vertical, are described. Type B indicates sightings with actual "generation" of UFO's, the number of secondary objects being indicated between parentheses. An (X) means that several objects were reported but that the exact number is unknown. References will be found in the text.

Typical Phases of UFO Behavior

at noon. Among the crowd was Professor Almeida Garrett, of Coimbra University, a scientist, who described the phenomenon in the following terms:

> It was raining hard, and the rain trickled down everyone's clothes. Suddenly, the sun shone through the dense cloud which covered it: everybody looked in its direction. *It looked like a disc, of a very definite contour.* It was not dazzling. I don't think that it could be compared to a dull silver disc, as someone said later in Fatima. No. It rather possessed a clear, changing brightness, which one could compare to a pearl. It looked like a polished wheel. This is not poetry. My eyes have seen it. This clear-shaped disc suddenly began turning. It rotated with increasing speed. Suddenly, the crowd began crying with anguish. The sun, revolving all the time, began falling towards the earth, reddish and bloody, threatening to crush everybody under its fiery weight. [Italics mine—Author.]

"How does one tie up chapter one with chapter two?" asks Inglefield.

> The explanation must be that a liaison existed between the visions and the final "sign." Was this liaison involved with the most vital of our religions—Christianity? Was the "sign" of the "dancing sun" a confirmation of the visions and their messages? Or was it—and this is a disagreeable thought—a gesture of mocking?

TYPE II SIGHTINGS: CLOUD CIGARS AND THE GENERATION OF UFO'S

Two ideas are commonly assumed in discussions of the observations of the Vernon type and, more generally, all events of Type II: the idea that they are extremely rare, and that they are typical of the 1954 French wave. Both are erroneous. Type II sightings have been associated with every important phase of UFO activity and have been reported in every country, from Portugal to Greece and the U.S.S.R., as well as Australia, New Zealand, South America and the United States.

It is true that sightings in this category are not numerous, but their character is such that they must be considered among the very best of the UFO cases. And their rarity is certainly not extreme, as evidenced by the fact that no less than thirteen are already known for the 1959–1964 period. These cases are detailed in the table on page 162.

Case 7 has been described earlier. This leaves us with twelve sightings, of which at least seven have never, to our knowledge, been published before. We will give résumés of these reports to clarify our definition of Type II.

Case 1. An object surrounded by smoke and a peculiar haze seemed to dive rapidly toward the ground. Suddenly four small objects sprang from it and climbed at a steep angle, apparently in formation. The course of the main object was southeast (30).

Typical Phases of UFO Behavior

Case 2. A reddish object with silvery shades was seen motionless in the western sky. It had the apparent diameter of the sun. Its shape was that of a fountain pen and it was tilted at an angle of about 45° with respect to the horizon. After three minutes the witness noticed the slight white tail that seemed about four times as long as the object itself. Shortly afterward it started moving and climbed into the clouds, going from west to northwest (30).

Case 3.

> Four strange glowing objects appeared over Broken Hill at about 10:30 P.M. on July 21st shortly after an unidentified flying object was sighted at Woomera rocket range. The screening of a film at the drive-in theatre had to be stopped as the patrons left their cars to watch the objects. Even the projectionist left his box. Mr. Brian Grosvenor, correspondent of the Australian Broadcasting Commission, noticed what he thought was a falling star. Then there was a fall-out of four glowing objects from the tail of the main one. These travelled in single file at low level across the sky and then faded from view. The main object, traveling at high speed, erupted then another ball of light and disappeared from view (163).

Case 4. A white object in the shape of a cylinder, compared to a baseball bat, reflecting sunlight and standing in a vertical position, moved slowly for about forty-five minutes. (This sighting carries a low weight because of the remote possibility that it might have been a balloon, even though it matches our definition of Type II-A.) (30)

UFO'S IN SPACE

Case 5. At 2:10 P.M. the first in a series of four very large objects was seen. At 40° elevation, it was surrounded by a white, luminous substance that resembled angel hair, and appeared as a dense sphere. One minute later a second one came into view. It resembled a piece of earthenware brilliantly lighted from the back and was surrounded by a blue glow. Two of the numerous witnesses shot color films, one of which was seen by official investigators but did not permit identification. The sighting remains in the "unidentified" category (30).

Case 6.

"Rev. Lionel Browning, an Anglican minister and Tasmanian Secretary of the World Council of Churches, and Mrs. Browning, observed in Cressy, Tasmania, a strange cigar-shaped airship accompanied by five smaller craft at 6:10 P.M. on Tuesday, October 4, 1960.

"'First we saw a large, dull-grey object about 300 feet long. It came at plane-stalling speed and seemed to pause,' said Mr. Browning, who estimated the speed of the ship at less than fifty miles per hour. The object was stationary for about thirty seconds. 'Then out of the clouds above and behind the ship, five or six small discs came shooting at terrific speed.'

"According to the minister, they were approximately thirty feet across and flat underneath with a dome on top. They 'came towards the ship like flat stones skipping along water.' The clergyman and his wife were reticent about releasing this sighting until they heard other local residents' reports. Mrs. Doris Bransden of Cressy said, 'It was a fantastic sight—like a lot of little ships flocking around a bigger one.' The aviation authorities stated there were no planes in the area at the time of Rev. Browning's sighting. It is a notable fact that the clergyman did not believe in the reality of flying saucers before this experience." This observation was discussed before the Australian Senate on October 18, 1960. (Quoted from [164].)

Case 8. Five miles from Beulah, Michigan, two youths in a car saw a bluish-white light going from southeast to northwest at the speed of a jet. Then the object stopped and came lower, rose again to about 20° elevation, came closer to the ground and was lost to view behind some trees.

A reddish glow then appeared and was observed for about two minutes, when the witnesses decided to drive to Beulah and came back with two other persons. They saw the object illuminating the countryside as a full moon and observed it for fifteen minutes. Then they drove on to Zimmerman Road, where they had a better view of the object. Inside the glow it produced they could see another sort of light similar to that of a rotating beacon. Five minutes later, a red object came from the direction of the forest, then a white one. Both were close to the ground and seemed to interchange positions. Then four objects appeared from behind the car and took part in the strange phenomenon.

Extremely puzzled, the four persons drove again to Beulah, came back with two additional witnesses and they all observed the original, beacon-like source of light and the glow. But they returned home without attempting to go closer to the strange object. When the three men came back that night to investigate, nothing was seen any more. All witnesses lived in Beulah, except one who lived in Benzonia (30).

Case 9. Two objects separate from each other, maneuver and reunite. The report is official rejected because "the maneuvers described do not fit any classical aircraft pattern"!

Case 10. From a cloud emerged twenty to thirty flying objects of various sizes, which flew in different directions; a majority of them, however, went toward the east. (Duration two minutes.) (166)

Case 11. A brilliant red oval object, emitting sparks at both ends, slowly descended behind some trees. Its center was white or yellow. It was seen by seven witnesses in different parts of the area. The exact place was on Massachusetts Highway 23, three-quarters of a mile west of the junction with Massachusetts Highway 20. Some of the witnesses could see the object from their cars for two miles. In all descriptions, the phenomenon is said to have been large and impressive (165).

Case 12. An oval object, emerald green, surrounded by a sort of glow, was seen hanging in the sky for ten minutes, after which the witness saw several smaller objects emerge from the large one, as it had assumed a vertical position. These small objects flew away and disappeared over the Channel (30).

Case 13. The best way to describe this sighting is to reproduce here the text of the letter written by the witness himself, a physiotherapist who resides in the state of New York:

Typical Phases of UFO Behavior

On April 11, 1964, my wife, two children and I were having a picnic supper on a hill 1,800 feet above sea level, about ten miles northwest of Homer, New York. It was 6:30 P.M. Several jet bombers had left vapor trails up high, traveling from west to east, but these trails quickly disappeared.

As I looked up in the sky a little to the northwest of us at about 6:30 P.M. there appeared what I thought was a very large jet trail from northeast to southwest. It was very white and wide and at the southwest end there was a break on the trail of about one mile. Then a very black spiral formation of what appeared to be smoke appeared, about one mile long. We remarked that the white trail was unusually wide for a jet trail and apparently the black portion looked dark because of the angulation of the glow of the setting sun behind the western hill several miles away.

The white vapor trail hung in the sky and gradually drifted to the south, slowly disappearing. Up to this point we were observing what we believed to be a normal situation, except for the abrupt ending of the white trail, the space and the continuation of the black spiral tip.

Approximately ten minutes had now passed and it suddenly occurred to me that the black spiral cloud had slowly moved to the west while the white trail had drifted south. Also, the cloud became much darker and we all observed this. At this point, I took my 6 × 25 binoculars to observe it and was shocked to see wisps of smoke actually streaming out of the black cloud... almost boiling out. It was now slowly approaching the distant stratus cloud formation silhouetted against the western hill. Suddenly the black cloud, still retaining its spiral shape, changed from the horizontal position to a vertical position with greater smoke activity and resembled a smoking plane slowly falling from the sky, at the same time assuming a shape not unlike a banana. Then it no longer seemed to be falling, but simply stopped and hung there for two or three minutes and then very slowly seemed to sink into the clouds and was obliterated. Every one of us observed this strange phenomenon plainly, with the naked eye.

After about three minutes had elapsed, while we were all wondering if our eyes had played tricks on us, my daughter suddenly exclaimed, "There's another one." It appeared as a horizontal pencil-shaped object. It was impossible to determine the length, but it could have been as large as a submarine. It moved from the left of the horizon to the right. We could not agree as to whether this was the original object or another rendezvousing with the first object, as this second sighting appeared to the left of where the first object became obliterated by the clouds.

As I was observing it with my binoculars, there was a flash of white light from the rear of it and it shot forward with incredible speed for a distance of about five times its length and as suddenly stopped, still maintaining the pencil shape, apparently hovering. My son described the incident as it happened while I watched it with binoculars. It became thick in the middle and, with a cloud of smoke emanating from it, shot backward as rapidly as it had gone forward, about the same distance. Again it hovered and then began to shorten in length until it appeared saucer shaped, fat in the middle. Then the most incredible part occurred... from the saucer shape it became almost perfectly round and slowly divided into two parts, one above the other, very much as a single cell does under a microscope. The top object slowly became smaller as it appeared to fade off in the distance, while the second object headed downward at a 45° angle toward the spot where we had seen the banana-shaped object disappear. At this point it divided in two again but the bottom object now assumed a vertical pencil shape while the top oval object slowly faded away. We realize the pencil shape could well be a disc observed from the side. Then the pencil-shaped object also faded from sight.

This whole episode took place in about forty-five minutes, and ended just about dusk. If it were not for the fact that all four of us observed this event I would hesitate to bring this to your attention.

HOVERING AND SPECIAL MANEUVERS: TYPE III SIGHTINGS

M. and Mme. Vitre, grocers on the Place Madeleine in Beaune, had just left the village of Meursanges (Cote d'Or) to go home by car. They had driven only a few hundred yards on Route D-111 when they noted through the window a luminous object flying at high speed. Quickly leaving their car, they called to the people at a nearby farm, and together they watched the maneuvers of the object. Their description is fascinating when we recall such a case as that of Frasne, two days earlier, or many others that are as good as identical.

"The object," they said, "stopped for an instant, came down slowly, balancing and changing color, throwing out yellow, orange and violent beams, and then resumed its course and disappeared behind the trees of a wood." Next to this group of trees, and east-southeast of Meursanges, is the village of Chevigny-en-Valiere. Here another witness described the Meursanges object, seen at the same time. Still farther to the east-southeast is the village of Palleau, four miles in a straight line from Meursanges and two and a half miles from Chevigny. At that moment M. Begin, a farmer at Chevigny, saw passing overhead, a round, green luminous object crossing the sky at high speed.

These observations from Meursanges, Chevigny and Palleau deserve special attention for several reasons.

First, though the witnesses at Chevigny and at Palleau knew one another quite well (both lived in Chevigny, a tiny village) they gave different accounts: the witness at Palleau, farther east, only saw "a green ball in rapid movement," while the one at Chevigny reported a complicated spectacle: slowing down, stopping, a "deadleaf" descent, and a profusion of varied colors.

Second, whereas the two well-acquainted witnesses described quite different phenomena, those who did *not* know each other—those at Meursanges and the one at Chevigny—described exactly the same sight. These two reports that are in agreement were from people *only a few miles apart*.

The observation made at Frasne, which is referred to in this quotation from Michel's excellent second book (115), was that of a round object emitting ocher-yellow and violent light, and flying straight at a moderate speed. As the witnesses, an industrialist and his friend, had stopped their car the object started to descend "with a jerky movement." It then stopped and started off toward the southwest.

The credit for recognizing such descriptions as different in nature from the majority of UFO reports undoubtedly goes to Michel. Unfortunately, the importance of this point has not yet been seen by other students of the problem, too often hypnotized by the immediate aspects of the cases and unfamiliar with the scientist's reflex of thinking in terms of classes. This applies especially to the American groups that do not lack data to conduct such an analysis, but fail to do anything beyond accumulating details.

In our analysis, descriptions such as those above fall into Type III. They are typical of a class of events that very clearly stand out from the general background of the reports which constitute the majority of the files. These events are often associated with an object of a definite shape (called "jellyfish-saucer" by Michel) that has been related in many instances to the production of electromagnetic disturbances and colorful luminous effects.

On October 3, 1954, inhabitants of Chereng, in the department of Nord, observed an object that flew at low altitude and great speed toward the Marque River, where it stopped, emitted what seemed to be sparks and descended. As the numerous witnesses ran toward the point at which it seemed about to land, the object gained altitude, still without making any sound. Forty minutes later, a person living at Marcoing, thirty-five miles south of Chereng, saw a luminous object which hung motionless in the air above Gouillet Woods: "It was circular, and red-orange in color. A little below this immobile object, and as though suspended from it, she saw a small spot of light with a kind of see-saw movement." The father of the witness, a policeman at Marcoing, several other policemen and their families (in all, twenty witnesses) continued to watch this phenomenon until, about 8:30 P.M., the object underwent a sudden transformation, the little spot of light vanishing while the ball assumed the shape of a cigar and left horizontally. According to police estimates, the altitude of the object at that time was about two thousand feet. Later investigation disclosed the fact that the phenomenon had been observed over a fairly large area at the moment of its arrival. These reports, exceptionally consistent, led to the belief that the object had come from the direction of Chereng, and was possibly the very cause of the sighting reported there a half-hour earlier. All these cars were carefully checked during our four-year investigation of the European files, and there is no question as to the genuine character of these reports. Consultation of collections of French newspapers or direct inquiry to the local authorities will show that we are indeed faced here with original reports that have not been distorted by specialized journals or groups of enthusiasts.

A few minutes after the Marcoing incident, and in the direction taken by the object, three residents of the town of Amiens saw a luminous ball of a brilliant orange color at low altitude, having the shape of a "mushroom hat." According to the report, "The upper part of the 'mushroom' appeared to vibrate as it changed color from violet to greenish, while short 'cables' of some kind hung from the bottom surface."

The sightings followed one another in the evening of October 3, always in the same northern region of France. Most of them involved objects in the shape of a "mushroom" or "half-moon" displaying typical Type III behavior. Such a motionless object was seen at 9:15 P.M. at Armentieres by dozens of witnesses. Ten minutes later, Jean Lecoq of Lievin observed an elongated object swinging slightly in the sky, at low altitude above the plateau of Lorette. He called other persons; soon one hundred witnesses were watching the phenomenon. They saw part of the object detach itself from the bottom of the rounded UFO. This little object descended rapidly to the ground, remained a few seconds in contact with it and rose again. After this maneuver the main object, reunited, took off toward the south.

Such series of events are not without parallel in other countries. For example, a sighting at Yaounde, Cameroun, on October 28, 1954, by numerous persons of that town, one of whom was the head of the hospital, refers to "an

Typical Phases of UFO Behavior

enormous, stationary disk, powerfully illuminated," which is described in detail in an official report as "mushroom-shaped and carrying beneath it a cylinder of a length equal to its own diameter, which was dangling from it."

On October 22, 1963, at 3:30 P.M., an object was seen for ten minutes at Ipswich, England, composed of a large bright part and a smaller one; it came from the northeast at a very high speed. After hovering for some time, turning and spiraling, it finally left toward the southeast. On August 12, 1963, at 8:30 P.M., a pear-shaped object was seen in several towns in the Black Country district in England. It was described by witnesses at the Birchills Power Station as a light from which smaller lights dropped or toward which they went up while the main object was motionless. On February 18, 1963 (in the morning), for a considerable length of time, objects were seen that displayed typical "aerial fight" behavior of the sort already illustrated in Jung's book (9). They were motionless at times; at other times they would rush toward one another at fantastic speeds, in apparent disorder, giving the impression they were going to crash. They were flat, metallic objects (30). This sighting took place in Maiden, North Carolina. Nine days later, on February 27, 1963, a large, crescent-shaped object was seen at Modesto, California. It was described as a large craft with portholes, which hovered, descended to an altitude of about one thousand feet and emitted for fifteen seconds a bright beam of light. There were seven witnesses (167).

On July 31, 1962, at 11:00 P.M., the Director of the Corrientes Airport at Camba Puntas, Argentina, and Dr. Gustavo Revidapte, a judge at Corrientes, saw a strange object coming toward the runway from the west. It emitted flashes of green, white and red light. Its altitude was of the order of nine hundred meters, and its brilliance was such that it was impossible to ascertain its shape. Six other persons, including several policemen, were called and observed the object as it stopped at the end of the runway, spinning and emitting beams of light. When the witnesses got into a truck and drove toward the object it left at great speed (168). On September 14, 1961, at 7:18 P.M., an object, white and circular, whose color turned to red, was seen for ten minutes at Osan Air Force Base in Korea. Its movement was irregular in speed and direction. At a certain moment it stopped completely, became very bright for two or three minutes, then rose vertically while changing color. When a jet plane came into the area the object started forward, made a ninety-degree turn and later turned again to continue on its original course toward the east-southeast. At that moment it was no larger than a star but was very bright and went faster than any aircraft; it suddenly dashed away and was lost to sight. The whole observation lasted twelve minutes. On September 2, 1961, at 11:40 P.M., several circular, silvery objects were seen for ten minutes at Albuquerque, New Mexico, moving from west to east with erratic movements. They gave the impression of reflected sunlight on a metallic surface. On two occasions they were released smaller silvery objects, of apparent diameter about one-sixteenth of the main objects.

On July 8, 1961, at 10:10 P.M., an orange-yellow object that looked like "an umbrella with a light below" was seen at Fairborn, Ohio, for ten minutes. The sketch given by the witness fits exactly the description of the "jellyfish" object in flight as given by the French observation of Milly-la-Foret and other classical cases. The UFO followed a straight line and disappeared toward the southwest (30).

The observation at Milly-la-Foret belongs to the series of October 3, 1954, that originated in the northern area of France. About 9:30 P.M., a witness living a few miles east of Paris had seen an object dividing itself into two luminous points like stars. These later reunited and, after a series of maneuvers scrupulously noted by the witness, left toward the south. At approximately the same time, four persons in Milly saw precisely the same sort of phenomenon, which they described as an object "in the shape of a half-moon" at first. But they soon realized that the moon was visible behind them; it was in first quarter two days later. After an interval of immobility, the object came lower and became more clearly visible as it approached the place where the four persons were standing. They described its shape then as "a kind of reddish cigar accompanied below by a small shining ring."

These are a few examples of typical behaviors of UFO's seen in all parts of the world. Any valid system of hypotheses concerning the UFO phenomenon should represent them, or at least not contradict the patterns, consistently observed, of their production. Until such a system of hypotheses is presented, however, these reports can only be defined objectively as elements of a class. As such, their scientific study is indeed permissible.

CHAPTER SEVEN

THEORIES AND HYPOTHESES

We leave now the scientific field to sum up the information obtained and compare it with popular theories commonly found in books or journals. We seem to have touched a grave problem, but our curiosity has not been satisfied. It is most clear that we have discovered in the structure of modern science a mechanism that would, in the event of an actual manifestation of extraterrestrial intelligence, probably prevent its recognition as such and would generate the exact type of emotional reaction we observe today. However, physical evidence to support the hypothesis that reports made by reliable observers are best explained as results of confrontation with extraterrestrial intelligence is not only missing; the purpose of possible visitations is still to be revealed. Fragmentary theories have been presented, which have tried to shed light on this point. We feel we should not conclude this book without reviewing them, even if they appear as mere speculations with little factual support.

AGREST'S THEORY OF EXTRATERRESTRIAL VISITATION IN PREHISTORIC TIMES

Because of the variety of their implications, theories that relate the UFO phenomenon to the older subjects of debate and reflection are of great human interest. These theories seem to receive more support from traditional texts and legends than from objective archaeological facts. Although often presented as unusual interpretations of religious beliefs, they do not generally contradict them.

According to Professor Agrest, a Russian physicist, "visitors" could have come to our planet, not from another world in our system, but from an inhabited planet of a distant star.* In an interview with P. Galkin and W. Chernin, published in (177), Agrest said that he felt these visitors may have landed in the Near East, where remains of puzzling ancient structures have been found. One of these is the Baalbek Platform, in the Anti-Lebanon Mountains, made of stone slabs weighing about two thousand pounds each and carried from a quarry at the foot of the hill. Professor Agrest claims that this theory, according to which the builders of these monuments were of extraterrestrial origin, is supported by four categories of traces or other indications:

(1) Tektites, mysterious glasslike stones which contain radioactive isotopes of aluminum and beryllium and are not older than a few million years, might be remains of experiments performed by the "visitors."

(2) Monuments of ancient art, especially the pictures

---

* Agrest's theory was favorably reviewed by George Ostroumov in (187).

showing "round head" figures in the French Sahara, could be images of "spacemen."

(3) Ancient religious traditions that speak of "gods" and "sons of gods" who descended to earth and of a man named Enoch, who was taken alive to Heaven, might be considered references to the same category of events.

(4) Ancient scientific treatises that seem to contain more than would be expected from primitive knowledge might reflect fragments of early teachings once handed to earthmen by the "visitors" and preserved in fragments.

Professor Agrest's hypothesis is certainly stimulating, but it could lead to grave pitfalls. It does not represent archaeological observations better than any speculation one could make a priori. Why did these unknown superior communities leave so suddenly, and why did they come in the first place? Why can we not explain the "incongruities" mentioned by Agrest (monuments, ancient knowledge) as remains of older terrestrial cultures rather than extraterrestrial? This theory also fails to explain the recurrence of UFO observations in historical and modern times. And it displays the same lack of imagination found in the Project Ozma theory, and calls for the same type of impractical decisions (e.g., listening to Epsilon Eridani and Tau Ceti on radio wavelengths).

The link between the celebrated tektites and the "visitors" seems to be especially weak; how could we relate biblical events, a few thousand years old, with the millions-of-years-old tektites? What happened between these two series of "extraterrestrial" interventions in earthly matters? Moreover, other theories of the origin of tektites exist, but Professor Agrest does not seem to take them into account, or try to disprove them.

References to "ancient knowledge" are commonly found in extrascientific literatures, and they are, as a rule, incompetently treated. Professor Agrest does not provide evidence of greater familiarity or personal experience with the subject than most of the modern popular writers, and he does not present, at least in the statements we have seen, specific examples of such "incongruities" that could lead to the idea that older, more knowledgeable civilizations preceded us on this planet.

The Agrest theory is a speculation of a type often presented by Western science-fiction novelists on the basis of arbitrary combinations of archaeological mysteries; Easter Island and Tiahuanaco, as well as other sites where monuments left by strange cultures have been found, have been associated with such ideas of "extraterrestrial visits" in prehistoric times. The myths of Mu, Atlantis and similar sunken continents are well known, and carry as much, or as little, weight as Agrest's theory.

MISRAKI'S THEORY OF EXTRATERRESTRIAL INTERVENTION IN RELIGION

Misraki's views, although of a similarly speculative nature, are the product of a more imaginative and more extensive study of basic writings of our civilization. Well-versed in traditional texts and a student of the origins of Christianity, he published in 1962 a system of hypotheses that covers modern UFO activity and relates it to fundamental writings. By so doing, he claims that he is able to receive support from two series of facts—the observations made in modern times, of the Fatima type, and some mysterious descriptions found in the Bible and a majority of basic writings made at the dawn of history.* His views are largely paralleled by those of the British author B. Le Poer Trench (182).

As had Agrest, the Soviet astronomer Kazantsev had suggested, before Misraki and Le Poer Trench, that angels could be men from space. In (178) it is remarked that this view finds serious corroboration in the Bible:

> According to Genesis 19:3 Lot took the two angels he met at the gate of Sodom to his house "and made them a feast, and did bake unleavened bread, and they did eat." But according to dictionary definitions angels are spiritual, ethereal beings. Angels who ate with Lot could not have been such beings.
>
> Rev. H. Wipprecht of Cobalt, Canada, says that the Bible's description of angels fits "intelligent beings" from other planets. In the Old Testament these "mysterious messengers" were said to regularly visit the Earth from the sky, and on occasion actually intermarried with human beings. The angels who married earth women could not have been "heavenly spirits" (179, 178).

Similarly, notes Le Poer Trench, we read in Gen. 18:4–5, 8:

> "Let a little water, I pray you, be fetched and wash your feet, and rest yourselves under the tree. And I will fetch a morsel of bread, and comfort ye your hearts,

---

* Misraki points out very clearly that the study of biblical events in the context of UFO phenomena would be an amusing but pointless game if attention upon such a relationship had not been focused by recent observations of the Fatima type. The idea that the UFO phenomenon and certain aspects of religion are inseparable in discussion of the Fatima case is basic in Misraki's system. His view here is much more specific than Agrest's, who studies traditions of the primitive period exclusively.

after that ye shall pass on: for therefore are ye come to your servant. And they said, so do, as thou hast said."

"And he took butter, and milk, and the calf which he had dressed, and set it before them; and he stood by them under the tree and they did eat."

In Gen. 6:4, this passage:

"There were giants in the earth in those days, and also after that, when the sons of God came in unto the daughters of men, and they bore children to them, and the same became mighty men which were of old, men of renown."

Misraki points out that the idea of the "spiritual" nature of angels did not appear in the teachings of the Church before the sixth century A.D., a relatively recent date. The Fathers of the Church had, until then, tended to consider the angels as physical beings.

According to Le Poer Trench, the Bible provides evidence that the "armies of God" were an extraterrestrial expedition coming from outer space:

"I have commanded my sanctified ones, I have also called my mighty ones for mine anger, even them that rejoice in my highness.

"They come from a far country, from the end of heaven, even the Lord, and the weapons of his indignation, to destroy the whole land." (Isaiah 13:3, 5)

In Misraki's interpretation, "Yahweh's Glory," the bright cloud that guided the Hebrews across the desert and later often hovered above Jerusalem and the Temple, is neither a mythical symbol used by poets, nor a product of superstitious imaginations, nor a supernatural entity, but a physical object and even, possibly, some type of craft capable of space travel. *Biblical events would be that series of facts, obviously exaggerated or distorted through human memories, that followed the contact between the "visitors" and primitive human congregations.* This contact did not happen by chance, but as part of a plan the "visitors" had concerning the development of civilized life on earth.

This view is startlingly specific; but it has been evaluated as a valid interpretation of the biblical text and is not in contradiction with the traditional teachings of the Church. The first part of Misraki's book (180) is concerned with quotations from the Bible and their interpretation in the author's view, as well as parallels to behaviors described by modern witnesses of UFO activity. Later, he generalizes his theory to include indications found in the majority of ancient documents. For example, he remarks, concerning the apparent disagreements among the gods, including Yahweh himself:

> It would seem that the Yahwist and Elohist tradition has been purposely censored in accordance with directions given by "celestial guides" of the Hebrews, who had very understandable reasons to conceal the fact that their leadership on our planet had been established in the midst of important disorders. We find nothing similar among the promoters of concurrent traditions.
>
> In narratives coming from all points of the globe, quarrels and disastrous fights are described at length. One finds mentions of dissensions resulting in ferocious battles, to which the convulsions of the crust of the earth gave a physical parallel.
>
> A Mediterranean gnosis taught that the world, i.e., the earth, had been created by Ialdabaoth, an incompe-

Theories and Hypotheses

tent 'demiurge' "who took himself to be God." Confronted with accumulating manifestations of his clumsiness, his son had to seize power violently in order to establish a new reign and repair his father's mistakes. This son, whose name is Sabaoth, has reigned ever since in Heaven. This tradition has left traces even in the Catholic liturgy; at every mass the congregation sings: *"Sanctus, Sanctus, Sanctus Dominus Deus Sabaoth, pleni sunt coeli et terra gloria tua."*

The Bible itself mentions this preliminary struggle for power in several books, a proof that the prophets themselves did not hold absolutely accurate the version given in Genesis. Isaiah 51:9 mentions "the generations of long ago," when Yahweh had to destroy Rahab, also named Leviathan, the dragon. Similarly Job 26:12 and several of the Psalms (74:14 and 89:10).

This fight, which preceded and established the reign of Yahweh over the earth, is found in the Judeo-Christian tradition in the episode of the Archangel Michael destroying the dragon.

In India, the Bhagavata Purana shows Vishnu, the Prajapati (progenitor), producing not light, a the biblical Elohim (Let there be light!), but darkness, error and utter tenebrae. And, adds the test: "Then, having contemplated this reprehensible creation, the Creator felt little admiration for himself." In order to repair such a sad beginning, Vishnu sent "wise men" with directions to create for him. But they neglected their duty and remained in motionless contemplation. Then, in order to put an end to this inertia, a young red god had to spring forth from the Prajapati's anger and to create the first human beings in place of his father.

Aztecs attributed their first creation to a couple, Ometecuhli and Omeciuatl, soon dethroned by younger, more active gods. In Assyria the dissensions between the early gods were accompanied with such vociferations that the universe was filled with it, and mountains collapsed.

From Greece comes the same voice; a legend, easily understandable, says that Ouranos (or Uranus)—the sky, space—fecundated his wife Rhea—the earth; we understand that life on earth has a "spatial" origin. But from that union were born abominable monsters; their father was horrified and sent them back into their mother's womb, another way of saying they were buried, and we find them now as fossils. Now Time (Kronos or Chronos—the Latin Saturn) takes the leadership; but Time "devours his children" and everything stagnates in an unproductive routine ("and the wise men, neglecting their duty, fell in contemplation instead of creating").

Later, we find the final landing of a strong new team led by Zeus (Jupiter, or Yod-Pater). All traditions celebrate his dynamism or "youth." His attributes, in Greece as in all other places, are synonymous with light, speed, power: fire, lightning, whiteness, solar radiance, eagle. The word Zeus, like the Latin *deus*, comes from the root *di*, common to our words "diurnal" and "divine." This is equivalent to the Indian "Red Child," the Persian "Solar Ormazd" (victor over Ahriman) and the Hebrew Archangel Michael (victor over the dragon). From then on, a new creation begins, and its object is man.

Are we to say that under this new reign everything is peaceful and quiet? Not at all; other dissensions appear, precisely about this new creature: man, whose appearance does not seem equally desirable to all. A narrative found by a man called Abu Zayd Al-Balkhi, in the margin of the Koran, gives us some indications about what may have happened in the mind of our predecessors; it reads:

"'I have the intention,' said God, 'to establish on earth a vicar.'" (This is how he designated man.) "But the angels, the companions of Iblis, then called Azazil, answered to him: 'Are you going to place on earth somebody who will introduce there corruption and will shed blood, when we, we do not cease to adore you?' But God answered: 'I know what you do not know'" (180).

Misraki's system, therefore, is complex and is not easy to realize at once with all its possible long-term developments and implications. It may contain errors in the interpretation of some documents; the texts themselves are subject to contradiction. The main events, however, and the essence of the documents are respected and even sometimes illuminated by this theory. What seems important here is the spirit in which Misraki treats the problem. This is a rational attempt to translate historical and prehistorical events into a pattern that can be interpreted in modern, technological terms. This standpoint is new and presents three advantages, complementary, in a way, to the three obstacles we found to acceptance of Agrest's theory. (1) It does not extrapolate from individual oddities found in the legendary or mythical side of traditional writings, but (2) considers them as historical documents relative to classes of events, and (3) treats their content in the light of a consistent analysis. Whereas the modern tendency is often oriented toward an interpretation of religious events as primitive legends or pure myths, Misraki's theory on the contrary treats them as real events produced by physical beings but distorted through the imagination of primitive writers. And it provides a possible solution to the mystery of modern UFO activity.

Misraki's ideas may not have been handled with all the necessary precautions the scientist would like to see observed. Even if this system does contain elements of feasible solutions to some of the problem the basic texts lay before us, it leaves certain contradictions unsolved.

It is of interest, however, to observe in what sense the problem of the UFO phenomenon in modern times has been related by knowledgeable and reliable writers to fundamental questions that puzzled man's imagination for ages.

FLETCHER'S "SCIENTIFIC THEORY"

In 1954, when the largest known wave took place over the entire planet, a number of interpretations and hypotheses were presented. Among them, G. Duncan Fletcher's theory was mentioned by numerous newspapers and has remained fairly popular.

Fletcher, vice-president of the Kenya Astronomical Association, suggested that UFO's were interplanetary ships sent to map the earth. Other hypotheses of the same general inspiration were published, in which the alleged visitors were said to be conducting other sorts of scientific missions.

The interest of such theories is limited; the existence of UFO's as material ships is not denied by them, but it is assumed that the communities that developed these machines are interested in scientific activities that duplicate precisely our present level of technology. This seems to be a very narrow view. Since the time of Fletcher's declaration (October, 1954) our own techniques of aerial mapping have greatly evolved and we would not expect now from vehicles carrying out a mapping mission on our planet the same behavior we conceived in 1954. Actually, one single ship orbiting the earth at several hundred miles' altitude could collect the necessary data after a few revolutions, if equipped with long-range optical instruments and means for memorizing this information of the type we are developing now for our own space probes. Such a ship, if covered with a material absorbent to light and radar waves and able to modify its orbit according to a programmed set of instructions, would completely escape detection. Besides, such an orbiter could be very small, and guided by remote control. If this is within the range of our present capability, we should not expect a "visiting community" to do less.

Instead of global mapping, detection of metals in the ground, search for materials or gathering of sociological data might be the purpose of such an expedition. But here again more efficient methods could be used. We are not able to find, in the arsenal of modern science, activities that would require such an extensive survey, made over a period of more than twenty years (earlier surveys, if any, were not extensive).

If we hypothesized that UFO's are indeed material vehicles, we would have to conceive of the 1954 French wave, for example, as an event involving an amount of planning and control equivalent to that of the landing in Normandy by the Allies in 1944. The entire 1954 wave, on a planetary scale, including transportation of the expedition from its place of origin to the environment of the earth, would represent something of the amplitude of World War II. By the standards of such a "community" this may be very small; if space travel was acquired long ago, such expeditions may be a matter of routine, and their execution relatively inexpensive. Still we reach the conclusion that UFO activity, if an artificial effect conditioned by rational thought, cannot have a purely "scientific" purpose as suggested by theories of the Fletcher type (mapping, search for minerals, etc.). Another argument against the Fletcher theory is that in the case of a scientific exploration one would expect to find far more specific activities associated with "landings," when the opposite situation seems to be the case.

MICHEL'S HYPOTHESES AND THE FEASIBILITY OF CONTACT

In his second book, Michel has summarized the hypotheses one could make concerning the purpose of UFO exploration and the attitude of the "operators" toward us. According to his theory, one of four main hypotheses may be true:

(1) At the time of space exploration, contact between races of different biological origins may be impossible, or may follow one-way channels parallel to the "contact" between a naturalist and the insects he observes; insects do perceive the contact but only on their level, and they are unable to participate in a voluntary exchange of information.

(2) Although possible, this contact may be systemically or temporarily avoided.

(3) The contact may already have taken place secretly.

(4) The contact may be openly realized on a "spiritual" level which is not perceptible to us; it is made on "their" mental level and remains invisible to us in our present state of consciousness. Similarly, mice may have eaten thousands of books without ever perceiving them for what they

are. Contact with superior communities might present situations of this general type.

The range of possibilities is so large that one should not reject alternatives 1 or 4 when the problem is considered *in abstracto*. But these speculations do not seem to correspond to the behavior of UFO's observed since 1946; in the present case, if we make the hypothesis that extraterrestrial intelligence is indeed responsible for the observed phenomena, we seem to be confronted with beings of human form that display many analogies with human psychology. Most of their "machines" have shapes that could almost have been designed by human engineers, and there is nothing in most descriptions, that could not be interpreted in technical terms. This is true even of the biblical events, as we have just seen, although they were long considered essentially supernatural and miraculous.

A limited number of observations, however, refer to behaviors almost indescribable in terms of our technology, and certainly do not lend themselves to simple interpretations. Among these are the "aerial fight" episodes already described at Basel and Nuremberg and quoted by Jung and most of the cases in Type III-D, including the observation in Arkansas City, Kansas. There, on June 19, 1956, at 12:10 A.M., a number of luminous objects with appendages were seen for several hours by Bryan Coyle, the editor of the *Arkansas City Traveler;* his wife; a Mr. and Mrs. Bradberry; and three policemen. Meanwhile witnesses in Wichita, Hutchinson, Eldorado and Wellington saw a large light dancing in the sky; the Hutchinson radar painted the movements of the object. Another very puzzling case is the Bismarack, North Dakota, episode, already mentioned.

Type III events, I imagine, could generally be interpreted by "believers" as maneuvers linked with some property of the propulsive power used by the machines. We would prefer to study them as manifestations of artificial intelligence (especially reports of "aerial fight"); but we have no real grounds on which to base such hypotheses at this time. Another mysterious phenomenon is, of course, the actual process of UFO generation and reintegration by Type II objects. For our part, however, if evidence is ever presented that we are visited by a superior community, we would be more impressed by the similarity of the reported features than by differences. We would be guided by these remarks in our judgment and would tend to conclude that, although his appraisal of the general problem is correct, Michel's idea of the nonfeasibility of contact may not be applicable in the particular case we are facing here.

THE LANDING AT KELLY

The landing at Kelly (a small town north of Hopkinsville) is a complete, well documented report, well handled by local authorities and the subject of an extensive investigation by the police and the Air Force. It is from this official report on the case, which contains some truly fantastic material, that the following is digested. We have found confirmation of several points through a person who was on the scene the very night of the sighting (153). Elements of information can also be found in the local newspapers and in the book of Dr. M. K. Jessup, *The UFO Annual*. The newspaper accounts were inaccurate in many cases; a civilian investigator, J. Sanders, has fortunately conducted an independent research and has published her findings (which parallel to a large extent those of the police) in the specialized journal edited by Gray Barker (158). These are the facts this series of investigations has established.

Three children and eight adults were present when the event occurred on the night of Sunday, August 21, 1955. They quite evidently lack the extraordinary wealth of imagination that would be necessary to contrive a fantastic story of such dimensions, but they also lack the ability to lie for the fun of it, or for publicity. It is a fact that a number of bullets were fired from the inside of the house, through the door and window screens, at something outside. It is also a fact that no special military device or equipment was being tested in the vicinity of the Sutton farmhouse, and it has been ascertained that no circus or wild animal show was in the area at the time of the sighting (181).

At seven in the evening, Billy Ray Sutton, the teen-age son, went out of the house to drink water from the well. When he returned, he said that he had seen a flying object land behind the farmhouse.

Nobody in the house thought much of this "object," and the idea that it must have been a shooting star seems to have prevailed. It was quite some time later, about an hour, that a creature was seen for the first time. According to several reports, it appeared first as "a strange glow." As it came towards the house, it could soon be seen as a "little man."

The creature's hands were raised as it moved closer to the witnesses. When it was about twenty feet from them, two of the men shot at the unknown entity. It somersaulted and disappeared in the dark. As the men came back inside the house, another creature, similar to the first one, appeared at the window and they fired again through the screen. It also seemed to be hit, and disappeared. Then the men decided to go outside, but as they did they saw another creature on the house, shot at it and knocked it over the roof. Another one was in a tree at some distance; it was also shot at. The creature *floated* to the ground; in her excellent article, Jacqueline Sanders remarks:

> They made direct hits on the "invaders." But bullets seemed to have no effect. When knocked down by a blast of Sutton's shotgun the uninvited guests would pop right up again and disappear into the darkness. Taylor told of knocking one of them off a barrel with his .22. He said he heard the bullet strike the creature, then whine as it ricocheted off! The little man tumbled to the ground, rolled like a ball.

Taylor fired about four boxes of shells with his .22 rifle; at about eleven, the Suttons gave up the idea of getting rid of the creatures; the visitors seemed to be invulnerable. The children were, of course, very much affected, and the women were extremely frightened. They all abandoned the house and drove to the Hopkinsville police station.

The agreement of all investigators—skeptics and non-skeptics alike—was complete on two points: the Suttons had not been drinking, and their extreme fright as they reached Hopkinsville was genuine. At the appeal for help more than a dozen state, county and city police officials arrived to investigate at about 12:30 A.M., led by Chief Greenwell. Jacqueline Sanders interviewed him and gathered the comments of the local policemen:

> All seemed impressed with the evident fright and sincerity of the highly excited family. A check with

Theories and Hypotheses

neighbors disclosed that they "were not a drinking family" and no evidence of drinking was found around the place. All the witnesses told practically the same story, with only minor variations, depending on what part of the house they were in at the time of the happening (158).

The police took immediate action and state troopers moved into the area. As one of the officers drove toward the farmhouse to join the search, he reported seeing several strange "meteors" that came from the southwest in the direction of the Sutton farmhouse. As he and his wife looked out of the car they saw two of them passing overhead with a loud "swishing" noise. The Suttons were so frightened that they would not reenter the farm before the police made a complete search. Investigators discovered several strange indications around the house, but no evidence that a craft had actually landed in the gully.

The descriptions of the creatures given in (158) and in (181) are in very close agreement. Considerable information was derived by the investigators from the Sutton family's observations, and this might be of interest to biologists, as a check of the coherency of the story. The eyes of the "entities" were large and apparently very sensitive. It was noticed that they always approached the house from the darkest corner. There was no pupil in the eye, no eyelid; when the witnesses turned on the lights outside the house, it seemed to prevent the creatures from coming toward the doors.

When they approached the witnesses, the creatures stood up with their hands in the air, walking slowly. When struck by shots they did not fall, but floated (from the roof, or from the tree, in the second occurrence) to the ground.

According to some of the witnesses they were not walking, but "seemed to float" toward them. The creatures were about 3½ or 4 feet tall, with huge eyes and hands, large pointed ears, and arms that hung almost to the ground. When asked about the clothing, the witnesses said the little men appeared to be "nickel plated" (158).

There is some doubt as to the precise number of these creatures. Accounts published by the press overestimated this number. From reading the Air Force report it seems that it might not exceed two or three. One of the witnesses remarked:

> I only know what I saw. I saw two of the men, or maybe the same one twice. I saw one about 10:30, and the other one around 3:30 A.M. That time I watched the little man for more than a minute (158).

The puzzling thing about this episode is that it seems to check with descriptions made by South American witnesses in 1954 and 1957 which have not been publicized by the press in the United States. The 1954 cases, especially, could hardly have come to the attention of the Sutton family.

Indeed, the three cases we have examined in detail—the New Guinea episode (Rev. W. B. Gill's sighting), the Fatima miracle and the landing at Kelly—give a new dimension to the UFO problem. I hope my reader will understand that they are quoted here not because of their sensational character, but because they are indeed among the most well-ascertained cases known, and in the hope that they will illustrate the anguish and deep concern serious researchers have encountered and define the context of scientific, objective discussion of the UFO phenomenon. They certainly make it easy to understand why so many persons have asked the question of the "origin" of the UFO's, and have proposed theories in which the alleged machines are not only spacecraft but come from planets outside the solar system. The next paragraphs will discuss this theory.

OBERTH'S THEORY OF THE EXTRASOLAR ORIGIN OF UFO'S

H. Oberth, well known for his contributions to the early development of rocket technology and connected engineering problems, has repeatedly claimed that UFO's are vehicles from another solar system. Others have also made this hypothesis, but they are often in disagreement over the exact origin of the "visitors"; the reader will often find the stars Tau Ceti and Epsilon Eridani associated with such speculations, simply because they are among the closest to the sun. There is very little ground to support these theories, especially when one begins to attach specific names to the hypothetical places whence such an expedition might have originated.

In our present view, there is no reason to assume that reports of UFO activity made in historical times refer to the same type of "exploration" as the modern or the biblical reports; a theory presenting the view that UFO's are material machines would gain in generality by avoiding this assumption. The identification of the sightings made in historical times with what we call here the UFO phenomenon weakens, undoubtedly, as one goes back in time. The fact that similar shapes are involved in both ancient and modern cases does not constitute a "proof" of identity as to their origin, since, on one hand, arguments of the type presented by Jung (the shape of the "saucer" as an archetype) would continue to hold and, on the other hand, the shape of the egg or disk is clearly optimal for space travel, and many "communities" might have arrived at the same concepts after following very different paths of technical experience. Similarly, the question of the exact origin in space is ill-defined; expanding civilizations might well establish colonies; we might even imagine that we are visited now by descendants of older terrestrial civilizations contacted by superior communities at a date so remote that no legend has recorded the event. Human imagination is rich and one has the right to use it in order to describe possibilities and suggest hypotheses. But the claim that such speculations correspond to the reality presently observed is merely a mockery of science.

The only document we have at the present time on which such a study could be tested is the graph of UFO activity over the past eighteen years. But early attempts made by several researchers to extricate the true signal from the noise and correlate the apparent periodicity of the function with astronomical events fail to present conclusive evidence of the Martian, or non-Martian, origin of the alleged visitors (the Martian solution being obviously the simplest and the most tempting). But only vague indications of a possible correlation have been presented.

THE RELAY ON THE MOON AND SAGAN'S HYPOTHESES

A Harvard astronomer, Dr. Carl Sagan, has repeatedly suggested that UFO's might muse the hidden side of the moon as a relay for a survey of our planet. He was not referring to the objects or phenomena we are studying in this book, but to hypothetical vehicles that would be the product of the technology of a superior community. His idea has tempted many students of the UFO mystery.

In support of this theory, it is often pointed out that a base of the visible side of the moon would be very convenient for surveillance of our planet, although space stations in orbit might have advantages in many cases. The reader interested in this controversy can consult the documents published in regard to plans for orbiting and lunar observatories; he will find that both proposals have advantages and inconveniences. A base on the moon would prove more advantageous for large colonies having a constant need for supplies. But there would be little reason to put such a base on the other side, since it would have to be mainly underground anyway and could be hidden easily from terrestrial telescopes even on the visible side. The only reason one could be led to prefer the invisible side would be to hide one's activities, if they involved huge constructions on the surface. But the craft going to or from the base would still be easily visible, or would leave clear traces on moon photographs, while all the advantages of direct optical survey of the earth would be lost.

Without going deeply into these "strategic aspects of the

UFO'S IN SPACE

question, we feel that UFO's if indeed material objects and if our conception of their reliability and performance is accurate, would have an excellent alternate solution if they wanted to keep a continuous watch on human activity: A machine in the shape of a disk or an egg, able to travel through space, is also able to travel through air or water. The bottom of our oceans would thus prove a splendid solution to the problem of a base, and certainly a much safer one than the lunar base. Let the reader compare the information we have on our spatial environment with the information we possess concerning our oceans, and see which is better known. We are likely to reach the moon long before we have means to reach the bottom of the Pacific Ocean safely, and there is little doubt that we will have less difficulty establishing a base on the moon than building even a small unit very deep in the water. In space, the range of visibility is many orders of magnitude greater than our ability to travel. Under the surface of the ocean, only a few feet can be explored visually, even with powerful searchlights. Most of our oceanic waters are so deserted that an object leaving or reentering the water would have a far greater chance of doing so unnoticed than a space vehicle racing through the night sky under the eyes of telescopes of dozens of satellite-tracking and moon-mapping stations. (Most of the sightings in our Type I-B could be interpreted in this context.) Although no serious indication shows that hypotheses of this type are tenable, a moon station to maintain our civilization under close watch is even less appealing.

A NEW SYSTEM OF WORKING HYPOTHESES

We should probably stop here, having shown that none of the present interpretations of the UFO phenomenon is fully satisfactory; we would thus stay on the safe side of the fence. However, we feel we must complete this chapter by stating where our own system of ideas tends to stand between the various theories we have reviewed. We are assuming, of course, that it is understood that the system is purely speculative in nature. We would summarize it under the following seven points:

(1) It is scientifically permissible to work under the general hypothesis that UFO's are material objects, not excluding the possibility of their being nonhuman vehicles. There is no reason only theories based on the idea that the senses of all witnesses have been abused should bear the stamp of scientific consideration. On the contrary, the hypothesis that the authors of reports have indeed been in visual contact with physical objects, possibly behaving under intelligent control, leads to an analysis of the UFO phenomenon that lacks neither objectivity nor consistency.

(2) Under such a hypothesis, the fact that the "controlling intelligence" could not belong to any of the communities which are present today on our planet would be shown by the permanence of UFO activity through changing phases of our technology and even, possibly, through early phases of our historical development.

(3) Historically, it would be difficult to determine a starting point for this activity, even if considered artificial in nature. The only fact clearly visible from the data we

have is that UFO activity almost ceased between 1914 and 1946 but was considerably renewed in May of 1946. It has been present ever since, with a significant decrease in amplitude since 1958.

(4) If the hypothesis that UFO phenomena are manifestations of a controlling intelligence finds serious confirmation in years to come, through research or otherwise, we feel that one should *then* accept the idea that UFO operators have been seen on the ground on several occasions.

(5) Under such circumstances, we would expect intellectual contact to be possible, owing to the fact that human concepts seem, in our observation, to be applicable to UFO behavior. But we would continue to reject the claim of particular individuals that they have been "contacted" and allowed to know the origin of the "visitors."

(6) In a discussion concerning the "purpose" of UFO activity we would point out:

a) that technological development on earth is now such that we are able, at least in theory, to reach any point in the universe which lies within our visual range, having thus overcome the handicap of creatures that can live only on the surface or very close to the surface of a planetary body;

b) that UFO activity was suddenly renewed after World War II, when both rocket and aircraft technology had reached a point where space travel could be realistically visualized;

c) that a particular peak of activity, quite unlike other waves, took place in 1957 when Sputniks I and II were launched into orbit.

(7) It is our opinion that a dispassionate, scientific debate could be established concerning the UFO phenome-

non, and that such a discussion could well be conducted within the boundaries set by rationalism for the purpose of objective acquisition of knowledge. The various points involved in the present arguments over the nature of this phenomenon could then be checked by reference to a system of catalogues of observations, very often of high reliability, that falls within the competence of the professional scientist. The existing files, kept up-to-date by official services in this country and by a few reliable amateurs abroad, would provide a basis for the establishment of a general investigation of this type. If, however, these documents and the underlying phenomenon they manifest should be neglected by professional scientists, only obscurantism and charlatanism would be encouraged. Such an attitude would lead to the generation of myths that could constitute a danger when the sociological impact of space exploration reaches its full strength.

Through UFO activity, although no physical evidence has yet been found, some of us believe the contours of an amazingly complex intelligent life beyond the earth can already be discerned. The wakening spirit of man, and the horrified reaction of his too-scrupulous theories: what do they matter. Our minds now wander on planets our fathers ignored. Our senses, our dreams have reached across the night at last, and touched other universes. The sky will never be the same again.

NOTE ON THE PROBABILITY OF CONTACT WITH SUPERIOR GALACTIC COMMUNITIES

THE FORMATION OF SOLAR SYSTEMS: THEORETICAL DATA

Present theories of stellar mechanics and physics provide, as far as we know, a good approximation of the laws of stellar evolution, and represent well visual and spectral observations. The evolution of the stars in space and time, their variations of color, temperature and chemical composition are described by these models.

Whether stars are formed by gravitational condensation of gas nebulae or by some other process is not yet clear, but it seems fairly well established that each star is not formed independently. Large "associations" are produced during the initial process and their elements move away from a common center. Today, most of the components of these large groups are so far apart that only careful studies of their proper motions can distinguish them from stars in the background and establish their common point of origin. Knowing this point of formation and the annual displacement, one can compute their ages. Stars are still being formed by this process.

In such associations, stars without companions are not the general case. The original mass of gas will often have distributed its angular momentum between the components of a multiple system and we observe double or triple stars, etc. Planetary systems seem to be generated because of similar physical processes. Angular momenta insufficient to allow the production of a binary system could be distributed between a central mass and a series of smaller condensations. When nuclear reactions start in the center of this mass, the new star radiates and the gaseous material is blown out of the system into space. From that point on, the planets cool and move freely in more or less definitive orbits, along with their smaller satellites, still integrating some dust material and exchanging small amounts of matter and energy with their environment and the solar corona.

Observation of planetary systems would therefore be a quite common experience if we had means of detecting the very small objects involved. But very often unseen companions of stars, when detected, may well turn out to be small stars of very low luminosity, and not planets.

PLANETARY SYSTEMS: OBSERVATIONAL DATA

The planets of our own system revolve, roughly speaking, in the same plane on elliptic (almost circular) trajectories with the sun as one of the foci. Their mass is small compared with that of the sun. However, the center of gravity of the solar system is situated outside the sun, at about one million kilometers from its center. The sun revolves around this point about twelve years, about the period of Jupiter, the heaviest planet by far. This phenomenon, as pointed out in (54), could be observed by extraterrestrial beings (for example, inhabitants of a hypothetical system around the star Proxima Centauri, the closest to us, would see the sun, as indicated below, from a distance of 4.5 light-years, and could detect an oscillation in its motion, if they possessed advanced astrometric techniques). Although it would probably remain impossible for them to see the earth or even Jupiter, they could discover the existence of our system as a consequence of this "waving" motion of the sun.

In recent years, this method has been used in a survey of neighboring stars and has led to the actual discovery of several unseen companions, among which could be planets. Using very delicate techniques of photometric

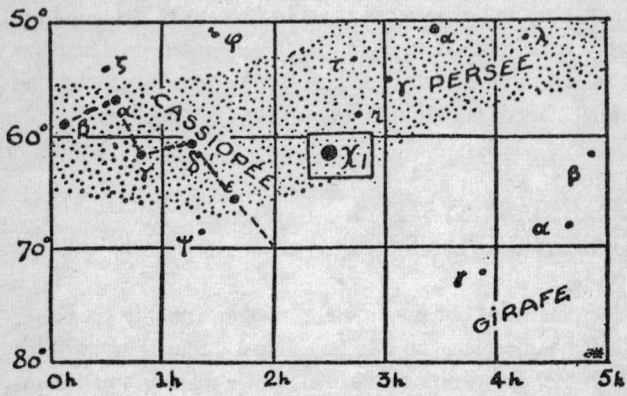

The sun seen the nearest star (Proxima Centauri) would appear as a star of the constellation of Cassiopeia. (After *L'Astronomie*, [54]).

Note on the Probability of Contact

measurement, P. Van de Kamp has been able to find displacements of the photocenter of these stars leading to the determination of systems in which the ratio of the mass of the companions to that of the central star is generally of the order of ten times the corresponding value in our system.*
These discoveries further confirm the words written by F. W. Bessel in 1844: "Light is not real property of mass. The existence of numberless visible stars can prove nothing against the existence of numberless invisible ones." This analysis was justified in 1862 when Alvan G. Clark, using the eighteen-inch refractor now at Dearborn Observatory of Northwestern University, discovered the companion of Sirius.

The fundamental difficulty, according to Van de Kamp, is that "a small perturbation such as would be expected from a planetary companion may be caused also by an unresolved binary whose photocenter falls close to the bary-center." A star is self-luminous, while a planet shines only by reflected light, but only conventional distinctions can be made between heavy planets and very small stars. Generally, an object of a mass of 0.05 solar mass is considered a borderline object (Russell, 1943, 1944); such an object would have a surface temperature of 700° K., of the order of some of the measurements taken by Mariner II of the atmosphere of Venus, and would be barely visible in the visual range of the spectrum.

---

* Knowing the distance d from the star to the center of gravity, the period of the revolution T and the magnitude of the star, from which is derived the total mass, the mean distance of the companion to the star is $a = \sqrt[3]{T^2}$ and the ratio of the masses is $\frac{m}{M} = \frac{d}{a}$. This ratio is $1/700$ in the case of the solar system; it is much higher in the systems actually discovered (see [57] to [62]). The smallest mass found is one-sixtieth of the solar mass for the third component of the visual binary 61 Cygni, discovered by Strand.

UFO'S IN SPACE

A sphere five parsecs (or sixteen light-years) in radius, with the solar system as its center, contains fifty-six stars composing forty-two systems, of which two are triple, ten double and thirty single. Among these nearby stars, the majority are faint, and less than a dozen are visible to the naked eye (Van de Kamp, 1955). Four of them undergo perturbations indicating the presence of unseen companions. The data relative to these stars are summarized below:

Name	α1950	δ1950	Distance (light-years)	Mass of Unseen Companion*	Period (years)
Barnard's star	17^H 55.4^M	+04° 33'	6.0		
Lalande 21185	11^H 00.6^M	+36° 18'	8.2	0.030	1.14
61 Cygni (Strand, 1943)	21^H 04.7^M	+38° 30'	11.1	0.016	4.90
BD + 20° 2465 = Ci 1244 (Reuyl, 1943)	10^H 16.9^M	+20° 07'	15.4	0.030	9.00

* solar masss = 1

But these indications must be considered carefully, in view of the fact that the observed perturbations, as mentioned earlier, might be caused by small stars rather than planets in certain cases. This list, however, does give an indication of what number of systems presenting conditions close to those of a planetary system can be expected in a given volume. It seems reasonable, on the basis of existing data, to take four as a probable minimum for the number of planetary-type systems in this standard volume, in addition to our own system, since the perturbations caused by bodies of a size comparable to that of our planets would be unobservable in the present state of astronomical techniques, and since considerations involving the fact that slowly rotating stars are likely to have planetary companions would lead to a higher estimate, possibly more realistic.

CONTACT WITH SUPERIOR GALACTIC COMMUNITIES

If we consider only space-traveling races that might have originated outside our solar system, the restrictions considered in Chapter 2 do not hold. As remarked by Dr. Lipp himself:

> Arguments like those applied to Martians above need not apply to races from other star systems. Instead of being a first port of call, Earth could possibly be reached only after many centuries of development and exploration with space ships, so that a visiting race would be expected to be far in advance of Man.

In our model, we would introduce a number of new parameters. Considering the fraction of eligible systems on which intelligent life has actually developed, we can give a new formula to express the number of races exploring space in a sample volume, and this will give, under our present assumptions, an upper limit of the number of space-traveling races which exist in this volume.

At a given time, one of these races has a certain quantity of information concerning us (possibly only observational data concerning our sun). We define the minimum level of information this particular race would have concerning a point at distance (d) in order to contemplate space travel to this point. From this, we can calculate the radius of the maximum volume of space that race could explore "physically" at a given time.

Obviously, some hypothesis should be made here concerning the levels of intelligence of these races, which need not be constant. However, in this approximation, we will consider that intelligence itself does not increase or decrease as times goes on, and that only the quantity of information or amount of knowledge every race possesses concerning its environment will vary. We can, for example, assume that the knowledge in question, for a given race, varies in proportion to a certain power of time, the coefficient of proportionality defining the type of intelligence of the race, which would be interpreted as an "intellectual development rate." We can then express completely the volume that can be physically explored by the race as a function of time and of this coefficient; similarly, we can calculate the age required for this race to be able to reach a point at a certain distance.

We would then have to take into account the rate of birth and death of such space-traveling races; we cannot expect to make contact with races for which the minimum age required to reach our system is larger than the expected lifetime of scientific civilizations. On the other hand, before we introduce this factor, we should know more about the volume of space to be considered. What physical reality could be attached to the exploration of the whole universe, or even of our galaxy? In the latter case, we would no longer be concerned with spherical volumes, and we should take into account the structure of the galaxy, its stellar population repartition and evolution.

No information on the total volume in which exploration

can realistically be considered is given in the literature. Dr. Lipp has only indicated that the probability of finding races occupying higher and higher levels in the intelligence spectrum was increased with the radius of the explored volume, but that the probability for these space explorers to ever find the earth was decreased. From that, we could be tempted to infer that the chance of being "visited" is more or less constant over the distance, the only change being in the "quality" of the visitors; UFO's from very distant places would occur just as often as UFO's from nearby stars, but they would be products of much more highly developed technologies.

We will now try to show another possible approach to this problem.

GALACTIC EXPLORATION IN THE VICINITY OF THE SUN

In (67) Sebastian von Hoerner says he expects "to find either a high activity in communication at shorter distances (200 to 300 parsecs) between civilizations of extremely long time scales, or very little if any activity at greater distances (600 to 1000 parsecs) from civilizations similar to our own." These estimates are justified in the light of an evaluation of the average distance to the ten nearest civilizations, expected to be of the order of 360 parsecs.

Here we do not limit ourselves to communication by radio signals, but consider all means of gaining information, not excluding physical travel (this may be more realistic, since the role of radio techniques as advanced means of communication can be expected to be of an extremely brief duration on our time scale); we can reformulate the problem of the maximum distance as follows:

Each race contained in a shell centered on our system has certain information concerning us that we can compute from considerations explained above. The total knowledge concerning our system and contained in the shell can also be expressed in mathematical terms. We cannot enter here into the details of this model; it is enough to say that as far as galactic exploration in the vicinity of our sun is concerned, it shows that the knowledge gathered by intelligent races situated at a distance (x) from us, and concerning our system, is related to a mean value of the product (age multiplied by development index), and varies in first approximation as the logarithm of the distance.

If we now consider, instead of the ideal "knowledge," the ability of these civilizations to communicate with us, or even to explore physically our system, we have to take into account the fact that such action will cost energy and that the difficulty of the experiment will be proportional to some power of the distance. When we express this idea in mathematical terms, we find that there exists an upper limit above which communication by conventional means with races of intelligence comparable to ours cannot be realistically considered, under our present hypotheses (in which we do not take into account colonies or a process of development of life that would not be random).

This upper limit, for plausible values of the different parameters involved, seems to be small compared to the radius of our galaxy, and this justifies the introduction of simple laws of proportionality and spherical approximations. From this new model we can also compute a new estimate of the average distance to the nearest civilizations.

Note on the Probability of Contact

We have already defined the fraction of existing systems which have actually seen the development of races able to travel through space. There is an obvious relation between this average distance, the upper limit of the volume considered and the total number of stars in this volume. For numerical values of the fraction defined above, ranging from one to one-tenth, the average distance to the six nearest civilizations ranges from five to ten parsecs. This is a more optimistic model than Von Hoener's estimate is (67), in which the average distance to the ten nearest civilizations is about fifty times larger, and ours is a more pessimistic view than Dr. Lipp's. Dr. S. S. Huang, of Goddard Flight Center, now at Dearborn Observatory, estimates that the number of inhabitable systems is about 3 to 5 percent of the number of stars; this leads to eight billion inhabitable systems in our galaxy. Our model is close to this estimate.

In the volume of realistic dimensions defined above we find a certain number of races exploring space. We will assume that the only purpose of these explorations is data collection, that both civilizations involved in contacts (if any) are sufficiently different and the duration of the contacts short enough to prevent "feedback" effects which would modify their rates of intellectual development. In order to keep our model free of extrascientific considerations, we will also assume that no colony is established by the visiting race. In this very simplified model, each civilization is allowed only one visit, for scientific purposes, and with limited contact, to another civilization.

We are not making a very restrictive hypothesis if we also assume that as soon as the knowledge a certain race situated in this volume has concerning our system is greater than a certain quantity, the actual sampling takes place.

What we are assuming here is simply that exploration of a system is conducted as soon as capability to travel to this point is obtained. The above problem can then be treated as a renewal process.

Consider the birth of a system able to support life. This birth occurs at a certain distance from the sun and a certain time elapses before life actually appears, depending on the physical and chemical conditions in the system, etc. If the system belongs to the total number of planetary systems that actually permit the development of intelligent life, a civilization will eventually develop on one or several planets and, assuming that the technician stage is reached within the lifetime of these civilizations, space travel will be acquired and exploration of space in the vicinity of the system in question will begin.

For this technical civilization to acquire sufficient knowledge concerning space travel and concerning our system to be able to sample the earth will require a certain amount of time; this we take as a random variable. During this waiting time other systems may be born and other communities may appear, possibly closer to us, and a new possibility of being visited is to be taken into account. But if we consider on one hand the average time between the birth of systems able to support life, and on the other hand the average time between actual samplings of our system, and if we assume the equilibrium has been reached and that steady-state has been realized, we can show that both average times tend toward the same limit, and this would lead to an estimate of inter-arrival time close to that found by Sagan, namely a visitation every one thousand years (7).

In a complete model, however, one should consider several facts that would increase the probability of visitation after a sufficient time. One would take into account the actual curve of the rate of star-generation for the different types as a function of time, when sufficient data exist from astronomical observations to permit this rate to be estimated. From results obtained through elementary models the expected number of samplings per time period seems to increase very rapidly as soon as the initial stages (during which no race has sufficient knowledge to contemplate travel to the sun) have elapsed. All the considerations involving possible feed-back effects or the foundation of colonies far from the original system, which should be introduced in the discussion but can hardly be formulated in mathematical terms in models of this type, would tend to increase the probability in favor of exchanges between these races.

LIMITATIONS OF THIS MODEL

This model is clearly bounded by our ignorance of certain physical laws which might be basic in the technology used by a superior community. In particular, we will point out that the idea of *travel* might undergo considerable variations as knowledge of natural mechanisms is expanded and new physical processes mastered. Most of our ideas about space and time still show the memory of centuries when the wind, the flow of water and the migration of animals and men were the sole illustrations of travel. Only much later was it discovered that physical forces such as electricity (for example, in the form of electrostatic charges) could "travel" in a way which was not easily understandable by *common sense*. Today, we know that people can communicate without actually walking toward each other, without being in visual contact or being connected by material objects such as wires. We can see what goes on in various parts of the world through television; we can even bring back scenes and voices from the past; we have extended our potentiality to travel beyond the immediate material world.

Although space travel as we imagine it (i.e., with some sort of rocket-propelled vehicle) is probably a basic step in the establishment of a technical civilization, it could by no means be considered an ultimate accomplishment. And the *common sense* idea that only propelled vehicles can bridge the gap between adjacent solar systems may well turn and to be as erroneous a view as our fathers' conceptions about the ether. The publicity given to some recent technical feats makes us forget too often that physics, not technology, holds the answer to the problem of space travel. Only when a general solution is found to the very grave questions physicists are debating now will it be possible to formulate satisfactory models for the rational exploration of the universe by scientific communities. The answer to some of the basic problems discussed here undoubtedly lies at this level.

Note on the Probability of Contact

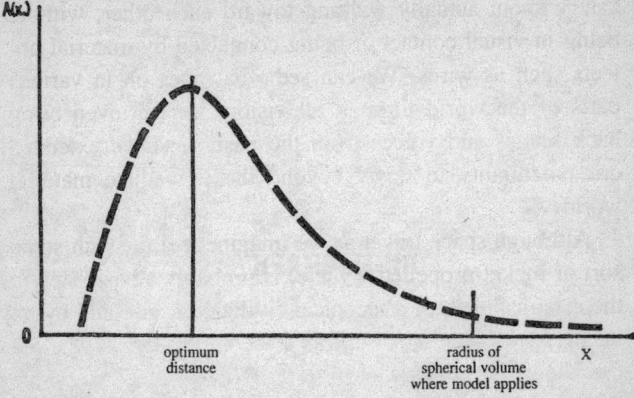

An estimate of the "ability" of a scientific community, situated at a given distance from our sun, to explore physically our system. The optimum distance is large enough to include a number of highly developed technical civilizations, and small enough to allow them to observe our sun and to contemplate actual space travel to our system.

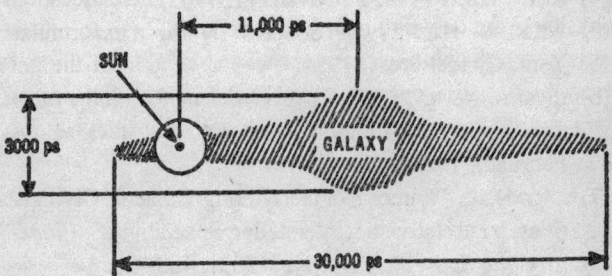

The position of the sun in our galaxy and the dimensions of the spherical volume within which could be situated about four million systems able to support intelligent life. The average distance to the six nearest civilizations would be ten parsecs in this model, in agreement with estimates published by S. S. Huang. The model formulated by S. von Hoener suggests a larger distance, while the calculations made by J. E. Lipp in the Project Sign report in 1949 were more optimistic.

BIBLIOGRAPHY

(1) *Denison Daily News*, January 25, 1878.
(2) KASANTSEV, A. "Did Ancients Meet Spacemen?" *Australian Flying Saucer Review*, Vol. I, No. 3 (September, 1960).
(3) *Domenica del Corriere*, May 27, 1962.
(4) *Austr. F.S.R.*, No. 7 (November, 1962).
(5) WILKINS, H.T. *Flying Saucers on the Attack*. New York: Citadel Press, 1954.
(6) DRAKE, W. R. "UFO's over Ancient Rome," *Flying Saucer Review* (London), Vol. IX, No. 1 (January-February, 1963).
(7) SAGAN, C. "Direct Contact among Galactic Civilizations by Relativistic Interstellar Spaceflight," *Planetary and Space Science*, XI (1963), 485–98.
(8) DRAKE, W. R. "Spacemen in the Middle Ages," *F.S.R.*, X, No. 3 (May, 1964), 11–13.
(9) JUNG, C. G. *Ein Moderner Mythus*, French trans. *Un Mythe Moderne*. Paris: Gallimard, 1961. Eng. trans. *Flying Saucers*. New York: Harcourt, Brace & World, Inc., 1959.

Bibliography

(10) *Guide de la France Mysterieuse*. Tchou, editeur a Paris, 1964.

(11) QUINCY, G. "Catalogue of 1,027 UFO Observations." Personal communication.

(12) *Paris-Presse*, November 10, 1954.

(13) ARAGO, F. *Oeuvres*, IX, 38.

(14) BUSCO, P. *L'Evolution de l' Astronomie au XIXeme siecle*. Paris: Larousse, 1912.

(15) FORT, C. *Lo!* Claude Kendall, 1931; New York: Holt, Rinehart & Winston, Inc., 1941.

(16) *Zoologis*, January, 1868.

(17) *L'Annee Scientifique*, XXIX, 8.

(18) *Astronomical Register*, XXIII, 205.

(19) *L'Annee Scientifique*, 1877, p. 45.

(20) *Knowledge*, December 28, 1883, p. 396.

(21) FORT, C. *New Lands*. Boni & Liveright, 1923; New York: Holt, Rinehart & Winston, 1941.

(22) *Lumieres dans la Nuit*. Collection.

(23) RIBERA, A. "What Happened at Fatima?" *F.S.R.*, X, No. 2 (March, 1964), 12–14.

(24) "Sky Phenomena at Fatima," *Austr. F.S.R.*, Vol. I, No. 3 (September, 1960).

(25) OPARIN, A. *et al* (eds.) *Proceedings of the International Symposium on the Origin of Life on the Earth* (Moscow). New York: Pergamon, 1960.

(26) *Science Digest*, October, 1962.

(27) *Cambrian Natural Observer* (Journal of the Astronomical Society of Wales), 1905, p. 35 and *English Mechanics*, pp. 86–100.

(28) *L'Astronomie*, 1909, pp. 519–20.

(29) *Journal* of the Royal Astronomical Association of Canada, November-December, 1913.

(30) Aerospace Technical Intelligence Center. Official files of the U.S. Air Force.

(31) *F.S.R.*, III, No. 6 (November-December, 1957).

(32) LABARTHE, A. S. and SICLIER, J. *Images de la Science-Fiction*. Paris: Editions du Cerf, 1958.

(33) FESENKOV, V. and OPARIN, A. *Life in the Universe*. New York: Twayne Publishers, Inc., 1961.

(34) ELIADE, M. *Cosmos and History*. New York: Harper & Bros., 1959, p. 44 *et seq*.

(35) EMMONS, G. T. *American Anthropology*, N.S. 13, 1911.

(36 SHKLOVSKY, I. S. *Intelligent Life in the Universe*. San Francisco: Holden Day.

(37) MORFILL, M. R. (trans.) *The Book of the Secrets of Enoch*. Oxford: Clarendon Press, 1896.

(38) HODGES, E. R. *Cory's Ancient Fragments*. rev. ed. London: Reeves and Turner, 1876.

(39) SCHNABEL, P. *Berossos und die Babylonish-Helleristische Literatur*. Leipzig: Taubner, 1923.

(40) FORT, C. *The Book of the Damned*. Boni & Liveright, 1919; New York; Holt, Rinehart & Winston, 1941.

(41) WEBB, T. W. *Celestial Objects for Common Telescopes*. New York: Dover, 1962.

(42) TISSERAND, F. "Notice sur les Planetes Intramercurielles," *Annuaire du Bureau des Longitudes*.

(43) HUTIN, S. *Les Civilisations Inconnues*. Paris: Fayard, 1961.

(44) MAETERLINK, M. *La Vie de l'Espace*. Paris: Fasquelle, 1928.

(45) HYNEK, J. A. H. Talk presented to the Hypervelocity Impact Conference, Eglin Air Force Base, Florida, April 27, 1960.

(46) MONTEMONT, A. DE. *Lettres sur l'Astronomie*. Paris: Armand Aubree, circa 1840.

(47) RICHARDSON, R. S. *Exploring Mars*. New York: McGraw-Hill Book Company, 1954.

(48) LEDERBERG, J. and SAGAN, C. "Microenvironment for Life on Mars," *Proceedings* of the National Academy of Sciences, XLVIII, No. 9 (September, 1962), 1473.

(49) FULTON, J. D. *Physics and Medicine of the Atmosphere and Space*, eds. BENSON, O. O. and STRUGHOLD, H. New York; John Wiley & Sons, Inc., 1960.

(50) HAWRYLEWICS, E., GOWDY, B. and EHRLICH, R. *Nature*, CXCIII (1962), 497.

(51) MASON, B. "Organic Matter from Space," *Scientific American*, Vol. CCVIII, No. 3 (March, 1963).

(52) LIPP, J. E. "Appendix D to Report Project Sign: Unidentified Flying Objects." U.S. Air Force, February, 1949.

(53) SALISBURY, F. "Accumulative Evidence Favors the Theory of Life on Mars," *Science*, Vol. CXXXVI, No. 17 (1962).

(54) PECKER, J. C. "Les Systemes Planetaires dans l'Univers," *L'Astronomie*, February, 1958.

(55) FLAMMARION, C. *La Pluralite des Mondes Habites*. Paris: Flammarion, 1862.

(56) DAUVILLIER, A. *Origin, Nature and Evolution of Planets*, 1947.

(57) *Reprints* from Sproul Observatory, Swarthmore College, Swarthmore, Pennsylvania.

(58) VAN DE KAMP, P. "The Astrometric Study of Unseen Companions of Single Stars, *Astronomical Journal*, Vol. LI, No. 7 (1944).

(59) ——. "Stars or Planets?" *Sky and Telescope*, IV, No. 2 (December, 1944), 5.

(60) ——. "Les Compagnons Invisibles d'Etoiles Proches," *L'Astronomie*, LXIV (1950), 393.

(61) ——. "Planetary Companions of Stars" (*Vistas in Astronomy*, ed. A. BEER, II, 1040). New York: Pergamon Press, 1956.

(62) LIPPINCOTH, S. L. "A Model of Our Stellar Neighborhood," Astronomical Society of the Pacific, Leaflet No. 377.

(63) VAUCOULEURS, G. DE. *Planetary Observations from Space Probes and Orbiters*, 1962.

(64) WHIPPLE, F. L. *Earth, Moon and Planets*. (Harvard Books on Astronomy) New York: Blakiston, 1943; Cambridge: Harvard University Press, 1963.

(65) REA, D. G. "The Darkening Wave on Mars," *Nature*, CCI (March 7, 1964), 1014.

(66) SCHATZMANN, E. *Origine et Evolution des Mondes*. Paris: Albin Michel, 1957.

(67) VON HOERNER, S. "The Search for Signals from Other Civilizations," *Science*, December 8, 1961.

(68) OPARIN, A. *The Origin of Life on Earth*. 3rd ed. New York: Academy Press, Inc., 1957.

(69) UREY, H. C. *The Planets: Their Origin and Development*. New Haven: Yale University Press, 1952.

(70) KRASOVSKIY. "Astronautics and Extraterrestrial Civilizations," *Izvestia*, May 4, 1961.

(71) HOYLE, F. *Nature of the Universe*. rev. ed. New York: Harper & Bros., 1960.

(72) ——. *Frontiers of Astronomy*. New York: Harper & Bros., 1955.

(73) SHARP, P. F. "The Search for Life beyond the Earth,"

F.S.R., VII, No. 6 (November-December, 1961), 12.

(74) BRACEWELL, R. N. "Communications from Superior Galactic Communities, *Nature*, CLXXXVI (1960), 670.

(75) HUANG, S. S. *The Problem of Life in the Universe and the Mode of Star Formation*. Publications of the Astronomical Society of the Pacific, LXXI (1959), 421.

(76) DRAKE, F. D. "How Can We Detect Radiotransmissions from Distant Planetary Systems?" *Sky and Telescope*, XIX (1959), 140.

(77) COCCONI, G. and MORRISON, P. "Searching for Interstellar Communications," *Nature*, CLXXXIV (1959), 844.

(78) SINTON, W. M. "Further Evidence of Vegetation on Mars," *Science* CXXX (1959), 1234.

(79) KUIPER, G. P. *The Atmosphere of the Earth and Planets*. Chicago: University of Chicago Press, 1952.

(80) SCHWARTZ, R. N. and TOWNES, C. H. *Nature*, CXC (1961), 205.

(81) KAZANTSEV, A. "The Tenth Planet," *Pravda*, January 5, 1959.

(82) LASSWELL, H. "Legal Aspects of Encounters with Living Forms." Astronautical Meeting, Washington, D. C., 1961.

(83) MARGARIA. "Possible Existence of Intelligent Beings." Astronautical Meeting, Washington, D. C., 1961.

(84) NOURSE, A. E. *Nine Planets*. New York: Pyramid Books, 1960.

(85) *Daily Express* (London), September 28, 1961, and *F.S.R.*, Vol. VII, No. 6 (November-December, 1961).

(86) GIRVAN, W. "The World of Dr. Menzel," *F.S.R.*, X, No. 3 (May-June, 1964), 29–30.

(87) TREPKA, A. "Uwaga! Latajace Spodki," *Skr Zydlata Polska* (Polish aviation magazine), No. 33 (August 13, 1958).

(88) SOUKHANOV. *Ogoniok*, No. 11 (March, 1958), p. 21.

(89) MILER, M. "Letajici Talire A Tisk," *Kridla Vlasti*, No. 18, (1958).

(90) United States Air Force. *Report*, Project Grudge. August, 1949.

(91) ———. *Special Report 14*, Project Blue Book. March 17, 1954.

(92) ———. *Final Report*, Project Twinkle. December 27, 1951.

(93) ———. *Report*, Project 9974 (Videon Camera). September 21, 1954.

(94) MICHEL, A. Personal communication.

(95) Collection of French newspapers.

(96) *Gazette de Lausanne*, April 20, 1951.

(97) *Tribune de Geneve*, March 13, 1951.

(98) *L'Astronomie*, 1951, p. 474.

(99) ATIC. Recently declassified report.

(100) *Ce Matin*, May 12, 1952.

(101) GARREAU, C. "Files of Early French Sightings." Personal communication.

(102) *Liberation*, June 18, 1952. With a drawing of the object.

(103) *L'Astronomie*, 1952. (Objets suspects)

(104) *Paris-Presse*, September 30, 1952.

(105) *Le Figaro*, September 29, 1952.

(106) *L'Astronomie*, 1954, p. 120.

Bibliography

(107) *Le Parisien,* October 29, 1954, and *Le Monde,* same date.

(108) Agence France-Presse. Dispatch of October 28, 1954.

(109) *L'Astronomie,* 1952. (Objets suspects)

(110) LE VERRIER, U. *Communication a l'Academie des Sciences.* Paris: July 2, 1849.

(111) *Le Parisien,* November 28, 1952.

(112) Keyhoe, D. *Flying Saucers from Outer Space.* New York: Holt, Rinehart & Winston, 1953, pp. 161–65.

(113) *L'Astronomie,* 1953, p. 477.

(114) *Liberation,* August 25, 1954.

(115) MICHEL, A. *Mysterieux Objets Celestes.* Paris: Arthaud, 1958. Eng. trans. *Flying Saucers and the Straight-Line Mystery.* New York: Criterion Books, Inc., 1958.

(116) *Sud-Ouest,* November, 1954.

(117) PLANTIER, J. *La Propulsion des soucoupes volantes par action directe sur l'atome.* Paris: Mame, 1955.

(118) RUPPELT, E. J. *The Report on Unidentified Flying Objects.* New York: Doubleday & Co., Inc., 1956.

(119) QUINCY, G. "Special Catalogue of Landings," Personal communication.

(120) KOESTLER, A. *The Sleepwalkers.* New York: Macmillan Co., 1959.

(121) MENZEL, D. and BOYD, L. *The World of Flying Saucers.* New York: Doubleday & Co., Inc., 1963.

(122) VALLEE, J. "How To Classify and Codify UFO Sightings," *F.S.R.,* IX, No. 5 (September-October), p. 9.

(123) *Young* (Australia) *Witness,* June 5, 1961.

(124) *Ball Lightning Bibliography, 1950–1960*. Science and Technology Division, Reference Department, Library of Congress; under sponsorship of U.S.A. Signal Missile Support Agency. Washington: 1961.

(125) *Newsweek*, June 16, 1958.

(126) "Temoins dignes de Foi," *Combat*, December 18, 1954.

(127) "Le Mythe des soucoupes volantes," *Combat*, December 29, 1954.

(128) "Les tremblements de Terre provoquent les soucoupes volantes," *Paris-Presse*, November 10, 1954.

(129) *Le Parisien-Libere*, October 28, 1954.

(130) "Un etrange phenomene," *Le Populaire*, October 22, 1954.

(131) GABEREL, J. *Rousseau et les Genevois*. 1858.

(132) "Les soucoupes volantes sont-elles fiction ou realtie?" *Tribune de Geneve*, November 6, 1954.

(133) MONTANDON, F. "Les tremblements de terre," *Geographica Helvetia*.

(134) LEBON, G. *La Psychologie des Foules*.

(135) FLOURNOY, T. *Des Indes a la Planete Mars*. Editions Alcan, 1900. English trans. *From India to the Planet Mars*. New Hyde Park: University Books, Inc., 1963.

(136) WEBER, E. *Satan Franc-Macon, La Mystification de Leo Taxil*. Paris: Julliard, 1964.

(137) "They Choose to Run," *Caper*, Vol. X, No. 5.

(138) GIRVAN, W. "Trained Minds," *F.S.R.*, X, No. 3 (May-June, 1964), 1.

(139) NORKIN, I. *Saucer Diary*. New York: Pageant Books, Inc., 1957.

(140) BETHURUM, T. *Aboard a Flying Saucer*. Los Angeles: De Vorss & Co., Inc., 1954.

(141) MANAS, J. H. *Flying Saucers and Space-Men*. New York: Pythagorean Society, 1962.

(142) KEYHOE, D. *Flying Saucers: Top Secret*. New York: G. P. Putman's Sons, 1960.

(143) *Aviation News*, February 18, 1951.

(144) Oklahoma newspapers.

(145) *The Flying Saucer Review's World Roundup of UFO Sightings and Events*. New York: Citadel Press, 1958, p. 103.

(146) *Calgary Herald*, November 6, 1957.

(147) *Indianapolis Star*, November 6, 1957.

(148) MICHEL, A. *Lueurs sur les Soucoupes Volantes*. Paris: Mame, 1954, p. 169.

(149) *Vancouver Suns*, October 5, 1959.

(150) *Lumieres dans la Nuit*, No. 62 (October, 1963).

(151) *UFO Investigator*, October-November, 1962.

(152) VALLEE, J. "A Descriptive Study of the 'Entities' Associated with Type-I Sightings," *F.S.R.*, X, No. 1 (January-February, 1964), 6–12 and X, No. 3 (May-June, 1964), 3–5.

(153) Radio reporter Andrew B. Ledwith.

(154) BLOECHER, T. "Saucer Landings and Little Men." Lecture, January 28, 1956.

(155) CARROUGES, M. *Les Apparitions de Martiens*. Paris: Fayard, 1963.

(156) *L'Astronomie*, 1954, p. 475.

(157) *L'Astronomie*, 1953, p. 477.

(158) SANDERS, J. "Panic in Kentncky," *Saucerian Review*, January, 1956, pp. 19–23.

(159) GONZAGA DA FONSECA, S. I. *Las Maravillas de Fatima*.
(160) INGLEFIELD, G. "Fatima: The Three Alternatives," *F.S.R.*, X, No. 3 (May, 1964), 5.
(161) "An Anglican Priest Contacts Pilots of an Unknown Craft over New Guinea," *Austra. F.S.R.*, Vol. I, No. 1 (December, 1959).
(162) VALLEE, J. "The 'Entities': The Facts and the Legend," *F.S.R.*, X. No. 3 (May, 1964), 22. Letter to the editor.
(163) *Austr. F.S.R.*, Vol. I, No. 1 (December, 1959).
(164) *Austr. F.S.R.*, Vol. I, No. 4.
(165) Independent reports from official files.
(166) *Manchester Evening Chronicle*, August 7, 1961. *F.S.R.*, Vol. VII, No. 6 (November-December, 1961).
(167) *Modesto* (California) *Bee*, February 28, 1963.
(168) CODOVNI *reports* for 1962.
(169) VERNE, J. "L'Eternel Adam," *Quatre Pas dans l'Etrange*, ed. G. H. Gallet. Paris: Hachette, 1961.
(170) ROSNY AINE. *Les Navigateurs de l'Infini*. Paris: Hachette, 1960.
(171) ASIMOV, I. *Foundation*. Hicksville, N. Y.: Gnome. French trans. J. Rosenthal. Paris: Gallimard, 1956.
(172) LEIBER, F. *Gather, Darkness!* New York: Berkley Publishing Corp. French trans. J. Herisson. Paris: Gallimard, 1958.
(173) RUSSELL, E. F. *Sinister Barrier*. New York: Paperback Library. French trans. R. and J. Rosenthal, *Guerre aux Invisibles*. Paris: Gallimard, 1952.
(174) HIGON, A. *Aux Etoiles du Destin*. Paris: Gallimard, 1960.

(175) VAN VOGT, A. E. *The Voyage of the Space Beagle*. New York: Macfadden-Bartell Corp. French trans. J. Rosenthal, *La Faune de l'Espace*. Paris: Gallimard, 1952.

(176) HYNEK, J. A. "Unusual Aerial Phenomena," *Journal of the Optical Society of America*, XLIII, No. 4 (April, 1953), 311–14.

(177) *Austr. F.S.R.*, Vol. IV, No. 1 (February, 1961).

(178) "Angels are Men from Space," *Austr. F.S.R.*, Vol. I, No. 3 (September, 1960).

(179) *Toronto Daily Star*, January 5, 1960.

(180) THOMAS, P. (pseudonym for P. MISRAKI) *Les Extraterrestres*. Paris: Plon, 1962.

(181) ATIC. *Report* on the Kelly-Hopkinsville case. 1955.

(182) LE POER TRENCH, B. *The Sky People*. London: Neville Spearman, 1960.

(183) DRAKE, W. R. *"Did UFO's Stop a War?" F.S.R.*, IX, No. 2 (March-April, 1963), 13.

(184) SANDERS, J. "Comments on Project Bluebook Special Report No. 14," *Saucerian Review*, January, 1956, pp. 34–41.

(185) GIRVAN, W. "Good Advice from the Past," *F.S.R.*, IX, No. 3 (May-June, 1963), 15.

(186) ALEXANDROV, V. *L'Ours et la Baleine*. Paris: Stock, 1958.

(187) OSTROUMOV, G. "Ideas are Overtaking Facts," *Izvestia*, February 5, 1961.

(188) LORENZEN, C. *The Great Flying Saucer Hoax*. New York: William-Frederick Press, 1962.

(189) VALLEE, J. *The Analysis of UFO Activity*. To be published.

(190) ZIGEL, F. YU. *Nuclear Explosion over the Taiga:*

Study of the Tunguska Meteorite. U.S. Department of Commerce, Temporary Building E, E. Adams Drive, Fourth and Sixth Street, S. W., Washington, D.C. 20443 ($.50).

(191) ROERICH, N. *Altai-Himalaya: A Travel Diary*, New York: Frederick A. Stokes Co., 1929, p. 361.

(192) *Times* (London), September 4, 1895.

(193) VALLEE, J. *How To Select Significant UFO Reports*. To be published.

(194) VALLEE, J. *Phenomenes Spatiaux Insolites*. To be published.

(195) "The New Zealand 'Flap' of 1909," *F.S.R.*, X, No. 6 (November-December, 1964), 32.

(196) HEYERDAHL, T. *Aku-Aku*. London: George Allen & Unwin Ltd.; Chicago: Rand McNally & Co.

INDEX

Aaland Islands, 62
Abilene, Texas, 189, 196
Adams-Anderson case, 77
Adamski, George, 124, 170, 175, 177
Addis Ababa, Ethiopia, 32
Adrianople, Turkey, 20
Aerial fight (see also Type III observations), 12, 72, 79, 90, 219
Aerial Phenomena Research Organization (APRO), 134, 161
Aerospace Technical Intelligence Center (ATIC), 16, 50, 59, 119, 120, 138
Africa, 79, 87, 103
Agobard, 7, 10
Agrest's theory, 223, 226, 231
Ahlgreen, General Nils, 61
Air Force, U.S., v, 21, 55, 106, 126, 130, 135, 150, 202
Aku-Aku, 114, 138
Alais meteorite, 48
Alamogordo, 68–69
Alaska, 73
Albuquerque, New Mexico, 75, 82, 220
Alvarez, Jose, 187
Amarillo, Texas, 188
Amiens, France, 94, 218
Anaxagoras, 41
Andrews Field, Washington, D.C., 76
Angel hair, 86
Angels, 24, 176, 226
Anita, Iowa, 141
Annales de Chimie et de physique, 14
Anti-gravity, 100, 159
Arago, François, 14
Archetypes, 242
Arkansas City, Kansas, 235
Armstrong, 70
Arnold, Kenneth, 1, 56–57, 67, 70
Arpi, Roman Empire, 4
Arras, France, 11
Asia, 75, 77
Asteroid Belt, 58
Astronomer Royal, 112
Atlantic Ocean, 16, 22, 28
Atlantis, 225
Atomic explosions, 68–69
Augermanland, Sweden, 13

275

Index

Australia, 57, 101, 146, 191, 209
Austria, 33
Aviation News, 182
Aztecs, 229

Baalbek Platform, 223
Bacchante, The Cruise of the, 18
Bakersfield, California, 70
Ball lightning, 21–22, 50, 76, 81, 129
Banning, California, 184
Barnard's star, 252
Basel, Switzerland, 12, 17
Baskatong, lake, Canada, 185
Baudelaire, 163, 167
Bayonne, France, 85
Beaune, France, 215
Beine, France, 84
"Beings," 4, 8, 30, 94, 96, 237–38
Belgrade, Yugoslavia, 25
Beljonne, 30
Bellocq, Paul, 87
Benevento, 10
Benton, Texas, 22
Bermudas, 31
Berzelius, 48
Bessel, F. W., 251
Beulah, Michigan, 206, 211
Beuscher, M., 70
Bible, 2, 59, 226
"Bintang," 30
Biot, France, 178
Bismarck, North Dakota, 88, 89, 235
Black Hawk, South Dakota, 88–89
Bocaranga, Africa, 87
Boise, Idaho, 73
Bone, Algeria, 84
Bonilla, José, 19
Boston, Massachusetts, 29
Bou-Hadjar, Algeria, 84
Bradytes, 18

Brahe, Tycho, 123
Brives-Charensac, France, 87
Broken Hill, Australia, 206
Brooke, Tom, 183
Brooksville, Maine, 71
Brosses-Tillots, France, 179
Brown, 15
Bruno, Giordano, 41
Buelta, Eduardo, 42, 160
Bushnell, D., 182
Byland Abbey, Great Britain, 11

Caerphilly, Wales, 29
Cairo, Egypt, 9
Camba Punta, Argentina, 219
Cambridge, Massachusetts, 71
Canada, 31, 37
Canadian, Texas, 188
Canals on Mars, 44
Cape Race, Canada, 22
Capiago, Chile, 16
Capitol, 84
Capocci, 15
Capodimonte Observatory, Naples, 15
Cardiff, Wales, 29, 31
Carlinville, Illinois, 18, 22, 36
Carrouges, 194
Casablanca, Morocco, 85
Casella, Jose, 178
Cavallo, Tiberius, 13, 145
Chaldea, 2
Chanute Air Force Base, Illinois, 141
Charlemagne, 10, 116
Chassin, General, 107
Chauvin, Professor R., 114
Chebar River, 2, 6
Cherbonnieres, France, 178
Chereng, France, 217
Cherns, Great Britain, 103
Chevigny, France, 216
Cheyenne, Wyoming, 102
Chicago, Illinois, 22, 36, 70, 80

276

Index

Chichester, 32
Chile, 16
Chiles and Whitted case, 74
China Sea, 22, 30
Christianity, 41, 207, 225
Chroniclers, 11
Cier-de-Riviere, France, 100
Cigar-shaped UFO's, 11, 17, 65, 73, 79, 86, 87, 91
Circleville, Ohio, 72
Ciry-le-Noble, France, 179
Clarion, Iowa, 70
Clarion, alleged planet, 171, 173
Clark, Alvan G., 251
Clark Airfield, Philippines, 74
Clem, Sheriff W., 187
Clessy, France, 180
Clifford, Alexander, 65
Clinton, North Carolina, 72
Cloud-cigars (see also Type II observations), 11, 17, 79, 86, 87, 90
Clouds of Mars, 47
Clovis, New Mexico, 189
Cocciatore, 15
Coimbra University, Portugal, 207
Cole, John F., 71
Comets, inhabitants of, 42
Companions, unseen, of stars, 249–251
Cone-shaped UFO's, 72
Consistency of UFO reports, 54, 170–171
Constantinople, Turkey, 20
Contact between galactic communities, 40, 49–53, 227, 234–235, 248, 253–255
Contactees, 124, 159, 170, 177
Copenhagen, Denmark, 63
Copernican system, 41
Corcelles-Neuchatel, Switzerland, 81
Corpus Christi, Texas, 206
Corva da Iria, Portugal, 204

Coyote Pass, California, 90
Cressy, Tasmania, 206, 210

Danville, Virginia, 206
Dayton, Ohio, 21, 59, 151, 153, 184
Dead-leaf motion (see also Type III observations), 17, 57, 80
Dearborn Observatory, Illinois, 251, 257
De Cuppis, 15
Delaware, Ohio, 73
Delingette, 30
Denham, G. B., 83
Denison, Texas, 1
Des Moines, Iowa, 77
Desvergers, 181, 183
Development index, 256
De Vico, 15
Devil, 24
Dewilde, Marius, 94–96, 125
Dimensions of UFO's, 70, 73, 127, 135, 201
Domnall Mac Murchada, 8
Dong Hoi, Annam, 30
Doolittle, General James, 64
Dover, G.B., 31
Drake, 4, 7, 9
Duclerc, Jacques, 11
Duluth, Minnesota, 101
Dyess Air Force Base, Texas, 189

Earthquakes, 12
Easter Island, 225
Egg-shaped UFO's, 187, 190
Egypt, 5, 9
Embrun, France, 14
Emmett, Idaho, 73
Enid, Oklahoma, 182
Enoch, 224
Enthusiasts, vi, 115, 203
Entities, 4–6, 23, 95, 193–198, 202, 237
Epping, G. B., 103

277

Index

Epsilon Eridani, 224, 241
Epstein, 2
Erbray, France, 195
Erchin, France, 195
Erfurt, 12
Eubank, Sid, 182
Europe, x, 56–57
Ezekiel, 2–4

Fairborn, Ohio, 220
Fargo, North Dakota, 76
Farmington, New Mexico, 79
Fatima, Portugal, 25, 32, 66, 110, 202–207, 225, 226, 240
Federal Bureau of Investigation, 56, 138
Fesenkov, 41
Finland, 62, 63
Flammarion, Camille, 18
Flash Gordon, 39
Flatwood, West Virginia, 181
Fletcher, G. D., 232, 234
Flodoard, 9
Florence, Italy, 73
Flournoy, Theodore, 168
Fontainebleau, France, 87
Fontenay, France, 195
Fontenelle, B. de, 41
Fontes, Olavo, 58
"Foo-fighters," 34, 66
Fort, Charles, 12, 15, 29, 30, 129
"Fort Salisbury," 28
Foussignargues, France, 99, 124, 177
France, v, 14, 36
Frankenstein, 38
Frasne, France, 215
Frenchmen, as a product of poisonous dust, 123

Gachignard, 125
Gaillac, France, 87, 140
Galaxy, 50, 248–261
Galileo, 122, 123

Gallup, New Mexico, 83
Garreau, Charles, 88
Garrett, Prof. Almeida, 207
Gascoyne, Dr., 148
Genelard, France, 179
Geneva, Switzerland, 15
Germany, 8, 33, 86
Germs of life, 41
Giants, 197, 227
Gill, Rev. W. B., 199, 240
Girvan, Waveney, 105, 115, 159
Gisors, France, 10
Glaisher, 15
Glenora, Canada, 190
"Golem," 38
Gorman case, 76
Grassy Plains, Canada, 190
Greek philosophers, 41
Green, Gabriel, 169–170
Greenwich, Great Britain, 13
Grimm, Jacob, 8
Grimoald, 10
Gueugnon, France, 180
Guiberteau, 20
Gulf of Mexico, 87

Hadria, 4
Halley, 12
Hallucinations, 38, 68, 103
Hamilton, Alexander, 22–24, 176
Harborside, Maine, 71
Harris, Dr., 31
Harvard, 112–114, 243
Hasselbach, Germany, 182
Hatton Garden, London, 14
Heaton Moor, G.B., 206
Helsinki, Finland, 63
Henderson, New York, 206
Hennezis, France, 195
Herschel, 43
Hess, Dr. Seymour, 80, 163
Heyerdahl, Thor, 114, 138
Highcliff, G.B., 206
Hiroshima, Japan, 69

278

Index

Hoaxes, 30, 38, 59, 102, 167–173
Holloman Air Force Base, New Mexico, 73
Homer, New York, 206, 213
Homunculus, 38
Huang, Dr. S. S., 53, 257
Hubbell, Nebraska, 32
Hunan, China, 2
Hungary, 8, 69
Hydrocarbons, 48–49
Hynek, J. Allen, viii, ix–x, 98, 126

Ialdabaoth, 228
Ichac, Pierre, 32
Incunabulum, 11
Inglefield, G., 203, 207
Inglis, 15
Intelligence in the universe, 40, 45–46, 253–255
Intramercurial planet, 15
Ipswich, G.B., 219
Italian Air Force, 131
Ivuna, carbonaceous meteorite, 49

Jacobson, Jacques, 185
Japan, 9, 22
Jellyfish-UFO, 217, 220
Jerusalem, 10
John Carter of Mars, 38
Journal of Natural History and Philosophy and Chemistry, 14
Julius Obsequens, 4
Jung, C. G., 8, 12, 110, 115, 128, 154, 167, 242
Jupiter, 46, 250

Kansas, 22–24, 36
Kazantsev, Alexander, 2, 26, 226
Keflavik Airport, Iceland, 101
Kelly, Kentucky, 101, 195, 198, 236–241
Kent, G.B., 73
Kepler, 122

Kermit, Texas, 187
Keyhoe, Donald, 87, 129, 161, 182, 183, 189
Kiess, 2
Kingsport, Tennessee, 33
Kirch, Gottfried, 145
"Kitsukawara Maru," Japanese ship, 185
Klagenfurt, Austria, 33
Kolobrzeg, Poland, 192
Koran, 230
Kutstown, Pennsylvania, 183

Labote, Henri, 2
"Lady of the Lake," 16
L'Aigle, France, 108
Lakeland, Florida, 141
Lake Tungting, 2
Lalande 21185, 252
Lamb, William C., 32
Landings (see also Type I observations), 18, 29, 64, 86, 90, 97, 103, 177, 183, 236–241
Lardner, Dionysius, 105
La Roche-sur-Yon, France, 82, 83
Las Cruces, New Mexico, 78
Las Vegas, Nevada, 189
Le Bourget Airport, France, 83
Lederberg, 47
Leipzig, Germany, 144
Leiria, Portugal, 204
Lenin, N., 157
Le Poer Trench, B., 5, 226–227
Le Roy, Kansas, 22–25, 36
Lethbridge, 29
Levelland, Texas, 187–189
Le Verrier, U., 16
Le Vigan, France, 86, 191
Lievin, France, 218
Life in the universe, 40–53, 258
Lille, France, 25
Lindsay, 31
Lipp, Dr. J. E., 49–51, 69, 253, 255, 257, 261

Index

Lisbon, Portugal, 204
Livy, 4
Llangollen, Wales, 29
Lock Raven, Maryland, 124
Lombard, Prof. A., 81
London, G.B., 13
Long, H., 183
Lorenzen, Coral, 129
Lot, 226
Louis I, the Debonair, 10
Lowell, 44
Lubbock, Texas, 124
Lugrin, France, 195
Lyons, France, 7, 10

Madisonville, Indiana, 82
Magonia, legendary region, 8
Maiden, North Carolina, 219
Mainbrace, NATO operation, 84, 85
Malaga, Spain, 79
Malmoe, 63
Manas, John, 173
Mandala, 122
Manila, Philippines, 73
Manitou Springs, Colorado, 69
Mantell, 72
Marcoing, France, 217
Marieham, Aaland Islands, 62
Mariner II, 47, 251
Marrakesh, Morocco, 85
Mars, 37, 47, 69, 156, 174
Marseilles, France, 19, 32
Martians, 51, 52, 94, 193, 242, 253
Martin, John, 1, 17
Massachusetts, 29
Matthew of Paris, 11
Mavrogordato, 20
McKinney, Texas, 183–184
Mebane, Alexander, 185, 187
Mediterranean Sea, 79
Melbourne, Australia, 17, 191

Melies, 38
Menzel, Dr. Donald H., viii, x, 4, 33, 68, 113, 124, 126, 129, 144, 152, 159, 175
Mercurians, 42
Mercury, 15, 46
Messier, Charles, 13
Metaphysics, ix, 173–176
Meteorites, 48–49
Meteors, 55, 68, 159
Metropolis, 38
Meudon Observatory, 17
Meursanges, France, 215
Mexico, 19, 36
Michel, Aime, x, 56, 88, 90, 92–93, 101, 128, 129, 130, 139, 149, 165, 179, 185, 216, 234–236
Middle Ages, 8
Midland, Texas, 189
Milly-la-Foret, France, 220–221
Mirages, 34, 68
Miserey, Bernard, 91
Misraki, Paul, 204, 225–232
Modesto, California, 219
Mongolia, 31
Montanus, 8
Mont-de-Marsan, France, 86
Montemont, A. de, 42–43
Montgomery, Alabama, 74
Monuments, 2, 223
Moon, 16, 46, 172, 243
Moore, Charles, 77, 163
Morocco, 85
Moscow, U.S.S.R., 57, 68, 75
Mouillon, M. G., 179
Mount Rainier, Washington, 56, 59
Mount Stromlo Observatory, Austr., 148
Mu, 225
Muroc Air Force Base, California, 71
Murray, Dr. A. H., 22

Index

Mushroom-shaped UFO's, 101, 218
Mythology, 66

Nagy, B., 49
Naples, Italy, 15
National Invest. Comm. on Aerial Phenomena (NI-CAP), 129, 152, 161
Nature, British review, 15
Neaufles-Saint-Martin, France, 10
Nemours, France, 87
Nevada desert, 189
New Albany, Miss., 206
New Guinea, 57, 198, 200–202, 240
New South Wales, 32
New Zealand, 32, 57, 103
Noise level, 55
Norkin, Israel, 172
Norland, Halifax, G.B., 103
North Atlantic Treaty Organization (NATO), 84, 107
Nuremberg, Germany, 12, 17

Oberth, H., 241
Ogoniok, Soviet review, 57
Ohio Northern University, 161
Oloron, France, 86–87, 140
Oparin, Soviet scientist, 41
Oradell, New Jersey, 191
Oran, Algeria, 84
Orchamps, France, 195
Orgueil meteorite, 48–49
Orion, 19
Orlac's Hands, 38
Osan Air Force Base, Korea, 220
Osborn, Ohio, 74
Osuma, Spain, 80
Ouranos, 230
Overkalix, Sweden, 61
Oxford, G.B., 13, 22
Ozma, U.S.A.F. project, 154, 224

Pacific Ocean, 185, 244
Palatka, Florida, 206
Palleau, France, 216
Papua, New Guinea, 199
Pasteur, L., 48
Pastorff, 15
"Patna," 17
Peking University, 2
Pepin the Short, 10
Persian Gulf, 17
Peru, 30
Peterborough, 29
Pharaoh, 5–6
Philalethes, 168
Philip the Good, 11
Philippines, 73, 74
Phu-Lien Observatory, Tonkin, 30
Pickering, 44
Planetary systems, 249
Poland, 8, 86, 192
Polar caps of Mars, 47
Polarimetric studies of Mars, 47
Poncey, France, 98, 100, 124, 176
Ponthierry, France, 124
Portholes, 74, 77, 219
Port Moresby, New Guinea, 89, 202
Porto Principal, Peru, 30
Posnansky, 2
Pouzou, France, 178
Praeneste, 4
Prague, 17
Prehistoric "visitations," 2
Premanon, France, 195
Prince of Wales, sons of, 18
Pringent, 86
Prodigiorum Liber, 4
Proxima Centauri, 250
Ptolemaic system, 41
Pythagorean Society, 173

Quarouble, France, 94, 125, 177, 195

Index

Quincy, G., catalogue of UFO events by, 32, 129

Rachewiltz, Prince Boris de, 5
Ragusa, Italy, 18
Rankin, Richard, 70
Rationalism, 175, 247
Reims, France, 9
Reliability of UFO reports, viii, 54–104, 126–132, 206
Religion, 2, 203–207
Remote control, 76
Rener, A. M., x
Reveillere, 20
Ribera, Antonio, 58, 79, 160, 203, 204–205
Richardson, 46
Richmond, Virginia, 69
Robots, 38
Rockfield, Wisconsin, 70
Roerich, Nicolas, 31
Roman Empire, 4
Royal Society, 13
Ruppelt, Captain E., 72, 115, 121, 128, 183
Russell, 251

Sabaoth, 229
Sagan, Dr. Carl, 4–5, 45, 47, 243, 258
Sahara Desert, Africa, 2, 131, 177
Saigon, S. Vietnam, 20, 75
Saint Airy Library, France, 11
Saint Albans Abbey, G.B., 11
Saint-Ambroix, France, 195
Saint Augustine, 41
Saint-Romain-sous-Gourdon, 179
Salisbury, Dr. Frank, 53
Sandia Base, New Mexico, 82
Satellites, artificial, 55, 137, 157, 246
Saturn, 42, 46, 171
Saucedo, Pedro, 185

Schaeden, Hartmann, 11
Schafarik, 17
Schmidt, 15
Science fiction, 38–39, 225
Scotland, 8, 36
Scutari, Albania, 21
Sea, UFO observations at, 8, 16–17, 20–21, 22, 28–29, 30, 79, 185
Segeberg, France, 19
Seville, Spain, 80
Shakespeare, 7
Sheneman, 183
Sidebotham, 15
Sign, U.S.A.F. project, 49, 261
Simon, Samy, 75
Siragusa, 170
Sirius, 19, 251
Sisterville, West Virginia, 22
Skyhook, balloon, 72
Smena, Soviet magazine, 2
Smith, Miss Helen, 168
Smith, Wilbert B., 115
Smithsonian Astrophysical Observatory, 130
Socorro, New Mexico, 189–190
Sodom, 226
Soukhanov, 57
Sounds, 70, 239
South America, 58, 77, 208
Southend, G.B., 29
Southern Cross, 20
Spain, 36, 58
Sperry, Captain W., 80
Spheres, 9, 28
Starovski, 195
Staveley, John, 14
Stockholm, Sweden, 61, 62, 65
Strand, 251
Strasbourg, France, 33
Stuttgart, Arkansas, 77
Sun, 15, 42, 43, 205
Sutton family, 237

Index

Sweden, 8, 13, 56, 60, 65, 77
Switzerland, 13, 15, 32–33, 64, 81
Sydney, Australia, 18

Taiga, explosion in, 26
Tammersfors, Finland, 63
Tangier, Morocco, 85
Tasman Sea, 32
Tassili, Sahara, 2
Tau Ceti, 224, 241
Taxil, Leo, 168
Tektites, 223
Tel Abib, 3
Teltown, Scotland, 8
Texas, 1, 22, 187, 200
Thann, France, 10, 84
The Hague, Holland, 74
Thutmose III, 5
Tiahuanaco, 2, 225
Time Machine, The, 157
Titan (satellite of Saturn), 46
Tombaugh, Dr. Clyde, 77, 78, 163
Tonkin, 30
Toompang, Australia, 146–147, 206
Topcliffe Air Force Base, Great Britain, 85
Tours, France, 89, 192
"Tromp," 33
Trouvelot, 17
Tschi Pen Lao, 2
Tulli, Prof. Alberto, 5
Tulsa, Oklahoma, 80, 182
Turkey, 79
Turquenstein, France, 101
Twin Falls, Idaho, 71
Types, definition of, 142–144
Type I, examples, 86, 98–100, 177–191
Type II, examples, 9, 11–12, 73, 79, 80, 84–85, 86, 87, 90–92, 208–215; table page 206
Type III, examples, 57, 69, 80, 81–82, 88–89, 215–221, 235

UFO phenomenon, definition of, 132, 142–143

V-rockets, 60
V-shaped UFO's, 82, 147
"Valentijn," 30
Van de Kamp, P., 251
Vannes, France, 98
Vatican, 5
Vaughan, Thomas, 168
Veillith, Raymond, 21, 165
Vence, France, 17
Venus, 47, 148, 174, 200, 251
Venusians, 170, 193
Verdun, France, 9, 11
Vernon, France, 90, 91, 139–140, 143, 149, 166, 208
Vogt, M., 58
"Vultur," 17

Waimera, New Guinea, 199
Wales, 29, 37
War of the Worlds, 39
Washington, 56, 57, 80
Waterford, Ireland, 64
Waves: before World War II, 31; in the United States, 36, 71; in France, 57, 90, 208; in Great Britain, 29, 36; in communist countries, 57, 69
Webb, 15
Welles, Orson, 39
Wells, H. G., 157
Westfield, Massachusetts, 206
White House, 84
White Sands Proving Grounds, New Mexico, 77, 189
Wilkins, 4, 11, 12, 13

Index

Williston, Florida, 183
Willoughby, Ohio, 183
Windsor Castle, G.B., 13, 145
Wings, 66, 82
Witharral, Texas, 187
Wolin, Poland, 192
Woomera, Australia, 209
Worcester, Massachusetts, 29
Wyalong, Australia, 146, 147

Yahweh, 227–229
Yaounde, Cameroun, 218
Yorkshire, 11

Zacatecas Observatory, Mexico, 19
Zamora, L., 176, 189
Zolotov, 27–28
Zurich, Switzerland, 12

EVERYTHING YOU'VE ALWAYS WANTED TO KNOW ABOUT EVERYTHING

Ballantine's Comprehensive Reference Books

Available at your bookstore or use this coupon.

___ **DICTIONARY OF FOOD AND WHAT'S IN IT FOR YOU**
by Barbara Levine Gelb   29479 3.95
The ingredients and nutritional values of your favorite foods.

___ **DICTIONARY OF MISINFORMATION by Tom Burnam**   32134 2.95
The world's #1 conversation starter and argument settler. Hundreds of categories!

___ **MORE MISINFORMATION by Tom Burnam**   29251 2.50
More of the same...

___ **THE NEW HANDBOOK OF PRESCRIPTION DRUGS Revised Edition**
by Richard Burack, M.D., F.A.C.P. & Fred J. Fox, M.D.   33422 3.95
Experts tell you what's in what you're using, and what they can—and cannot—do.

___ **DICTIONARY OF COMPOSERS AND THEIR MUSIC**
by Eric Gilder & June G. Port   28041 3.25
Every listener's companion guide to major composers and their works. "Splendidly thorough!"—*Bookviews*.

___ **THE BOOK OF KEY FACTS by The Queensbury Group**   28044 3.25
The world's most important information, events and discoveries.

BB BALLANTINE MAIL SALES
Dept. AL, 201 E. 50th St., New York, N.Y. 10022

Please send me the BALLANTINE or DEL REY BOOKS I have checked above. I am enclosing $.................(add 50¢ per copy to cover postage and handling). Send check or money order—no cash or C.O.D.'s please. Prices and numbers are subject to change without notice. Valid in U.S. only. All orders are subject to availability of books.

Name_____

Address_____

City_____State_____Zip Code_____

Allow at least 4 weeks for delivery.   AL-32

27 million Americans can't read a bedtime story to a child.

It's because 27 million adults in this country simply can't read.

Functional illiteracy has reached one out of five Americans. It robs them of even the simplest of human pleasures, like reading a fairy tale to a child.

You can change all this by joining the fight against illiteracy.

Call the Coalition for Literacy at toll-free **1-800-228-8813** and volunteer.

Volunteer Against Illiteracy. The only degree you need is a degree of caring.

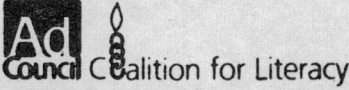

Ad Council · Coalition for Literacy

LV-3

THIS AD PRODUCED BY MARTIN LITHOGRAPHERS
A MARTIN COMMUNICATIONS COMPANY